World Economics

Book Ser

Volume 1

Piketty's *Capital in the Twenty-First Century*

The **World Economics Association (WEA)** was launched on May 16, 2011. Already over 13,000 economists and related scholars have joined. This phenomenal success has come about because the WEA fills a huge gap in the international community of economists – the absence of a professional organization which is truly international and pluralist.

The World Economics Association seeks to increase the relevance, breadth and depth of economic thought. Its key qualities are worldwide membership and governance, and inclusiveness with respect to: (a) the variety of theoretical perspectives; (b) the range of human activities and issues which fall within the broad domain of economics; and (c) the study of the world's diverse economies.

The Association's activities centre on the development, promotion and diffusion of economic research and knowledge and on illuminating their social character.

The WEA publishes books, three journals (*Economic Thought, World Economic Review and Real-World Economics Review)*, a bi-monthly newsletter, blogs, holds global online conferences, and is about to launch its Textbook Commentaries Project.

Website http://www.worldeconomicsassociation.org/

Piketty's *Capital in the Twenty-First Century*

Edited by

Edward Fullbrook and Jamie Morgan

ISBN 978-1-84890-157-5

Published by College Publications on behalf of the World Economics Association
College Publications
Scientific Director: Dov Gabbay
Managing Director: Jane Spurr

http://www.collegepublications.co.uk

Original cover design by WEA
Printed by Lightning Source, Milton Keynes, UK

Contents

Introduction: the Piketty phenomenon

Jamie Morgan [Leeds Beckett University, UK]
Edward Fullbrook [University of the West of England, UK]

All the contributors to this collection agree that Thomas Piketty's *Capital in the Twenty-First Century* is an important book because it has placed the problem of wealth concentration and income inequality centre stage. In so doing it has served to restructure the questions we ask. Most especially, can humanity afford the ultra-rich? Pre-Piketty it was unacceptable to raise this question in polite society. Yet it was Adam Smith, not Karl Marx, who among economists first warned of the dangers of not asking it.

> Upon this disposition of mankind to go along with all the passions of the rich and the powerful, is founded the distinction of ranks and the order of society. Our obsequiousness to our superiors more frequently arises from our admiration for the advantages of their situation, than from any private expectations of benefit from their good-will. Their benefits can extend but to a few; but their fortunes interest almost everybody... Even when the order of society seems to require us to oppose them, we can hardly bring ourselves to do it. [And] This disposition to admire, and almost to worship, the rich and the powerful, and to despise, or, at least, to neglect, persons of poor and mean condition, though necessary both to establish and to maintain the distinction of ranks and the order of society, is, at the same time, the great and most universal cause of the corruption of our moral sentiments. (Smith, *Theory of Moral Sentiments,* 1759/2000: pp. 73-4, 84)

For Smith, what to do about wealth concentration depended on whether its existence contributes to a desirable social order, whether the activities that lead to its concentration create unintended social benefits, and whether human nature can be relied upon (in conjunction with institutional initiatives from the state) to limit its adverse consequences for society.

In Smith's time classical political economics defined itself with reference to the creation of an economic surplus that could then be *distributed* in different ways. Neoclassical economics, especially the variety that constitutes today's mainstream, takes an altogether different route. Its theoretical focus on scarcity and allocation and its methodological focus on linear mathematics has marginalized concern with the distribution of income and wealth, and compartmentalised the economic, the political and the social

Furthermore, under its marginal productivity theory of distribution of income and thereby ultimately of wealth, any real-world distribution is implicitly "justified" and not to be regarded as a cause of concern as it was with Adam Smith. Moreover, looking beyond the neoclassical paradigm it has, following Kuznets, been assumed that long-term development reduces inequality. It is no wonder then, given the justified and transient interpretations, that the enormous upward redistributions of wealth and income that have taken place over the last forty years and that Piketty and others document have been in the main ignored.

But now, like a bolt of lightning from the winter's sky, Piketty's book has changed that. Socially it is now acceptable and professionally almost acceptable to talk about the huge upward redistributions, including, like Adam Smith, their undesirability and even the possibility of reversing them. Thanks to Piketty's book the economics profession has already entered into a process of refocussing its discourse, maybe even rethinking its ethics, processes that leave in doubt who and what will be tomorrow's mainstream.

There are two primary dimensions to *Capital in the Twenty-first Century*, the empirical and the theoretical. It is the first, with its massive foregrounding of the recent and acute upward redistributions, that has made the book both a publishing and an intellectual sensation.

Piketty's capital collates and synthesises data on wealth and income drawn primarily from tax data and national accounts. This means that the data is conditioned by the methods used to calculate particular categories (e.g. National Income) from what is reported. So as with any empirical project, Piketty's is restricted in terms of history and method. Nonetheless Piketty's data base is broadly transnational. His most 'complete' data, running over two centuries, is for France, Great Britain, and the USA, followed then by particular countries in Europe and extending only to data for the rest of the world, in which he has some confidence, from the 1980s.

Assured of the world's attention because of his monumental and momentous display of empirical data, Piketty, inevitably perhaps, ventures a theoretical interpretation of the causes of the redistributions and concentrations that he documents. Early in his book he proclaims what he calls the First and Second Fundamental Laws of Capitalism. As you will see from this collection there is wide disagreement as to both the significance and meaning of these "laws". The first is that "the share of income from capital in national income " is "the rate of return on capital" times the "capital / income ratio" (p.52). But, as Piketty acknowledges, this "is a pure accounting identity" rather than a "law" in the sense that the word is used in science. His second law states that in the long run the capital / income ratio will equal the savings rate divided by the growth rate (p. 166). Because Piketty sees the saving rate in the long run increasing relative to the growth rate, his two "laws" together predict that over time the capital / income ratio will increase and with it so will the concentration of wealth and income.

These dynamics, if true, mean that the capitalism system intrinsically leads to acute inequality. Piketty claims on the basis of his data that these dynamics are a deep structural tendency in capitalism and that the mid-Twentieth-Century decline in inequality in core countries was an anomaly to this tendency because of the destruction of wealth by the two world wars and because of what have proved to be time-limited institutional breaks in the form of post-war consensus. The dissolution of that consensus in the 1970s has, says Piketty, resulted in a return from the 1980s onwards to the long-term tendency expressed in his "laws". Furthermore Piketty says the situation seems set to extend through the Twenty-First Century and will do so globally, creating a return to a 'patrimonial capital' ownership structure of a wealthy and powerful elite, which can only be corrupting for social and political cohesion. Since the problem is pervasive to capitalism and is global in extent, Piketty advocates a progressive global tax on capital to offset the tendency for wealth to accumulate and concentrate in the hands of a few. *Inter alia*, he assumes this progressive taxation will reduce the drive amongst the wealthy to use their positional power (whether as a way to earn income within the upper echelons of corporations or as a way to defend returns to capital from ownership of investment assets) to augment their wealth.

Although *Capital in the Twenty-First Century* is a data-led exercise committed to seeking and amassing the best available evidence in a way that the author considers quite different than is typical of much of current mainstream economics, the work is also substantially shaped by its concepts and theoretical framework. Crucially, the dynamics of Piketty's "laws" hinge to a significant degree on the concept or concepts of "capital", a word which the author uses synonymously with "wealth". The hypothesis that wealth tends to concentrate to a high degree and the plausibility of this as a *deep structural tendency* of capitalism is rooted in the basic assumptions that are necessary to animate the relations between aspects of the formulae. In this collection, the potential problems with the concept of capital are most thoroughly explored by Galbraith, Varoufakis and by Fullbrook (but also more briefly by almost all of the contributors; notably Baker, Beker, Ghosh, Hillinger, Hudson, Pettifor and Tily, and Syll).

James Galbraith deconstructs the first "law" in order to demonstrate that it is not based on a consistent concept of capital but refers only to current financial valuations of net assets. Yanis Varoufakis extends the logic of this critique to other aspects of Piketty's laws. Both authors demonstrate that Piketty's dynamics need not result in a long-term tendency for wealth to concentrate in capitalism. The formulae, they argue, are deterministic and mis-specified.

Edward Fullbrook argues that as a quantitative order market-value has a Boolean metric rather than the Euclidian one assumed by Piketty and neoclassical economists generally. The Boolean structure means that in the real-world Piketty's equations work quiet differently from how he thinks and that the combination of political manipulation and financialization accounts for the recent radical redistributions of wealth and income. Fullbrook also argues that the-one-percent implicitly understands the Boolean structure of market-value, and that this understanding contributes to its ongoing success at redistributing wealth and income.

A general point that emerges from the papers is that Piketty's concept of "capital" is misleading rather than merely differing from various received usages of the word. One needs to carefully distinguish between capital as something that facilitates the production of goods and between forms of capital that do not. If one does not make this distinction, then one can say little about capital's role in the production of material wealth. One can only track changes in the financial valuation of a range of wealth assets and demonstrate variations in ownership of those assets – which is essentially what Piketty has done. Though a timely exercise and in the eyes of many an extremely important one, it is not an explanation of the processes of capitalism and offers little beyond empirical description of wealth and income inequality. It can say little about why these variations arise in particular manifestations of capitalism.

Though one might not be saying a great deal about why wealth and income inequality arise, one can of course appear to be doing so, and it is here that many of the contributors locate some of their critique of the popular success of Piketty's *Capital.* These matters are most thoroughly addressed by Robert Wade, Michael Hudson and, again, by Varoufakis. The laws which Piketty hypothesizes allow him to make some quite specific claims regarding changes in wealth and income that would appear discursively quite different without his mathematical architecture. Claiming a deep structural tendency and being able to transform many and potentially counter-moving valuations of categories of wealth assets into specific single numbers, which one then expresses using the term "capital", provides the book with a clear and headline friendly message because of its determinism. It is primed for publicity because of its simple equations and simple message. Moreover, the world was primed for that message because the book, whilst not new in focusing on wealth and income inequality, was timely in appearing in the aftermath of the Great Recession, a period during which the left, middle and right have become concerned with the perception of wealth. However, for that determinism to hold requires a basic inconsistency: Piketty is required to fall back on some simple assumptions rooted in neoclassical production functions (see also Ghosh, and Pettifor and Tily). Here the comforting determinism of the underlying economic theory sits uncomfortably with the simultaneous claim that institutions affect the returns to capital and labour.

If institutions matter, then there can be no confident assertion that a given returns structure is explained by the neoclassical production function. Piketty thus makes use of a form of economics theory that sits uneasily with his own comments regarding today's mainstream economics. In doing so his work remains conventional and so is not an immediate challenge to traditional orthodoxy and this "weakness" renders it more widely palatable as a publication – augmenting its potential for success *because of* its theoretical shortcomings. It also follows that the form and focus of the theoretical impasse affects how one views Piketty's prognosis. This is so in two senses. First, if there is a tension between the deterministic aspects of Piketty's laws and his claim that institutions matter *and* there is a problem with the way the laws are misleading and miss-specified, then, on both accounts, any attempt to extrapolate from the laws across the whole of the new century becomes problematic. Second, in so far as the laws create a focus on an aggregate of wealth and place this in a global context, the whole approach can mislead one into thinking that the *only* solution to any arising problems of wealth concentration and of wealth and income inequality must also be in the aggregate, that is a global tax on capital. However, if the causes of concentrations and inequality are more specific and are varied then one can address them in more varied and specific ways. These issues are most thoroughly dealt with by Baker, Colander, Galbraith and Wade (as well as Hudson).

Dean Baker provides data for the US that establishes that only some economic sectors accounted for increases in profit shares prior to the Global Financial Crisis. Those were (putting aside the housing bubble) the financial sector, the retail sector and private provision of public services. Each can be addressed on the basis of the actual characteristics that lead to a rise in profit share. Galbraith, on the basis of his own longstanding work (including the University of Texas Inequality Project), and also Wade, make the similar point that it is through specific policies aimed at key characteristics of modern capitalism, such as financialisation, that one actually addresses the sources of unjustifiable increases in particular sources of wealth. Both authors then link their arguments to the broader Keynesian issues of wages and of aggregate demand.

David Colander essay places the problem of extreme concentrations of income and wealth in the context of the work of John Stuart Mill. Rather than approaching distribution problems through taxation, Colander proposes doing so though changes to the legal and institutional frameworks that have created today's mal-distributions.

So a range of the contributors emphasise that one can avoid the difficulties of coordinating and implementing a progressive global capital tax by being more targeted in ones goals. Wealth concentrations and wealth and income inequality remain central issues, but they are central issues that can be considered based on different strategies that build from more developed, more consistent and, most crucially, more empirically based theoretical frameworks. That this can be the case does not, however, prevent some of the contributors considering how one might constructively build on Piketty's tentative proposals. Richard Parker, for example, provides an extended account of seven ways one might build support for a more egalitarian-centred consensus in academia, in regional and global organizations, and in politics. He compares this process with the conditions that paved the way for an acceptance of a version of Keynesianism in the US. Heikki Patomaki meanwhile, with reference to his longstanding work on a financial tax and on a global Keynesian policy structure, considers the different ways one might facilitate the transition to a workable version of a global tax on capital.

Ann Pettifor and Geoff Tilly, giving special importance to government interest rate policies, consider Piketty's findings beyond the "deterministic straitjacket" from which he views economic history.

Lars Syll attacks, head on, Piketty's reliance on the robustly falsified marginal productivity theory of distribution and which now "functions as a legitimizing device of indefensible and growing inequalities."

Claude Hillinger's paper argues that Piketty's claim, accepted uncritically by many reviewers of his book, to have offered a theory of the evolution of a capitalist economy is a case of having conflated mere assertion with theoretical construction. He concludes that Piketty's book "does not have a theory in any formal sense of that term."

Jayati Ghosh's paper, drawing on the two-Cambridges capital controversy, broadens Piketty's consideration of the resurgence of patrimonial capitalism.

Victor Beker's paper, after considering reasons for the book's remarkable success, analyses the difference between inequality and poverty, and relates Piketty's finding to the Kaldorian model of economic growth.

Finally, we come to the contributions of Richard Koo, Merijn Knibbe, and Alicia Puyana Mutis. Koo and Knibbe pursue lines of argument that are quite different from other contributions. Koo offers an alternative explanation for the shifts in returns on capital identified by Piketty for the Twentieth Century. He argues that the shifts can also be accounted for by national and global Lewis Turning Points (LTPs). An LTP is a point where labour migration as urbanization of the population is completed. Up to this point capital has a potential for greater returns because wages are suppressed. So the transition beyond a national LTP triggers a reduction in the return to capital, but only if there is no possibility of transferring some of the production process to places where the LTP has not yet been achieved. Knibbe, meanwhile, explores Piketty's original dataset and attempts to reproduce some of its findings using the Netherlands. In so doing he highlights some of the consistency problems of the System of National Accounts (SNA) approach. Puyana, provides a constructive critique of Piketty based on Mexico as a case study. She clearly establishes how the period of neoliberal policy has not been one that fits easily with a narrative of technological efficiency (of the kind one would expect based on neoclassical production functions). It has simply been one of increasingly exploitative institutional practices within an economic system.

So what is the long-term significance of Piketty's *Capital in the Twenty-First Century* likely to be? Will it still be read in ten, twenty or fifty years' time, or even at the end of the Twenty-First Century across which it extrapolates? It seems more likely that it will be *referred to* more than actually read. It will be referred to as the text that set in motion a historically important debate that rapidly exceeded the book's framework. Its data content will be remembered more than its theoretical and policy content.

Piketty would probably not be surprised by such an outcome, given that he appears to have intended his book to be primarily an empirical contribution rather than a theoretical one. Even if its theory turned out to be true rather than false, it is not the kind of book one would read and reread in order to tease out nuances of that theory or to seek fresh inspiration based on its deep content.

What is already certain about the publication of *Capital in the Twenty-First Century* is that as a world intellectual event, its impact, rightly or wrongly, outranks that of every economics book and paper published since 1936. The editors of this collection were both amazed and delighted by the alacrity with which its large global cast of high-profile economists accepted on very short notice our invitation to contribute. The result of their efforts is a book that not only enriches Piketty's, but that also, because of its theoretical substance, will be discussed for at least as long.

References

Piketty, T. (2014) *Capital in the Twenty-First Century* London: Belknap Press

Smith, A. (1759/2000) *The Theory of Moral Sentiments* New York: Prometheus Books

The Piketty phenomenon and the future of inequality

Robert H. Wade [London School of Economics and Political Science, UK]

Economists and other social scientists tend to study "problems". Issues not studied tend to be seen as "natural". "Poverty" and the "poor" are problems, the subject of a vast social science literature. Inequality, income concentration, the behaviour and influence of the super-rich tend to be treated as part of the natural order of things, warranting no more than marginal social science attention. We have a "poor economics" but no "rich economics".

Mainstream economists have tended to emphasise the need for inequality as a source of incentives for effort and creativity, from which the whole society benefits; and to agree that higher taxes on the rich and increased aid to the poor are likely to hurt economic growth.

Willem Buiter, former professor of European economics at the London School of Economics and currently chief economist, Citigroup, succinctly expressed a common nonchalance: "Poverty bothers me. Inequality does not. I just don't care" (2007). The Nobel Prize economist Robert Lucas was more aggressive: "Of the tendencies that are harmful to sound economics, the most seductive, and in my opinion, the most poisonous, is to focus on questions of distribution" (2004). Earlier the famous neoliberal economist Ludwig von Mises declared his love for the anti-egalitarian, anti-democratic message of Ayn Rand's *Atlas Shrugged*. He wrote to Rand in 1958, "You have the courage to tell the masses what no politician told them: you are inferior and all the improvements in your conditions which you simply take for granted you owe to the efforts of men who are better than you" (in Frank, 2012: 147).

Conservative politicians have long celebrated inequality and trickle-down economics. Prime Minister Thatcher assured her public, "It is our job to glory in inequality and to see that talents and abilities are given vent and expression for the benefit of us all". Prime Minister Blair, of the center-left, told one interviewer: "If you end up going after those people who are the most wealthy in society, what you actually end up doing is in fact not even helping those at the bottom end."

The US Republican Party has been committed to defending the interests of the wealthy over those of ordinary families. The biggest tax cuts presided over by President George W. Bush were on income from investments and on heirs to large fortunes: the top rate on dividends fell from just under 40% to 15%, and the estate tax was eliminated. The Republican tax plan during the second Obama administration would enable someone living off investment income to pay no federal tax at all. In Britain, the Conservative Party's Prime Minister David Cameron vetoed the idea of a "mansion tax" on the grounds that "our donors will never put up with it" (Eaton, 2014).

Many in the business world have welcomed this relaxed attitude towards the rich. Bernard Arnault, CEO of the French luxury group LVMH, boasted in 2000 (when he was said to be the 10th richest person in the world), "Business, especially international ones, have ever greater resources, and in Europe they have acquired the ability to compete with states.... Politicians' real impact on the economic life of a country is more and more limited. Fortunately" (quoted in Halimi 2013).

A publishing sensation

Thomas Piketty's book, *Capital in the Twenty-First Century,* was published in English translation in March 2014. As of April and May 2014 the book hit number one on Amazon's best-seller list (including fiction). BookData reports that UK sales in the eight weeks following late April were 14,445. The Economists' Bookshop, next to the London School of Economics, says it has never sold so many non-fiction hardbacks in the first months of publication. The nearest competitor is Steven Hawkings' *A Brief History of Time*, from 1988. An economist friend who mentioned his occupation to his London taxi driver was surprised and pleased to be asked whether he had read this book by a Frenchman named Piketty. Yet Piketty's is no bedside reading: its 685 pages weigh 1.1 kilos.

Its success makes that of the earlier, slimmer (only 330-page) book about the *costs* of inequality, Richard Wilkinson and Kate Pickett's *The Spirit Level: Why More Equal Societies Almost Always Do Better*, look almost modest. *The Spirit Level* has sold "only" between 250,000 and 300,000 copies in 24 languages since publication in 2009. The publicity storm around *Capital* will die down; the question is whether the book will remain in the pantheon or disappear when – if – robust economic growth returns.

How can we explain the book's astounding success? One obvious reason is a slew of extravagant reviews, some very favourable, others deeply hostile. Martin Wolf of the *Financial Times*, one of the world's most influential economic commentators, described it as "an extraordinarily important book" (2014a). Paul Krugman, Nobel laureate in economics and columnist for the New York Times, hailed it as "awesome", "truly superb", "the most important book of the year – and maybe of the decade" (2014b). John Cassidy in the *New Yorker* said, "Piketty has written a book that nobody interested in a defining issue of our era can afford to ignore" (2014). Other reviewers trashed it. Clive Crook's review on *BloombergView* was titled "The most important book ever is all wrong" (2014a). Allister Heath's in *The Telegraph* described it as "horrendously flawed" (2014).

Beyond the review pages, four main reasons for the book's success stand out. First, the book makes a carefully documented challenge to the belief that inequality is not a problem for public policy attention (Wade, 2007, 2011, 2012, 2013, 2014). Second, the Great Crash of 2008 and its aftermath – when surges of unemployment and underemployment went with surges in senior executive remuneration and in the share of the top 1 percent in national income growth – boosted the salience of inequality as a "problem" in political debate; so the ground for the book's uptake was already prepared. Third, it clarifies, objectifies, legitimizes and provides a kind of catharsis for heightened middle-class anxieties during the Great Recession since 2008. Finally, the book is in important ways reassuringly conventional in its analysis and prescriptions, and so less threatening to familiar ways of thought. At the end I discuss the future of inequality, and an intellectual and policy agenda.

The book challenges dominant beliefs about elites and inequality

Piketty challenges the earlier-described insouciance about inequality in an easy-to-read but authoritatively scientific way. His central point is that viewed over centuries income and wealth have tended to concentrate in the top few percentiles of the population, with only modest restraint from self-equilibrating mechanisms like social mobility.

The long term trend has been checked from time to time by some combination of (a) wars, depressions, hyperinflations, (b) highly progressive tax rates, and (c) high growth of productivity and population. The first two have lowered the rate of return on capital ownership; the third has raised the rate of economic growth and so raised the rate of growth of average incomes.

Thanks to these forces, the middle decades of the twentieth century, from the 1930s to the 1970s, saw an exceptional inequality decline in the West. But in "normal" conditions, including the period since the 1970s, the tendency to rising inequality re-emerges. The owners of capital (broadly defined, to include land, real estate, as well as factories and financial assets) accrue a rising share of national income, the suppliers of "labour" accrue a falling share. Piketty suggests that many developed economies in the past few decades have been moving up towards (but remain some way short of) levels of income and wealth inequality last seen in the early twentieth century. He further suggests that the much higher levels of inequality in today's "emerging markets" will persist rather than subside unless strong policy measures are taken to rein them in or unless they experience wars, depressions or hyperinflations.

Moreover, Piketty's and other data show that income and wealth concentration typically increases the higher the position in the hierarchy: within the top 1% of the population the top 0.1% have a disproportionately large share; within the top 0.1% the top 0.01% have a disproportionately large share. This pattern fits Zipf's Law, which characterizes not just income distributions but also city size distributions, word frequency distributions, and more.

Why does income and wealth concentration increase the higher towards the top? One reason is that the rate of return on fortunes *increases* with the size of fortunes. Another is inheritance, as fortunes are passed from generation to generation – fortunes not just in material assets but also in the self-confidence learned from being brought up as a superior in social hierarchies. Piketty draws on the novels of Jane Austin and Balzac to show how inheritance dominated income distribution – and marriage strategies – in the eighteenth and nineteenth centuries.

The upshot is that money begets money, and the more money the more begetting (Henwood 2014). In Piketty's phrase, "The past devours the future". The future may see a return to the "patrimonial capitalism" of the eighteenth and nineteenth centuries, in which income distribution is substantially shaped by the distribution of inherited wealth. This is a society at complete odds with understandings of the good society shared across most of the western political spectrum today.

However, Piketty's data show that Northwest European countries and Japan have experienced much less increase in concentration at the top than the US, UK and other Anglo countries (also tiny Iceland: Sigurgeirsdottir and Wade, 2014). In the former, incomes of the middle class and the poor have increased faster than in the Anglo countries, while their economies grew more or less as fast and levels of material well-being for ordinary people kept pace.

From this we can conclude, first, that the trend towards rising concentration is not quite as hard-wired into capitalism as most (but not all) of Piketty's book says. Policies, institutions and politics – all changeable – have more of a role in income distribution than the more fatalistic passages say. Second, more equal economies are not necessarily less dynamic, and more unequal economies are not necessarily better at raising mass living standards, contrary to default thinking. In other words, Anglo levels of income concentration are not necessary for a well-functioning society.

That being said, pointing to Europe as a place of significantly lower income and wealth concentration than the US raises a data problem. Gabriel Zucman's new research suggests that the fraction of European wealth hidden away in tax havens is substantially higher than the fraction of American income and wealth, which reflects higher rates of tax on top incomes and capital gains in Europe and therefore a stronger incentive for concealment. So European income and wealth concentration may be relatively higher than the tax return data suggests, as compared to the corresponding adjustment for the US. Zucman finds that the overall numbers for income and wealth concealment are huge – around 8% of global wealth of households is held in tax havens, most of it unrecorded, and most of it owned by residents of developed countries, especially Europeans (Zucman, 2013).

As these findings suggest, one can raise plenty of queries (nit-pickettys) about Piketty's data, especially about trends in wealth concentration, which is the most original part of the data set. *The Financial Times* launched an assault on Piketty's main conclusions, saying in an editorial that errors and data problems "seem to undermine his conclusion that wealth inequality is rising in the US and Europe"; indeed, "undermine his thesis that capitalism has a natural tendency for wealth to become ever more concentrated in the hands of the rich" (*Financial Times*, 2014a).

However, the *Financial Times* conclusions have been substantially rejected by former World Bank economist Branko Milanovic, who knows as much about the data as anybody and has worked independently of Piketty (Milanovic, 2014, 2011). A re-analysis of Piketty and the *Financial Times* comes to conclusions close to Piketty's and far from the *Financial Times'*. It turns out that the *Financial Times* did not make allowances for several changes in the methodology used to measure wealth distribution in Britain over time (related especially to the difference between tax return data and household income survey data, the latter underestimating income and wealth at the top by even more than the tax return data). So it took at face value – without adjusting for the methodology changes – that the wealth share of the top 10% in the UK did fall, *in reality*, by 12 percentage points during the 1970s and by another 11 percentage points in 2005-06. Piketty made the adjustment for the changes in methodology, and found a much higher wealth share in the top 10% (Elliott, 2014).

The *Financial Times* emerged with a bloody nose, having also ignored its own coverage of other indicators of income and wealth concentration such as soaring prices of high-end real estate, booming market for luxury goods, and bubbling market for equities. In May 2014 Christie's contemporary art auction in New York returned the world's highest ever auction total for one day: $744mn; enough to build quite a few schools and hospitals (Barker, 2014).

Some critics dismiss the *future* relevance of the trends Piketty identifies, on two grounds. First, the intense rate of technological change (internet, mobile telecoms, digital economy) will accelerate economic growth in the West to the point where growth stays above the rate of return to capital; and this will drive income and wealth concentration down "by itself". Second, the whole world economy will grow faster thanks to growth in the "emerging markets", and this too will help to keep the concentration of income and wealth down. The message is, "this time is (or will be) different" (Worstall, 2014). But we have heard this message during every boom, and most insistently between 2000 and 2008.

Inequality became a heated topic after 2008

Piketty's challenge on its own cannot explain the book's success, because his broad findings are not new. Sharp increases in inequality in developed countries since the late 1970s, especially in the United States but also in other Anglo countries (including New Zealand: Rashbrooke 2013), have been well documented by others, though less comprehensively and without much data on wealth as distinct from income. They include Larry Mishel and co-authors at the Economic Policy Institute in Washington DC, who have documented rising income inequality in the US in periodic publications since the late 1980s. James K. Galbraith and colleagues at the University of Texas, Austin have used data on wages to examine trends in distribution since the 1960s, across developed and developing countries. As have Anthony Atkinson at Oxford and Gabriel Palma at Cambridge. The popular Nobel Prize-winning economist Joseph Stiglitz drew on a lot of existing evidence of fast-rising inequality for a recent book, *The Price of Inequality*, published in 2012; but it did not take off in the way that Piketty's has. With these and other cases in mind, I published an essay in 2012 called "Why has income inequality remained on the sidelines of public policy for so long?" (Wade, 2012; also Wade, 2014.)

Timing matters. Had the book been published before 2008 it would have been much less successful. So the second reason for *Capital's* success is that inequality and concentration had already risen up the public and political attention cycle by the time of its publication in early 2014. Many Americans, who used to dismiss concern about inequality as "the politics of envy", were stung by the excesses of Wall Street and dismayed that they could no longer borrow against rising house prices; and began talking of inequality more negatively than for decades. President Obama declared inequality to be "the defining challenge of our time" (Obama, 2013). Pope Francis tweeted that "inequality is the root of social evil" (quoted in Brown, 2014). The World Economic Forum's panel of global risk experts ranked "severe income disparity" as the second equal global risk over the next decade (World Economic Forum, 2012). The Occupy Protests framed the issue as the "top 1% vs. bottom 99%", as they occupied key sites in nearly a thousand cities in more than 80 countries in 2011-12 under the banner of "We are the 99%". Even Alan Greenspan, the former Fed chairman who calls himself a life-long libertarian Republican and devotee of Ayn Rand, has recently cited inequality as the "most dangerous" trend afflicting America (Tett, 2014).

Prominent figures among the super-rich hit back, furious at this questioning of their role in society as job creators for the common good, innovators for social betterment, and problem-solving philanthropists (Konczal, 2014). Prominent Wall Streeters accused President Obama of "demonizing" and "persecuting" the rich. Stephen Schwarzman, CEO of Blackstone Group (an American multinational private equity firm), declared that proposals to eliminate tax loopholes for hedge funds and private equity managers were "like when Hitler invaded Poland in 1939". Venture capitalist Tom Perkins wrote to *The Wall Street Journal*, "I would call attention to the parallels of Nazi Germany to its war on its 'one percent', namely its Jews, to the progressive war on the American one percent, namely the 'rich'" (both quotations in Krugman, 2014a). A sizable section of the American public supported the wealthy in their push-back out of anti-government sentiment. The Tea Party insurgency – financed largely by billionaires – preached that government measures of progressive taxation and social protection undermined the moral fabric of society by enabling some to free-ride on the hard work and creativity of others. By 2010 Friedrich von Hayek's *The Road to Serfdom* stood at 241 on the Amazon best-sellers list, exceptional for a book first published almost 70 years before. It was propelled to these heights by seethingly conservative TV hosts advertising it as a guide to what the Obama government was trying to do to America through its efforts to reduce the great divides in access to health care, health status and life expectancy (Farrant and McPhail, 2010).

The book clarifies, objectifies and legitimizes middle-class anxieties after 2008

The third reason for *Capital*'s success is that it objectifies and legitimizes the anxiety that has pervaded large swathes of western societies since 2008. And crucially, it does so from within a conventional capitalist discourse; Piketty is not an outsider, a member of a heterodox sect who can easily be dismissed. His work serves the same purpose as a psychotherapist – it helps people to recognize that their experiences and feelings are legitimate.

The World Economic Forum's *Global Risks 2012* reports, "*On an unprecedented scale around the world*, there is a sense of receding hope for future prospects. Gallup polling data in 2011 reveal that, globally, people perceive their living standards to be falling, and they express diminishing confidence in the ability of their government to reverse this trend. This discontent is exacerbated by the starkness of income disparities" (2012: 18, emphasis added).

In the US, only 36% of respondents in 2011 said economic globalization is a positive development, down from 60% in 2001. A Gallup poll in 2011 asked respondents in many countries the question, "Does globalization bring more problems than it solves?". In Western Europe, 59% agreed or agreed strongly; in Asia and Pacific, 64% agreed or agreed strongly.

Employment in the US has been increasing since early 2010; but four mostly precarious, low-skilled jobs have been created in hotels, restaurants, healthcare and social assistance for every new job in manufacturing (Norris, 2014).

In Britain the Labour Party since 2012 has campaigned under the banner of "the cost of living crisis", meaning the long stagnation of middle-class incomes, uncertain career prospects for middle-class children, and job growth biased, as in the US, to internships, part-time and minimum-wage activities (the "precariat").

In Germany, according to Markus Pohlmann, professor of sociology at Heidelberg University, "For the older generation [of managers], there was a kind of social pact by which the search for a consensus tempered the overriding obligation to pursue profit. That concept has vanished. Today it is the principle of human capital that prevails, according to which every individual is responsible for his or her own fate" (quoted in Cyran, 2013). The president of the powerful Federation of German Industry, Michael Rogowski, explained in 2005, "Labour has a price, just like pork. In the business cycle, prices are high when pork is hard to come by. Where there is a lot of pork about, prices fall" (in Cyran, 2013).

In the Eurozone the adult unemployment rate in Spain has been over 20 percent for three years, in Italy over 10 percent; and the biggest economic bloc in the world has languished in recession since 2008.

The other side of the zeitgeist is rage against the rich, fuelled by daily revelations of corporate wrongdoing combined with immense personal enrichment and immunity from prosecution. In 2009-12 some 93% of the increase in US national income accrued to the top 1% – in a stable democracy, not a kleptocracy like Equatorial Guinea (Klitgaard, 1991).

Anger and anxiety about living and employment conditions feed into a concatenation of other sources, including immigration, obesity, failing public health services, failing public schools, bankers' bonuses, unaccountable governments, dead-end Congress, globalization, terrorism, Islamic threat to our way of life, Russia swallowing its neighbors, "rising powers" challenging western rule, and weird weather. Every day in 2014 has woken to another intake of bad news.

In this context *Capital* has the appeal of a dystopian novel like *Nineteen Eighty Four* and *Brave New World*, by indicating the destination we are headed for if we do not change now. In that future the wealthy lift off from the rest of society and perpetuate their wealth from generation to generation like the nobility of old.

Then, having painted a dystopian future, the book ends with catharsis: an escape route to a fairer and more stable world. The trend of rising concentration at the top is not destiny; it can be changed by political choices, short of wars, depressions, and Apocalypse. The past need not devour the future (see below).

The book remains reassuringly conventional

A fourth reason for the book's success is that its basic "lens" or paradigm is reassuringly conventional. If the book had been called *Capitalism in the Twenty First Century* it would have been less popular, for "capitalism" easily slides to Marx, while "capital" has generally positive connotations. Even so, when a top-level executive of Deutsche Bank in London entered the office of a researcher and spotted *Capital*, he spat out, "Regurgitated Marxism!", leaving the researcher convinced he should not be seen around Deutsche with the book in hand (personal communication, June 2014).

Like neoclassical economics in general, the book concentrates on income and wealth distribution and says little about production – about the structure of power relations in the world of employment, notably between the owners and managers of capital and the rest. One does not have to be a Marxist to see that these power relations in production are a prime cause of pre-tax income distribution. To the limited extent that Piketty tries to *explain* income and wealth distribution he uses a fairly standard neoclassical marginal productivity explanation for distribution below the top one percent, and a sketchy "grab everything you can" for the latter. Thomas Palley comments, the mostly neoclassical framing "creates a *gattopardo* opportunity whereby inequality is folded back into mainstream economic theory which remains unchanged" (2014). *Gattopardo* refers to the famous line in *The Leopard*, "For things to remain the same, everything must change".

Piketty's re-distribution policy solutions – including a wealth tax – are also of a comfortingly conventional neoclassical kind (though they call for a much stronger redistribution of market income than has been achieved through current rates of tax progressivity, wage subsidies and social assistance). Had Piketty emphasised "pre-distribution" – changes in institutions and policies to make *pre-tax* income distribution less unequal, including in corporate governance law and trade union law – he would have been seen as more radical, more threatening, more marginal (Baker, 2011).

The costs of inequality

It is striking that in the course of more than 600 pages, Piketty devoted almost no attention to *why* inequality matters. That would mean asking questions like: when are the rich too rich? When do the social costs of reducing their share outweigh likely social benefits?

For reasons suggested earlier, these have been largely taboo topics. But recently researchers in the International Monetary Fund – a pillar of global orthodoxy – have published findings about the macroeconomic costs of inequality (Ostry et al., 2014), findings which Martin Wolf of the *Financial Times* describes as "strikingly clear" (2014b). First, *countries with higher inequality tend to experience lower and more volatile growth*; countries with lower inequality tend to experience higher and less volatile growth, other things being equal. Second, *there is little if any trade-off between redistribution and growth*; so the growth costs of redistribution measures (like higher taxes) are typically less than the growth benefits of lower inequality.

The implication of the IMF's and other evidence is that current levels of inequality in the Anglo countries make it difficult to achieve *adequate economic growth with financial stability* (unless by the unsustainable German route of repressed wages plus large export surpluses). High and rising income concentration generates savings glut at the top and underconsumption below. Governments are constantly tempted to engineer credit and asset booms. Credit remains too cheap and debt remains too high, and central banks then become reluctant to damage the debt-heavy economy by tightening monetary policy. Meanwhile *fiscal* tightening is hobbled by political paralysis and visceral rejection of "Keynesianism". When the boom turns to bust, governments and central banks try to ease the ensuing hangover with loose monetary policy. But the bust is likely to usher in a "balance sheet recession", when households and firms labour under far too much debt relative to income, as in Japan through the 1990s and 2000s and much of the West since 2008. Balance sheet recessions are difficult to escape from, because the chief objective of households and firms becomes to pay down debt; so private demand shrinks and monetary policy becomes ineffective. It can take years for the deleveraging process to be complete enough for economic growth to resume without riding on the back of more borrowing and still more financial instability. As *The Financial Times'* Wolfgang Munchau says about Europe gripped by a balance sheet recession (which very low interest rates have not cured), "The most likely trajectory is a long period of slow growth, low inflation, and a constant threat of insolvency and political insurrection" (2014:13).

Wilkinson and Pickett's *The Spirit Level* (2009) pulls together evidence on social and health costs, under the headings of life expectancy, child mortality, obesity, homicides, imprisonment rates, mental illness, teenage births, social mobility and trust. Using samples of more than 20 "advanced" economies and the fifty US states (the social mobility index is excluded for US states), it finds that the levels on all these variables correlate fairly closely with levels of income inequality, much closer than with average income. (It measures inequality as after-tax-and-benefit income of the richest 20 percent over the poorest 20 percent, or the Gini coefficient.) The striking finding is not just that health and social problems are more frequent among the poorer people in the more unequal societies; the overall burden of these problems is much higher in the more unequal societies.

Lawrence Katz's recent research finds that US generational educational inequality is higher than almost all other industrialized countries, measured as the inverse of the percentage of adults who have a higher level of education than their parents; and that educational inequality has increased (the proportion with education at higher levels than parents is lowest in the 25-34 year old cohort). (Katz, 2014; Porter, 2014)

Political scientists have found a startlingly high degree of "representational bias" or "representational inequality" in recent US politics. The finding is all the more dramatic because the "median voter" model (public policy responds to the preferences of the median voter in a well-functioning democracy) has been almost as central to political science as the competitive market model to economics. Martin Gilens summarizes: "Under most circumstances, the preferences of the vast majority of Americans appear to have essentially no impact on which policies the government does or doesn't adopt" (2012:1). More specifically, when the preferences of the wealthy differ from those of the general public (on economic, financial, social welfare issues), public policy reflects the preferences of the wealthy, except in rare moments of radical social movements, such as the two "big bangs" of US social welfare policy in the 1930s and 1960s.

Research across European countries also finds a high degree of representational bias in favour of the wealthy. But it is typically less than in America, the difference probably reflecting more public financing for candidates, parties and media in Europe and therefore somewhat less dependence on private donors (Rosset et al., 2011; Mandle, 2004).

On both sides of the Atlantic we seem to be caught in a vicious circle, such that economic inequality generates inequality of governmental responsiveness, producing policies which favour the wealthy and disfavour poorer citizens, most of the time (Bartels, 2008; Hager, 2009). Breakaway nationalism, alienation, and antagonism to immigrants, minorities and governments are the all too common responses. Long ago Louis Brandeis (justice of the US Supreme Court from 1916 to 1939) urged: "We must make our choice. We may have democracy, or we may have wealth concentrated in the hands of a few, but we can't have both."

Wealth concentrated in the hands of a few reinforces institutional arrangements which keep sluicing pre-tax incomes upwards, often by enabling interlocking elites to create self-serving arrangements for themselves (far from "free markets"). Think of the elite networks of Wall Street, Washington, big agriculture, big energy, big universities (Brooks, 2014; Wedel, 2009). These privilege-protecting networks extend far beyond national boundaries, and coordinate national politics to advance the interests of the owners and managers of capital in high profits and low taxes, everywhere. The "mega-regional" trade deal currently under negotiation called the Transatlantic Trade and Investment Partnership (TTIP) is a case in point. Corporations on both sides of the Atlantic, including European giants like Siemens and France's Veolia, are pressing for new privileges to take direct action against states that dare to threaten their profits by protecting employment, the environment and health rights. The deal is intended to strengthen the ratchet under corporate profits; to boost western business' "ability to compete with states" and limit "politicians' real impact on the economic life of a country", in Bernard Arnault's approving words.

Another part of the same syndrome is expanding acceptability of tax avoidance and wealth concealment. Rich people at London dinner parties boast that they pay almost no tax anywhere; and their tax lawyers boast that they can ensure this result with no risk of penalties (personal communications, June 2014). They seem entirely untroubled by the social implications of their actions. Zucman's research reported earlier testifies to the magnitude of this behaviour.

The future of inequality

For all the recent national and global attention to inequality, the chances that it will be curbed to a significant degree appear to be slim. The policies and institutions of the post-war decades which helped to drive inequality down – including high upper-bracket tax rates, laws protecting trade union bargaining power, financial sector constraints, capital controls, fixed exchange rates, and Left political parties which were left-wing (in contrast to today) – could not have happened without *elites being deeply fearful* of mass unrest, based on fresh memories of the Depression and war, strong trade unions, and the nuclear-armed Soviet Union providing an apparently plausible alternative to capitalism. As these fears waned, higher capital mobility generated competition between jurisdictions to offer favourable conditions, including "light touch" regulation, free capital mobility, privatization (of housing, energy, transport, children's homes, adult social care), anti-union laws, pro-CEO-remuneration laws, and tax cuts on the rich and rises in indirect taxes (including the energy and water fees customers pay to the now-privatized utilities).

To the extent that western elites after the 1970s identified inequality as a problem, they domesticated it as "poverty"; reducing inequality meant reducing poverty. The middle-class professionals who staff the commentariate, the higher offices of state and the agenda-setting organizations like the OECD, the IMF and the World Bank are comfortable talking about helping "the poor", "the other"; and all the major religions, as well as secular humanist philosophy, enjoin help for "the (deserving) poor". Providing universal access to basic services and safety nets allows them to airbrush away the larger distribution structure. For if that larger structure is presented as a problem, then they themselves are part of the problem. Reducing inequality might mean taxing them and lifting up those not far below in the hierarchy, reducing the gap – threatening their status.

This helps to explain why self-styled centre-left parties have in recent decades made a tactical choice not to emphasise dangers of rising inequality. In the words of Roger Liddle, one of the principal strategists of the British New Labour Party:

> "In the mid-1990s, the leaders of New Labour made a fundamental policy choice. In government [they had been out of government since 1979] they would not explicitly prioritise a lessening of inequalities between top and bottom. Instead their social justice priorities would be to tackle poverty, worklessness and economic and social exclusion.
>
> Several reasons were clearly important in Labour making this choice.... [First, a sense] that intellectually Thatcherite neoliberalism was triumphant, and that the post-war welfare state consensus had irretrievable broken down and could only be rebuilt on a basis that incentivised (and did not penalise) hard work at all levels of society.
>
> [Second], New Labour ... seized on the discourse of globalisation to provide a deeper intellectual rationale.... New Labour portrayed globalisation as an inexorable force of nature beyond political control – making irrelevant old egalitarian and interventionist social democratic responses

> and requiring a thorough rethink of the means of achieving social justice, if not a redefinition of its goals" (2007: 2).

But it was not just a matter of tactics. Leading centre-left figures really did believe in a moral society similar to that of conservatives: one in which, to quote two British theorists of the "Third Way", "the key to justice as fairness can be seen in terms of the procedural securing of *opportunities* rather than a substantive commitment to patterned relative *outcomes*" (Buckler and Dolowitz, 2000, emphasis added).

Another leading intellectual on the British centre-left, Will Hutton, likewise defines "fairness" as rewarding individuals in proportion to the amount of discretionary effort they deploy to achieve socially useful results, provided they actually achieve them. The aim of a centre-left government should be to make access to riches dependent on "talent, effort and virtue", as distinct from making outcomes more equal (Hutton, 2010).

But for all that it has been vital to the center-left's defence for ignoring inequality of outcomes, the rationale for prioritising equality of opportunity over outcomes bears little scrutiny. Research shows children of wealthy parents have far wider market opportunities than children of poor or middle-class parents, through multiple channels (Summers, 2014; Boucher, 2013).

An agenda

The key lesson from Piketty's book is that, at present and likely future levels of income and wealth concentration, capitalism is losing its core claim to legitimacy – that it provides incentives for hard work, entrepreneurialism and innovation while at the same time it defends individual liberties and ensures a sufficiently equal distribution of material benefits to sustain a social compact between classes and protection to those near the bottom of the income scale. The evidence is fairly clear that income concentration at or above present Anglo levels tends to depress economic growth; worsens public health and a range of social problems across the society, not just among the poor; and strengthens political capture by the rich, whose policy preferences tend to reinforce income inequality. The evidence is also fairly clear that inequality can be reduced without the societal costs of doing so outweighing the societal benefits.

Piketty's main proposal – a global wealth tax – is easily dismissed as utopian. *The Economist* sniffs that "Mr Piketty's focus on soaking the rich smacks of socialist ideology, not scholarship" (*Economist,* 2014). But it is not as utopian as might be thought at first glance. The US government taxes citizens wherever they live and work in the world. In recent years the government has elicited "cooperation" from several key foreign jurisdictions, notably Switzerland, to comply with US standards and hand over bank details of American citizens. A global wealth tax could build on this cooperation (Crook, 2014b). A necessary condition is a global registry of wealth similar to land registries, which countries have had for centuries. Recording who owns the world's equities and bonds would make tax evasion a lot more difficult (Zucman, 2013).

Also, national governments could feasibly do more to tax wealth than at present without waiting for international cooperation across tax jurisdictions – and then cut income tax or value-added tax (Morgan and Guthrie, 2011). For example, the UK tax system presently encourages people to own big houses, because high value houses are taxed (by Council Tax) much less as a proportion of their market price than cheap ones (Dixon, 2014). It would be quite feasible for the government to levy a flat percent of the price of the house; or at least place an extra levy on Council Tax for houses owned by "non-doms" who live in the UK but are not domiciled for tax purposes. New York City's former mayor Michael Bloomberg pays property taxes on his $20 million London house of a mere $3,430 a year. The government should also place an extra levy on empty properties, which currently enjoy a Council Tax *discount*. The latter is particularly egregious, because – in wealthier parts of London – houses and apartments have become a place for the world's super-rich to park their money at an annual rate of return of 10 percent, rather than a place to live. The minimal tax paid by those treating real estate like a global reserve currency gets reflected in failing public services, including a school capacity shortfall in London projected to be 90,000 places by 2015 (Goldfarb, 2013).

However, the focus on wealth distribution does miss an important point. If we take Piketty's figures at face value and put aside Zucman's evidence on income and wealth concealment, then only about a third of the income of the top 1% (in US) is capital income; two thirds is "labour" income – e.g. super-salaries and super-bonuses. Trends in market income distribution (before tax) are driven more by the determinants of labour income distribution than wealth distribution, so far. Remedies for soaring income concentration have to tackle labour income concentration, which is not directly hit by wealth taxes.

To have a hope of reversing the trends we must aim to limit the scope for the owners and managers of big capital to control society in their search for higher productivity and expansion into new areas of geographic and sectoral commercialization. That means rejecting or reframing a set of commonplace ideas that have served to obscure this fundamental point. They include: economics is a value-neutral study of choice in conditions of scarcity (DeMartino and McCloskey, 2014); the economy is a self-equilibrium system into which the state sometimes "intervenes", often dysfunctionally; more equality of "opportunity" can substitute for more equality of outcomes; "labour" is a commodity, as in "labour has a price, just like pork"; austerity is expansionary, as in "Austerity is the only cure for the Eurozone", in the words of German Finance Minister Wolfgang Schauble (2011); financial markets, including currency markets, "get the prices right", in the same way as normal goods markets; more equality of income is to be achieved by "redistribution" through the tax and benefit system and not by "predistribution" to change the policies, laws and institutions that shape market income; and finally, "we must go beyond left and right".

Finance must be curbed, but in simple ways, not in the manner of the Dodd-Frank Act, whose 848 pages contain holes big enough to drive a coach and horses through. The core de-financialization prescription is simple: end the subsidies to banks thought too big to fail (the Bank of England calculates that the world's 29 most significant banks received around half of their profits from these subsidies in 2002-2007); and more broadly, "force banks to fund themselves with equity to a far greater extent than they do today", with a true leverage ceiling no greater than 10 to one (Wolf, 2014c; also Alcaly, 2014).

The danger in the current orgy of law- and rulemaking around finance and monetary policy is not only that it makes things too complex to work. It is also that it focuses on only one wing of the bird. The other more neglected wing is the global monetary system. The magnitude of the booms in housing and other asset markets through the 2000s in the US and southern Europe could not have occurred without giant current account deficits and accompanying capital inflows. The protracted recession in the Eurozone since 2008 has been caused in significant part by Germany's chronic black hole of demand, in the form of ballooning current account surpluses, which in 2014 might amount to 8 percent of GDP; yet the German government holds up Germany as a model for others to emulate.

The magnitude of the booms over the 2000s in many other countries could not have occurred without vast short-term capital carried from low interest rate countries to countries with inflation-fighting high interest rates, thereby appreciating the currency of the latter and worsening their current account deficits (Wade, 2009). (Iceland is a classic case: Sigurgeirsdottir and Wade, 2014.) The *Financial Times* highlights the problem in an editorial which begins, "The past couple of months have been one of those rare and precious times when foreign exchange markets move the way they are supposed to" (*Financial Times,* 2014b).

No amount of Dodd-Frank-type financial regulation could have done much to check the destabilizing effects coming from unreformed international capital markets.

So regulation of the financial sector must be complemented by substantial reforms in the global monetary system aimed at limiting the size of current account imbalances and limiting the movement of exchange rates in the wrong direction. This means further legitimizing national governments' use of quantitative restrictions on capital mobility, and moving to "a system of managed flexible exchange rates which aims for a rate that is consistent with a sustainable current-account position" (UNCTAD, 2009:127).

At a more abstract level of analysis, we must reframe the whole discussion of state and market, in at least two ways. First, change the prevailing narrative of "deregulation" as "more free market" and "regulation" as "more state". Even people on the left use this framing, as in: "We need regulation to curb the dangers of free markets." But it is misleading. The issue is not regulation or deregulation, because there is no such thing as a free or unregulated market. The crucial but neglected question is: regulation to benefit whom, regulation in line with broadly shared social values or in line with the preferences of the wealthy elite? The call for "market deregulation" is often a smokescreen; it tends to conceal continuing state actions (policies and institutions of the "pre-distribution" kind) that directly and indirectly drive money and power up. Second, insist that "market" means not only private (profit-maximizing) companies but also social enterprises, cooperatives and limited liability low-profit companies; and insist that public bodies outsourcing contracts weigh not just the cheapness of the bid but also the benefits of mutualism, permanence and participation. An expanding sector of social enterprises and low-profit companies is a bottom-up means of limiting the power of capital to control society.

But at least in the United States and the United Kingdom, the twin centers of global finance and setters of global rules, much of this agenda will remain written on sand until there are tighter limits on private spending for political parties, candidates and electoral advertising. Without tighter limits on private spending democratic politics will continue to produce strong representational bias in favour of the wealthy, as wealth begets influence and influence begets wealth. Yet when the UK Committee on Standards in Public Life published "Political Party Finance: Ending the Big Donor Culture" in November 2011, and the prime minister presented it to parliament, the report died on the day of presentation. None of the parties wanted to run with its proposals for limiting the role of big donors.

So we come back to the essentially political question: if the inequality-reducing measures of the 1930s to the 1960s came about because governing elites were fearful, what kinds of threats might induce a similar response today? The system we call "capitalism" has demonstrated a striking ability to adapt, and within its capacious boundaries are varieties a lot less prone to rising inequality than the Anglo variety has been. But pessimistic news about reining in Anglo inequality comes recently from Amazon. For years Hawkings' *A Brief History of Time* held the record for least number of pages read (on e-books); the average reader quit around page 16. Piketty has broken the record; the average reader quits around page 12 (http://online.wsj.com/articles/the-summers-most-unread-book-is-1404417569).

References

Alcaly, R., 2014, "The right way to control the banks", New York Review of Books, June 5-18, p.59-60.

Baker, D., 2011, *The End of Loser Liberalism*, Center for Economic Policy Research, Washington DC.

Barker, G. 2014, "The shark is dead but the price has a bite", Financial Times, July 2, p.10.

Bartels, L., 2008, *Unequal Democracy: The Political Economy of the New Gilded Age*, New York: Russell Sage Foundation.

Boucher, J. 2013, "We can't ignore the evidence: genes affect social mobility", *Prospect*, November 14.

Brooks, D. 2014, "America's new right", New York Times, June 11.

Brown, A., 2014, "Pope Francis condemns inequality, thus refusing to play the game", Guardian, April 28.

Buckler, S. and P. Dolowitz, 2000, "Theorizing the Third Way: New Labour and Social Justice", Journal of Political Ideologies 5, no.3: 301-20.

Buiter, W., 2007, Economists Forum, *Financial Times*, Feb 14.

Cassidy, J. 2014, "Forces of divergence", *New Yorker*, March 31.

Crook, C. 2014a, "The most important book ever is all wrong", BloombergView, Apr 20.

Crook, C. 2014b, "Piketty's wealth tax isn't a joke", BloombergView, May 11.

http://www.bloombergview.com/articles/2014-05-11/picketty-s-wealth-tax-isn-t-a-joke

Cyran, O. 2013, "The social partnership breaks up", Le Monde Diplomatique (English), October, p.10-11.

DeMartino, G. and D. McCloskey (eds), 2014, *Oxford Handbook of Professional Economists' Ethics*, Oxford University Press.

Dixon, H. 2014, "How to fix Britain's housing crunch", *International New York Times*, June 9, p.18.

Eaton, G., 2014, "Stuck on a burning platform", New Statesman, 20-26 June, p.9.

Economist, 2014, "A modern Marx", May 3.

Elliott, L., 2014, "That's rich: FT critic of Piketty accused of errors of his own", *Guardian*, 30 May, p.12.

Farrant, A. and E. McPhail, 2010, "Does F.A. Hayek's *Road to Serfdom* deserve to make a comeback?", Challenge 53 (4), July-August, 96-120.

Financial Times, 2014a, "Big questions hang over Piketty's work", editorial, 27 May.

Financial Times, 2014b, "Currencies and global growth", editorial, September 12.

Frank, T., 2012, *Pity the Billionaire*, London: Harvill Secker.

Gilens, M. 2012, *Affluence and Influence*, Princeton University Press.

Goldfarb, M. 2013, "London's great exodus", *New York Times*, October 14.

Hager, N. 2009, *The Hollow Men: A Study in the Politics of Deception*. Craig Potton Publishing, Nelson, New Zealand.

Halimi, S., 2013, "Tyranny of the one per cent", *Le Monde Diplomatique (English),* May.

Halimi, S., 2014, "A world run for shareholders", Le Monde Diplomatique (English), June.

Heath, A. 2014, "Thomas Piketty's best-selling post-crisis manifesto is horrendously flawed", The Telegraph, Apr 29

Henwood, D., 2014, "The top of the world", Bookforum.com, April/May.

Hutton, W. 2010, *Them and Us: Changing Britain – Why We Need A Fair Society*. London: Little, Brown.

Katz, L. 2014, "America's jobs and inequality challenges", Harvard Business School, April 10, at hbs.edu/faculty/conferences/2014-business-beyond-the-private-sector

Klitgaard, R., 1991, *Tropical Gangsters*. Basic Books.

Konczal, M. 2014, "Studying the rich", Boston Review, April 29.

Krugman, P., 2014, "Paranoia of the plutocrats", *New York Times*, January 26.

Krugman, P. 2014b, "Wealth over work", New York Times, March 23.

Liddle, R., 2007, "Creating a culture of fairness. A progressive response to income inequality in Britain", Policy Network, London, December.

Lucas, R., 2004, "The industrial revolution: past and future", *2003 Annual Report Essay*, Federal Reserve Bank of Minneapolis, May.

Mandle, J. 2004, "The politics of democracy", *Challenge*, Jan-Feb, 53-63.

Milanovic, B., 2011, *The Haves and the Have-Nots.* Basic Books.

Milanovic, B., 2014, "My view on Piketty's critique by the FT", Mike Norman Economics, May 25.

Mirachi, J. 1988, cartoon, *New Yorker* , September 26.

Morgan, G. and S. Guthrie, 2011, *The Big Kahuna: Turning Tax and Welfare in New Zealand on its Head,* The Morgan Foundation, Wellington.

Munchau, W., 2014, "Europe faces the horrors of its own house of debt", Financial Times, 16 June.

Obama, B., 2013, speech to Town Hall Education Arts Recreation Campus, 4 December.

Norris, F. 2014, "American confidence is finally growing, but there's a catch", New York Times, June 28-29.

Ostry, J. et al., 2014, "Redistribution, inequality, and growth", IMF Staff Discussion Note, SDN/14/02, International Monetary Fund, Washington DC.

Palley, T. 2014, "The accidental controversialist: deeper reflections on Thomas Piketty's 'Capital'", at www.thomaspalley.com/?p=422, April 25.

Perkins, T., 2014, letter, *Wall St Journal*, January 24.

Piketty, T. 2014, *Capital in the Twenty-First Century*. Cambridge: Harvard University Press.

Plender, J., 2014, "The crisis shows moral capital is in secular decline", *Financial Times*, 10 June, p.13.

Porter, E. 2014, "For many, education is hardly equal", International New York Times, 10 September, p.15.

Rashbrooke, M.(ed), 2013, *Inequality: A New Zealand Crisis*, Bridget Williams Books, Wellington.

Rosset, J., N. Giger, J. Bernauer, 2011, "Political representation of the poor and economic inequality: a comparative analysis". Paper for 3-Lander-Tagung, Basel, 13-14 January.

Schauble, W., 2011, "Austerity is the only cure for the Eurozone", *Financial Times*, September 5.

Sigurgeirsdottir, S. and R. H. Wade, 2014, "From control by capital to control of capital: Iceland's boom and bust, and the IMF's unorthodox rescue package", *Review of International Political Economy*, 21 (4): 1-31.

Stiglitz, J., 2012, *The Price of Inequality*. Penguin, UK

Summers, L., 2014, "The rich have advantages that money cannot buy", *Financial Times*, June 8.

Tett, G. 2014, "An unequal world is an uncharted economic threat", *Financial Times*, 5 September.

UNCTAD, 2009, *Trade and Development Report, 2009*, Geneva.

Wade, R. H., 2007, "Should we worry about income inequality?", in *Global Inequality*, ed. D. Held and A. Kaya, 104-31. Cambridge: Polity.

Wade, R.H., 2009, "From global imbalances to global reorganizations", *Cambridge J. of Economics*, 33: 539-62.

Wade, R. H., 2011, "Global trends in income inequality: what is happening and should we worry?", *Challenge*, September-October, 54-75.

Wade, R. H., 2012, "Why has income inequality remained on the sidelines of public policy for so long?", *Challenge*, 55, 3, May-June, pp.5-20.

Wade, R.H. 2013, "How high inequality plus neoliberal governance weakens democracy", Challenge, 56 (6): 5-37.

Wade, R. H., 2014, "The strange neglect of income inequality in economics and public policy", in Giovanni Andrea Cornia and Frances Stewart (eds.), *Towards Human Development: New Approaches to Macroeconomics and Inequality*, Oxford University Press, pp. 99-121.

Wedel, J. 2009, *Shadow Elite*. Basic Books, New York.

Wilkinson, R. and K. Pickett, 2009, *The Spirit Level*, Allen Lane.

Wolf, M., 2014a, "'Capital in the Twenty-first Century' by Thomas Piketty", *Financial Times*, April 15.

Wolf, M., 2014b, "A more equal society will not hinder growth", *Financial Times*, April 23.

Wolf, M., 2014c, "Call to arms", *Financial Times*, September 4, p.11.

World Economic Forum, 2012, *Global Risks, 7th edition*.

Worstall, T., 2014, "Why Thomas Piketty's global wealth tax won't work", *Forbes*, 30 March.

Zucman, G., 2013, "The missing wealth of nations: Are Europe and the U.S. net debtors or net creditors?", *Quarterly J. Economics*, 1321-64.

Egalitarianism's latest foe: a critical review of Thomas Piketty's *Capital in the Twenty-First Century*

Yanis Varoufakis[1] [University of Athens, Greece and University of Texas at Austin, USA]

1. Introduction

> "The rich... divide with the poor the produce of all their improvements. They are led by an invisible hand to make nearly the same distribution of the necessaries of life which would have been made, had the earth been divided into equal proportions among all its inhabitants and thus without intending it, without knowing it, advance the interest of the society, and afford means to the multiplication of the species." Adam Smith, *The Theory of Moral Sentiments*, Part IV Chapter 1

> "For he that hath, to him shall be given: and he that hath not, from him shall be taken even that which he hath." Mark, *King James Bible*, 1611, 4:25

Adam Smith's optimism and its vulgar neoliberal reincarnation, the 'trickle down effect', are thankfully on the back foot these days, steadily losing ground to a more 'biblical' narrative (see Mark 4:25 above[2]). The Crash of 2008, the bailouts that followed, and the 'secular stagnation' which is keeping the wage share at historic lows (at a time of conspicuous QE-fuelled, bubble-led, asset-price inflation), have put paid to the touching belief that the 'invisible hand', left to its own devices, distributes the fruits of human endeavour more evenly across humanity.

---

[1] Thanks are due to Joseph Halevi, for steering my thinking, and to James Galbraith for commenting extensively an earlier draft. Errors are, naturally, mine

[2] Of course when Mark was prognosticating that more will be given to the 'haves', and taken away from the 'have nots', he was not referring to wealth, but to understanding, wisdom, propriety. Still, the quote fits recent wealth and income dynamics so well that it would seem a pity not to employ it in this context.

The commercial and discursive triumph of Thomas Piketty's *Capital in the Twenty-First Century* symbolises this turning point in the public's mood both in the United States and in Europe. Capitalism is, suddenly, portrayed as the purveyor of intolerable inequality which destabilises liberal democracy and, in the limit, begets chaos. Dissident economists, who spent long years arguing in isolation against the trickle-down fantasy, are naturally tempted to welcome Professor Piketty's publishing phenomenon.

The sudden resurgence of the fundamental truth that the best predictor of socio-economic success is the success of one's parents, in contrast to the inanities of human capital models, is undoubtedly uplifting. Similarly with the air of disillusionment with mainstream economics' toleration of increasing inequality evident throughout Professor Piketty's book. And yet, despite the soothing effect of Professor Piketty's anti-inequality narrative, this paper will be arguing that *Capital in the Twenty-First Century* constitutes a disservice to the cause of pragmatic egalitarianism.

Underpinning this controversial, and seemingly harsh, verdict, is the judgment that the book's:

- chief theoretical thesis requires several indefensible axioms to animate and mobilise three economic 'laws' of which the first is a tautology, the second is based on an heroic assumption, and the third is a triviality;
- economic method employs the logically incoherent tricks that have allowed mainstream economic theory to disguise grand theoretical failure as relevant, scientific modelling;
- vast data confuses rather than enlightens the reader, as a direct result of the poor theory underpinning its interpretation;
- policy recommendations soothe our ears but, in the end, empower those who are eager to impose policies that will further boost inequality;
- political philosophy invites a future retort from the neoliberal camp that will prove devastating to those who will allow themselves to be lured by this book's arguments, philosophy and method.

2. Conflating wealth with capital

Teaching economics to undergraduates requires, as a first step, 'deprogramming' them. To relate properly the concept of economic rent, we must first expunge from students' minds the everyday meaning of 'rent'. Similarly, with economic (as opposed to accounting) cost, profit etc. But perhaps the hardest concept to convey to students is that of capital.

To understand what capital means in the context of either classical or neoclassical economics, students must leave outside the seminar room's door their preconception that capital means 'money' or assets expressed in money terms. Instead, they need to embrace the idea of capital as scarce goods that have been produced so as to be enlisted in the production of other goods; "produced means of production" as we keep repeating hoping that repetition will help free our students' thinking from their urge to conflate a firm's or nation's (a) capital and (b) the total value of its marketable assets.[3]

Professor Piketty has no such need to deprogram his readers. For he is himself defining capital as the sum of the net worth of all assets (excluding human skills and labour power) that can be sold and bought courtesy of well-defined property rights over them, measured in terms of their net market price (minus, that is, of any debt liabilities). From this prism, aggregate capital (of a person, a company or a nation) is the sum of the market prices of not only robotic assembly lines and tractors but also of assets like shares, stamp collections, paintings by Van Gogh, the equity that people have in their house (i.e. its price minus any outstanding loan on it).[4]

Deprogramming our students so that they can tell the difference between capital and wealth, in a manner that Professor Piketty eschews *vis-à-vis* his readers, is hard and dispiriting work which we would rather avoid doing. But

---

[3] Taking students further from capital as 'produced means of production' to Karl Marx's idea that capital is, besides steam engines and harvesters, a 'social relation' between people, requires a degree of de-programming that most lecturers have no time to effect.

[4] Professor Piketty chooses not to include consumer durables in his 'capital' measure. So, washing machines do not count and nor do cars, unless they have become antiques and can be sold by auction to some collector.

we do it with good cause: for without such de-programming, it is impossible to introduce an audience to anything resembling a coherent theory of production and prices.

Collecting stamps is a romantic and, in many ways worthy, pursuit. It can also be quite profitable. Similarly with art collections. Or a garage full of Ferraris. Nevertheless none of these assets can be enlisted as inputs into some production process. Even if a photographic book is to be published depicting such a collection, we need machinery, paper, ink etc. to produce it. Capital goods (in the sense of 'produced means of production') must be blended in with human labour to produce the album. Otherwise, however splendid the collection may be, it will not produce anything beyond itself.

In short, production and growth depends on material or physical capital. And while capital is a form of wealth, a great deal of wealth is not a form of capital; i.e. it is not an input into any production process generating hitherto non-existent commodities. Thus, the growth of an economy cannot rely on wealth. It needs a *particular* kind of wealth: capital goods. So if we conflate capital with wealth, our theory of production will suffer to the extent that we will have wilfully misspecified a key input, mistaking all increases in wealth as increases in capital's contribution to the production process.

In 2010, many rich Greeks escaping the crisis that had just engulfed their country took their savings to London and bought princely homes in Belgravia and Holland Park, bidding up London's house prices in the process. Inadvertently they boosted Professor Piketty's measure of the UK's aggregate capital. But if an econometrician were to use this measure in some aggregate production function of the British economy, expecting an uptick in GDP, she would be mightily disappointed and would find it impossible to estimate her model's parameters properly. While Professor Piketty can argue that his definition of capital is logically consistent, it is nevertheless incapable of helping us understand the link between capital and GDP, or between increases in the stock of capital, its 'price' and growth; a link that is, as we shall see below (see Section 3), crucial for Professor Piketty's own narrative.

Once a problematic definition of aggregate capital is embedded in an analysis, the problems spread out to the definition of the return to capital. When a capital good has a physical form, we more or less know its material utility since it is a technical matter to work out, e.g., how much electricity an electricity generator produces per hour per given quantities of diesel. But what is the return to an art collection that the collector is not auctioning off? Or to an owner-occupied home in which a family insists on living? Indeed, what is the rationale of treating (as Professor Piketty must do, to remain consistent with his wealth-capital conflation) the income of a stamp collector from trading in stamps as a return to capital (and not as income from work) while the super-sized bonuses of money market traders are counted not as returns to capital but, instead, as... wage income?

Naturally, Professor Piketty knows this all too well. So, why has he chosen to conflate capital and wealth? One plausible answer is that his primary concern was to present an empirical study that tracked the evolution of Western civilisation's wealth and income distributions, so as to show that inequality is spreading like a forest fire since the 1970s, reverting to 19th Century levels and trends. To do this he had no need to refer to aggregate capital at all (which is, also, impossible to quantify). However, Professor Piketty is an ambitious man and wanted to do more: he wanted to prove, as a mathematical theorem, the proposition that this historical trend of increasing inequality is capitalism's 'natural' tendency.

To achieve this proof, he needed to talk about capital as an input into the production process; as the engine of the growth that determines a society's future wealth (and, therefore, the 'laws' of the wealth distribution's evolution). Alas, this required a demonstration that his wealth-metric is interchangeable with a reliable capital-metric; a demonstration that is impossible and, therefore, never appears in the book's many pages.

Summing up, Professor Piketty's capital is a metric of wealth. A hugely important metric indeed since, in any society, relative wealth determines the relative power between those who have oodles of it and the rest who do not. Adam Smith, one may recall, made his name with a magnificent book that attempted to explain "the nature and causes of the wealth of nations". So, why did Professor Piketty not attempt to emulate the great Adam Smith, mainstream economics' patron saint, given that he, in essence, wrote a large volume on the... wealth of nations? Why did he, instead, choose the title of another classic book, *Das Kapital*, that does not reflect in the slightest the contents of his own book or the method of his approach?

One explanation is that Smith did not offer a theoretical link between capital and wealth creation that can have much currency in 21st Century debates.[5] A second explanation is that Smith, as the quotation at the beginning of this article reveals, had precisely the opposite perspective to that of Professor Piketty on the prospects of wealth inequality. In contrast, Marx's epic narrative on capitalism's remarkable capacity to create, simultaneously, untold wealth and unprecedented misery resonates much better with Professor Piketty's message; namely that capitalism, left unchecked, has a 'natural' tendency toward creating vast, destabilising inequality. It is therefore entirely possible that *Capital in the Twenty-First Century* had the ambition to warn a complacent society (including its über-bourgeoisie), as apocalyptically as *Das Kapital* had done in the 19th Century, about capitalism's self-defeating tendencies while, at once, rejecting Marx's analytical method, and of course his political program.

3. Professor Piketty's three economic 'laws'

To avoid following Professor Piketty in conflating wealth (W) with capital (K), and rates of return to investment in capital goods (r) with the rate at which dollar-valued wealth begets more dollar-valued wealth, the present section will be narrated in terms of a different notation that is consistent with Professor Piketty's assumptions (unlike his own notation that is designed to conflate W and K). So, where he mentions capital (K), conflating it with wealth measured at its market value, I shall refer explicitly to the latter as

[5] Indeed, Adam Smith understood perfectly well how hard it is to combine a theory of growth with a theory of the distribution of income. Indeed, Varoufakis, Halevi and Theocarakis (2011) demonstrate that this combination (i.e. a grand theory that explains both growth and distribution) is not just difficult to construct: it is, rather, impossible. We also argue that Smith, cognizant of this impossibility, chose to 'fix' his income distribution by assuming that wages are determined exogenously vis-à-vis the market mechanism (and set equal to subsistence levels defined in the realm of biology and, possibly, of social norms). (See Varoufakis et al, 2011, Chapter 3.)

wealth (W); and where he speaks of 'returns to capital', which he denotes as r, I shall use the Greek letter ρ which I shall define as the ratio of income accruing to wealth (R) over aggregate money-valued wealth (W).

Three are the 'laws' of capitalism postulated in, and making up the theoretical backbone of, *Capital in the Twenty-First Century*. The first 'law' ties together the preponderance of wealth in society's total income (ω) to its own returns per unit of income (x) and to its capacity to reproduce itself (ρ).[6] The second 'law' attempts to explain the same preponderance of wealth (ω) by linking it to net savings and growth. Finally, the third 'law' depicts the manner in which unequal wealth distributions beget even more unequal wealth distributions *via* the inheritance mechanism. In more detail:

'Law' 1: $\omega = x/\rho$, where

- ω = W/Y is the share of Wealth (W) of aggregate income Y (e.g. GDP)
- x = R/Y is the ratio of income accruing to Wealth (R) over aggregate income Y; and
- ρ = R/W is the income accruing to Wealth (R) per unit (or $1) of Wealth (W)

'Law' 2: ω rises if σ>g [or $\frac{\dot{\omega}}{\omega} = \sigma - g$] where

- σ = s/ω
- s = S/Y with S representing net aggregate savings
- g = is the proportional rate of change, over time, of aggregate income Y; i.e. $g = \frac{\dot{Y}}{Y}$

'Law' 3: ω rises in proportion to ψ-e•d [or $\frac{\dot{w}}{w} \propto \psi - e \cdot d$] where

- ψ = i/Y is the ratio of aggregate inheritance transfers (i) over aggregate income Y
- e = W_d/W_a is the ratio of wealth owned by people at the time of their death (W_d) over the mean wealth of those alive (W_a)
- d = the death rate

[6] Professor Piketty's own notation denotes my ω and x as β and α respectively.

In the Introduction I referred to the first 'law' as a tautology, to the second as reliant on a contestable assumption and to the third as trivial. That 'Law' 1 is an identity, empty of theoretical content, is self-evident,[7] as is the claim that 'Law' 3 is a simple codification of the inevitable feedback of wealth disparities when the rich bequeath their wealth to their offspring.[8] In this sense, 'Law' 2 is the theoretical 'workhorse' that energises Professor Piketty's analysis, animating his wealth dynamics with the indispensible help of a theorem (which I discuss in the next section) concerning the relationship between variables W and ρ in 'Law' 1.

'Law' 2 pivots on a crucial assumption:

An economy's aggregate net savings (S) feed fully into increases in aggregate wealth (W) (i.e. $\dot{W} = S$). Then and only then $\frac{\dot{\omega}}{\omega}$ = σ-g; i.e. the rate of growth of wealth's share of total income shall equal the difference between:

(i) the ratio σ of aggregate savings (S) over aggregate wealth (W) *and*
(ii) the economy's growth rate $g = \frac{\dot{Y}}{Y}$.

Put simply, only when net savings equal new wealth will an excess of savings per unit of wealth (σ) over and above the growth rate (g) cause the preponderance of wealth in society's total income (ω) to rise over time.[9]

The above suffices to put together, in summary form, the main analytical argument that is the foundation of Professor Piketty's book:

---

[7] Dividing both the numerator and denominator of ω = W/Y with R we get (W/R)/(R/Y). 'Law' 1 obtains from re-arranging (W/R)/(R/Y) as (R/Y)/(R/W).

[8] As long as older people's average wealth is higher than average wealth (i.e. d>1), increases in an economy's wealth preponderance (ω) boost inherited wealth per unit of overall income (ψ) that, in a never-ending cycle, reinforces ω thus increasing ψ which magnifies ω etc.

[9] Note that, by definition, $\dot{\omega} = \frac{Y \times \dot{W} - \dot{Y}W}{Y^2} = \frac{\dot{W}}{Y} - g\frac{W}{Y}$. If we then assume that $\dot{W} = S$, it turns out that $\frac{\dot{\omega}}{\omega} = \frac{S/Y}{\omega} - g = \frac{\frac{S}{Y}}{\frac{W}{Y}} - g = \frac{S}{W} - g = \sigma - g$ where s=S/Y

> We live in a low growth (g) era. Courtesy of 'Law' 2, net savings boost the wealth-to-GDP ratio (ω) because savings as a percentage of total wealth (σ) rise faster than the economy's growth rate. 'Law' 1 then kicks in. As the wealth-to-GDP ratio (ω) rises, the already wealthy acquire access to a higher rate of return to their wealth in proportion to existing wealth (i.e. ρ rises). This means that the returns to wealth also increase *vis-à-vis* national income (i.e. x rises in sympathy). Finally, 'Law' 3 ensures that the wealth-inequality-multiplier described above becomes a wealth-inequality-accelerator as inheritance permits the creation of dynastic wealth concentrations which add fuel to the inferno of in-egalitarianism. So, given the trends established during the past three decades, with savings rates at 10% and growth no more than 1.5%, capitalism's current steady state is pushing us to a situation where wealth will exceed six times GDP and the proportion of GDP that will be going to those living off wealth (as opposed to wages) will be at least one third.[10] This is an unsustainable tendency that operates like a time bomb in the foundations of liberal democracies.

Undoubtedly, those of us already convinced that global capitalism is on an unsustainable path find the above verdict plausible. Alas, lowering one's analytical guard just because one likes the offered analysis' epilogue is fraught with danger (e.g. a powerful backlash from the supporters of even greater inequality), not to mention unworthy of an inquisitive mind. Looking

---

[10] To see how these numbers are derived, we need to inspect the steady state of the differential equation time-path in 'Law' 2. If we assume $\Delta W_t = S_t$ then we can re-write this assumption as
$W_{t+1} = W_t + S_t$. Dividing both sides by $Y_{t+1} = (1 + g_t)Y_t$ we get:
$\omega_{t+1} = \frac{W_{t+1}}{Y_{t+1}} = \frac{W_t + S_t}{(1+g_t)Y_t} = \frac{1}{(1+g_t)}[\omega_t(1 + \sigma_t)]$ or $\omega_{t+1}/\omega_t = \frac{1+\sigma_t}{1+g_t}$.
In other words, in discrete time, the steady-state condition $(\omega_{t+1} = \omega_t)$ requires that $\sigma_t = g_t$ or $s_t/\omega_t = g_t$. If, as Professor Piketty suggests, our era is one in which growth is stuck at 1.5% (g=0.05) and savings ratios are stabilising at 10% of GDP (i.e. s=0.1), then global capitalism tends towards $0.1/\omega_t = 0.015$ or $\omega_t = 6.67$. Plugging $\omega_t = 6.67$ into 'Law' 1, and assuming as Professor Piketty does that the rate of return to wealth ρ is approximately 5% (i.e. ρ=0.05), then it turns out that x=0.33. This means that wealth's monetary value will tend to 670% of GDP while non-wage income (accruing to wealth assets) stabilises at one third of GDP annually.

once more at the logical structure of Professor Piketty's argument, its flimsiness becomes clear quickly.

Two are the conditions that must hold for the above storyline to hold together. One pertains to 'Law' 2 and boils down to the requirement that, as mentioned above, net savings must transform themselves, without any 'leakages', into new wealth. The second one is that, in the context of 'Law' 1, increases in ω must give rise to, or at least be consistent with, increases in ρ and in x. Below I refer to the first condition as Professor Piketty's 1st Axiom and to the second condition as his Theorem.

> **Axiom 1:** (i) All net savings become new wealth. (ii) There can be no new wealth unless there are positive net savings from which to materialise.[11]

While this axiom seems plausible, the question is whether it is consistent with the particular definition of wealth at hand. In times typified by a glut of savings (e.g. the billions of idle dollars and euros currently 'parked' with Central Banks or in zero-interest bearing accounts) and wildly fluctuating real estate prices, it seems a little *risqué* to presume that there are neither any leakages in the process transforming net savings into fresh wealth nor any instances when wealth is created in the absence of new net savings.

For example, consider Europe's periphery today, with its collapsed house prices and catastrophic falls in aggregate wealth *at a time when net savings are increasing* (as the private sector is de-leveraging). This observation should cast serious doubt on the notion that net savings translate automatically into greater wealth, as should the memory of long periods prior to 2008 when asset price inflation managed substantially to inflate wealth even though net savings were zero or even negative (e.g. in Ireland or in the

[11] Axiom 1 is somewhat reminiscent of Karl Marx's 'Fundamental Theorem' which states that all profit stems from surplus labour value and no profit can be realised in the absence of surplus labour value. Of course, Marx's proposition came in the form of a genuine theorem that Marx attempted to prove (and whose proof ended up particularly controversial, as it sparked off the so-called 'transformation problem' – see Varoufakis *et al.* 2011, Chapter 5). In Professor Piketty's case, all we have is a mere axiom that is not even discussed in any great detail, buried as it is inside the unfolding narrative.

UK during the 2001-2008 period). In other words, it is neither true that *all* new wealth springs from net savings nor that without net savings there can be no new wealth.

One possible rejoinder to the above is that wealth cannot be created out of nothing. Tell this, if you dare, to the army of financial engineers whose job is, daily, to add to paper wealth by manipulating existing bundles of debt. Of course one will rightly claim that this is not 'real' wealth. Be that as it may, this is an argument that became unavailable to Professor Piketty the moment he chose to define wealth as the sum of the net market value of all assets, excluding human skills, labour power and consumer durables. Toxic derivatives are, thus, part of his wealth stock and, for this reason, his Axiom 1, underpinning 'Law' 2, is clashing with our experience of really existing, financialised capitalism.

Another potential retort by Professor Piketty is that his 'laws' pertain only to the long run. Resisting the understandable urge to quote John Maynard Keynes regarding the fate of us all in the long term, it is an empirical fact that the 'deviations' mentioned above, which contradict his first axiom, lasted almost as long as the central empirical finding central of his book; namely, that ρ has been rising since the 1970s. If these four decades have been sufficiently long to establish his main 'empirical regularity', they are long enough to qualify as a long-term deviation, and thus refutation, of his first axiom.

Let us now turn to the second condition or prerequisite for Professor Piketty's main argument to remain valid: a positive relationship between the market value stock of wealth, W, and its self-reproductive rate, ρ (=R/W). Without this positive relationship, 'Law' 1 cannot demonstrate, as the author wants to do, that income inequality is also rising. Indeed, even if the wealth-to-GDP ratio increases, it might also be true that the return to wealth per unit of wealth (ρ) falls (as long as it is falling faster than x, the ratio of returns to wealth and GDP). Unwilling to leave that possibility open, and thus blunt his powerful storyline, Professor Piketty wants to find solid theoretical grounds in order to argue that, along with ω, x and ρ have a 'natural' tendency to rise too. Only to do this, he needs a model of ρ.

The problem with ρ, as explained in the previous section, is that its numerator (R) conflates too many disparate income streams (e.g. the proceeds from trading in junk CDOs, the profits of a factory owner, the income of a stamp collector from buying and selling stamps) while excluding other income streams that ought to be relevant (e.g. bankers' salary bonuses). This conflation makes it difficult to conjure up a model that delivers a coherent theory of ρ's fluctuations.

One of the, admittedly lesser, problems with this conflation is that it makes it next to impossible to compare Professor Piketty's theoretical results to those of other political economists who focus, as they should, on capital (as opposed to wealth) in an attempt to tell a story about its rate of return r (as opposed to ρ). For instance, Karl Marx famously and controversially predicted, on the basis of his assumption of an increasing organic composition of capital (or capital utilisation per unit of output), that the rate of return to capital, or the profit rate, would be in a secular decline (the infamous 'falling rate of profit' hypothesis). Confusingly, it is perfectly possible to have a macro-economy in which both Marx's r falls in the long term while Piketty's ρ is rising in the long term. Similarly with John Maynard Keynes' 'euthanasia of the rentier' hypothesis, which proposes a negative relationship between K and r, and prognosticates that a society that mechanises and automates production will be typified by a falling r. This hypothesis too can be reconciled with a rising ρ. After all, has ρ not been rising inexorably since 2008 while r (at least in its guise as the Central Banks' real overnight interest rate) has hit the 'lower zero bound'?

None of these qualms seem, however, to have impeded Professor Piketty's commitment to telling a determinate story regarding the determination of his ρ, as a prelude to 'closing' his model of wealth and income dynamics in a manner reinforcing his argument that ω, ρ and x (see 'Law' 1) have a tendency to rise all at once. In a spectacular, and stunningly unacknowledged, move, the purpose of which is to provide him with the missing theory of the determination of ρ, he shifts surreptitiously from his ρ to the economists' r (be they neoclassical, Marxist or Keynesian). All of a sudden (around p.216), his rate of return to money-valued wealth is treated as if it were the rate of return to the type of physical capital goods that one comes across in standard neoclassical textbooks. Why? Because Professor

Piketty wants to borrow from the latter their determinate theory of r, his hidden assumption being that r and ρ are either the same or highly correlated.

4. The slide to vulgar neoclassicism

Honouring a long tradition of mainstream economics (and corporate accounting for that matter), according to which the modeller's ends justify his underlying assumptions, Professor Piketty picks the one aggregate production function in neoclassical textbooks which delivers the relationship between K and r that he needs – and which he uses to tie up his wealth (W) metric with wealth's rate of reproduction (ρ). His pick is the CES (constant elasticity of substitution) aggregate production function that can deliver K and r values that move in unison as long as the elasticity of substitution of capital and labour in the production of given units of output is greater than one.

Suppose that aggregate output:

$$Y = \left\{\alpha K^{\frac{\varepsilon-1}{\varepsilon}} + (1-\alpha)L^{\frac{\varepsilon-1}{\varepsilon}}\right\}^{\frac{\varepsilon}{\varepsilon-1}}$$

where α is an exogenous share parameter and ε is the elasticity of substitution between capital input (K) and labour input (L) for the production of the same output. The first order derivative of output w.r.t K. i.e. the marginal product of capital (MP_K), equals $\alpha(K/Y)^{(-1/\varepsilon)}$.

> **Theorem:** The rate of return to capital, r, is determined by its marginal productivity and, thus, $r = \alpha(K/Y)^{(-1/\varepsilon)}$.

The proof of this standard neoclassical theorem requires two familiar axioms that, intriguingly, never get much of a mention in *Capital in the Twenty-First Century*:

Axiom 2: Aggregate capital K is an independent variable in the determination of the rate of return to capital r (in the sense that r is not necessary in the measurement of K).

Axiom 3: Labour has, in the following sense, precisely zero bargaining power in the determination of wages and employment levels: Wages are determined *as if* by some large-scale, economy-wide auction in which workers pile up the labour services they want to rent out and allow employers to bid for them, settling a wage that (i) reflects labour's marginal product and (ii) clears the labour market. Then, given that equilibrium wage, employers choose freely how much labour, or employment, to hire; i.e. they select the point on their labour demand curve that corresponds to the equilibrium wage.

Even with Axioms 2 and 3 in place, sufficing to prove Theorem 1, to have any relevance to the preceding analysis of a society's wealth dynamics, the above results must be augmented by Axiom 4:

Axiom 4: K equals (or is highly correlated with) W and r equals (or is highly correlated with) ρ.

Of course, Professor Piketty does not need to make Axiom 4 explicit as he has already subsumed it by adopting K and r to refer, respectively, to W and ρ throughout his book. With this sleight of hand, and the rest of the axioms in place, he can now argue that:

$$\rho=r=\alpha(K/Y)^{(-1/\varepsilon)}=\alpha(W/Y)^{(-1/\varepsilon)}=\alpha\omega^{(-1/\varepsilon)}.$$

Substituting into 'Law' 1 (see previous section), he finds that $x=\alpha\omega^{(\varepsilon-1)/\varepsilon}$. All he now needs in order to complete his narrative is Axiom 5 below:

Axiom 5: The elasticity of substitution (ε) in our economies' production function exceeds unity.

Indeed, if $\varepsilon>1$ then ρ,ω and x all rise together, as Professor Piketty believes is capitalism's innate tendency. And what does $\varepsilon>1$ mean? At $\varepsilon=1$, the production function is of the Cobb-Douglas kind. This will not do, as such 'technology' would result in an inverse relationship between K and r. But when $\varepsilon>1$, production technology is moving toward a linear type where labour and capital can be substituted for one another at a constant rate and K and r rise or fall together. Moreover, although this is not mentioned by Professor Piketty, it can be shown that the larger ε the more the economy grows in a steady-state (see Klump and Preissler, 2000).

With the underlying model now in full view, it is possible to assess its assumptions one by one.

Axiom 1 is impossible to fathom given Professor Piketty's definition of wealth (W) and its returns (R) while Axiom 4, we have already seen (see the previous section), is hardly defensible by any school of economic thought, including the neoclassical mainstream. Axiom 5, on the other hand, is the least problematic,[12] if one is prepared to adopt Axiom 2 which is, in fact, an axiom that neoclassical research programs *must* make even though it has been shown to be logically incoherent.

Why is Axiom 2 logically incoherent? Because, as the so-called Capital Controversies revealed in the 1960s, aggregate capital (K) cannot be measured independently of its rate of return (r), in which case r cannot be said to be determined by the first order derivative of Y w.r.t K. (see Harcourt, 1972, and Cohen and Harcourt, 2003). The reason why neoclassical theorists ignore this 'small' logical difficulty, and habitually adopt Axiom 2, is that their only alternative is to abandon their neoclassical research program (e.g. to switch to a theory of production like that of Luigi Pasinetti[13]) which endows them with tremendous discursive power in the academy.[14] It would take a truly heroic disposition to do this. Professor

---

[12] Axiom 5 is the least problematic in this analysis. If we *had* to adopt a CES aggregate production function, we might as well opt for an elasticity value large enough to capture the fact that, in the real world, it is often impossible smoothly to substitute labour with capital while affecting output.

[13] See Pasinetti (1977,1983).

[14] For an analysis of the sociology of knowledge behind this 'choice', see Chapter 1 in Varoufakis (2013).

Piketty sides with them, in sticking to a neoclassical production function but, intriguingly, chooses to misrepresent the meaning and outcome of the Capital Controversy debates, rather than to ignore them (as is the neoclassical 'practice').[15]

Of Professor Piketty's five axioms, Axiom 3 is the most revealing since it shows his economics to be not merely neoclassical but a species of antiquated, vulgar neoclassicism. By assuming wage-taking firms and workers, on the one hand he succeeds in determining ρ in a manner that is consistent with a rising ω and x but, on the other hand, he is paying the hefty price of assuming:

(a) the impossibility of involuntary unemployment[16] (i.e. of recessions or even mild depressions, like the one Europe is now experiencing or the 'secular stagnation' we encounter today in the United States, the UK and Japan); *and*

(b) the perfect incapacity of labour to bargain collectively or to exert extra-market influence in the wage and employment determination process.

Run-of-the-mill, junior economists, who just want to 'close' some inconsequential neoclassical model and publish it in some run-of-the-mill journal (e.g. in the pursuit of tenure), can be excused for adopting Axiom 3. However, Axiom 3 has been surpassed by enlightened members of the mainstream a long time ago and to such an extent that the economics mainstream itself now rejects Axiom 3 as too uncouth. For instance Akerlof (1980, 1982) and Akerlof and Yellen (1986) showed that it is perfectly possible for involuntary unemployment to persist in neoclassical models. All it takes is an admission that wages and unemployment levels influence

[15] In his only refernce to the Cambridge Capital Controversies the author tells his reader that the objection to the neoclassical aggregate production approach had to do with a dislike of capital-labour substitutability (when the objection concerned the logical fallacy of needing to determine r before measuring K so that r can be determined). He also states, as a matter of fact, that the neoclassical argument won the argument (which, of course, it did not).

[16] Even a cursory inspection of Axiom 3 reveals that, as wages equal marginal productivity and employers are free to choose the level of employment on their labour demand curve, there can never exist a single worker willing to work for the going wage but unable to find a job.

labour productivity, a terribly uncontroversial and highly plausible assumption. Moreover, as Varoufakis (2013, Chapter 2) demonstrates, even a small degree of bargaining power on the part of a collective of workers (e.g. a trades union, an informal association) suffices to throw off the labour demand curve not only the actual levels of wages and employment but even the wage and employment *targets* of both workers and their employers. In short, *any* level of involuntary unemployment, especially when combined with *some* bargaining power in the hands of labour, radically undermines Professor Piketty' theory of income distribution.[17]

The question thus becomes: why did the author of a major treatise on global inequality adopt Axiom 3? Why did he ignore not only the compelling objections of dissident economists but also forty years of neoclassical efforts to instil a modicum of realism into neoclassical models? Does he not recognize that, as a long-standing social democrat (which Professor Piketty certainly is), he may have a certain difficulty explaining (even to himself) his:

- assumption that involuntary unemployment cannot prevail,
- unqualified adoption of Say's Law,
- implicit rejection of the notion that investment is influenced by aggregate demand,
- supposition that savings adapt to investment (rather than then the opposite); *and his*
- espousal of the type of supply-side economics that caused so much damage upon the poor whose plight his book is, ostensibly, passionately concerned with?

I have no doubt that Professor Piketty is fully aware of all of the above but, nevertheless, opted for a particularly vulgar form of neoclassicism that jars terribly with his own social democratic pedigree. The next section offers an explanation of this peculiar choice.

---

[17] Galbraith (2000) shows the importance of industry-specific labour rents.

5. Why, oh why?

Controversial assumptions have a *raison d' être* only if there is no other way (i) to generate some desired hypothesis or (ii) to 'close' one's model. In the case of Professor Piketty's controversial axioms (see previous section), it is clear that (ii) must have been his prime motivation. For if he simply wanted to make the point that wealth inequality tends to reproduce and reinforce itself, he needed none of his problematic axioms.

It is, demonstrably, a simple matter to prove that when the rich have a higher propensity to save than the average person, the chances are that their share of wealth will be rising. As long as they save more than the poor and receive total income (wage income plus returns to their wealth) well over and above the average citizen's income, the rich will find themselves on a perpetual escalator that guarantees them a constantly increasing share of aggregate wealth. And even if they enjoy *less* than half of aggregate income, it is still possible to show that their wealth share will be rising as long as their marginal propensity to save is considerably greater than that of the poorer citizens.[18] In short, none of the modelling tricks that left Professor Piketty

[18] Let γ equal the rate at which the wealth of the rich grows in relation to aggregate wealth, or

$\gamma = \frac{\Delta W^R}{\Delta W} = \frac{s^R(Y^R+R^R)}{s(Y+R)} = \xi\frac{M}{N}$ where,

W^R is the wealth of the rich

Y^R is the wage income that the rich receive

R^R is the unearned income the rich receive from owning wealth assets

s^R is the propensity to save of the rich

ξ equals s^R/s – i.e. is the ratio of the saving propensity of the rich *vis-à-vis* society's average propensity to save

$M = Y^R + R^R$ is total income of the rich

$N = Y + R$ is society's total income (from both labour and from owning wealth)

For the wealth distribution increasingly to favour the already rich, i.e. for γ>1, ξ>1 is a necessary but not sufficient condition. If M>N, then γ>1 and so the wealth distribution will be increasingly unequal, favouring the rich; that is, if the wealthy receive more than 50% of total income, and save more than average, they will own an increasing portion of society's wealth. But even if the rich receive less that 50% of societal income (i.e. if M<N), wealth will concentrate increasingly in their hands as long as $\xi > \frac{M}{N}$. For example, if the rich enjoy 40% of total income, but they save more than 12.5% of their income, when the average citizen saves only 5%, then the rich can expect to own a greater and greater portion of total wealth.

open to serious criticism in the previous section are necessary in order to show that wealth inequality tends to reinforce itself.

So, why? Why base such a weighty treatise, as *Capital in the Twenty-First Century* clearly is, on shaky theoretical foundations? If I were allowed to speculate on this question, I would be tempted to outline two reasons. One is expediency. Professor Piketty's analysis allowed him to come up with some very catchy numbers; e.g. the 'result' that when the rate of return to wealth is at its historic average of around 5%, there is a tendency for wealth to grow to more than six times the level of GDP and for income accruing to wealth to converge to one third of GDP (see note 9). This is the stuff that contributes to headlines that journalists and the wider public are eager to consume. But to come up with these numbers, and then argue that they are reflected in the empirical data, the author had to 'close' his model; he had somehow to snatch determinacy from the jaws of radical indeterminacy. And if this requires incorrigible assumptions that are ill equipped to sustain the cold light of critical analysis, one may be tempted to assume that the wider public will never know or care. Catchy numbers, in combination with excellent marketing, are bound to over-rule any objections like the ones appearing in this journal in general and in the present paper in particular.

A second, related, reason has to do with a penchant for staying clear of some fascinating, but also all-consuming, debates within political economics. To give a flavour of this, consider the only decent alternative to Professor Piketty's axioms. Without Axioms 2 and 3, for example, he would have to choose between (or some combination of):

a) the aforementioned sophisticated neoclassical theorists' models of efficiency wages and endogenous involuntary unemployment
b) analyses along the lines of Richard Goodwin and Luigi Pasinetti that demonstrate the permanence and indeterminate nature of cycles unfolding on the two-dimensional plane of growth and income distribution (see Taylor, 2014)
c) Keynes' argument that aggregate investment is perfectly capable of driving employment and aggregate income, while being *driven* by aggregate employment and income, thus giving rise to multiple

macroeconomic equilibria some of which involve permanently high unemployment, secular stagnation etc.

While (a), (b) and (c) would furnish Professor Piketty with narratives significantly more sophisticated and nuanced than his vulgar neoclassical framework, there is one thing they share that, one suspects, makes them terribly unattractive to him: they are radically indeterminate models, in the sense that they cannot offer determinate answers to the question "what will the wage share be given all the microeconomically relevant data?"

In conclusion, Professor Piketty chose a theoretical framework that simultaneously allowed him to produce catchy numerical predictions, in tune with his empirical findings, while soaring like an eagle above the 'messy' debates of political economists shunned by their own profession's mainstream and condemned diligently to inquire, in pristine isolation, into capitalism's radical indeterminacy. The fact that, to do this, he had to adopt axioms that are both grossly unrealistic and logically incoherent must have seemed to him a small price to pay.

6. Explaining the 'aberration'

Professor Piketty's empirical findings confirm the widely acknowledged fact that wealth inequality rose exorbitantly during the 19th Century but began to ebb in the 1910s, continuing its slide during the two world wars until the time the Bretton Woods system caved in. Since then, it has resumed its upward trend. If his analytics are taken for granted, accepting that inequality must normally rise and rise, then the bulk of what Eric Hobsbaum described as the Short Twentieth Century (1914-1989) manifests itself as an 'aberration'; a departure from capitalism's 'natural' tendency to boost ω at a rate maintained through the operations of ρ.

To explain this remarkable 'aberration',[19] spanning at least one sixth of the 20th Century, Professor Piketty refers his reader to the effects of the two

[19] Other authors have delved into Professor Piketty's empirics more diligently, and in greater detail, than I – see for example Galbraith (2014). My focus will, instead, be on explanations the author gives for the observed 'aberration'.

world wars on the politicians' commitment to egalitarianism, the imposition of strict capital controls by the New Dealers (which later spread worldwide under Bretton Woods), the positive effect of trades unions on the wage share, of fiscal policies that civilised society *via* progressive income taxation, etc. Undoubtedly, these factors forged a more equitable distribution of income and wealth. However, one might have expected from Professor Piketty an explanation of why these policies and institutions were in place after 1949 and why they survived until 1970 but not afterwards.

Why, for instance, were the New Dealers, as Galbraith (2014) reminds us, intent on, and capable of, preventing (both during and especially *after* the war had ended) the creation of multi-millionaires? Why were Republican administrations in the United States (e.g. under President Eisenhower) or Tory governments in Britain (e.g. under Harold Macmillan) uninterested in reversing the decline of inequality and adopting the trickle-down fantasies that prevailed after the 1970s under both Democrat and Republican, Tory and Labour (or European social democratic), administrations? Were the exogenous shocks that pushed capitalism into a more egalitarian posture occasioned by a visitation of an 'exogenous' ethical spirit upon the high and mighty, perhaps one brought on by the war? Or could the answer, instead, lie in some deeper dynamic at work that is as endogenous to capitalism as the latter's tendency to enrich the already wealthy? And could an argument be made that the said dynamic fizzled out in the 1970s for reasons that are in no sense 'natural'?

Professor Piketty, rather than attempting to tackle such questions, seems eager to transcend them by implying that the factors which caused the '20th Century aberration' had an exogenous expiry date. Once the latter arrived, inequality returned to its long-term equilibrium path. At the very least, it is comforting to note that his ironclad empirical determinism maps fully into his analytical determinism (as outlined in the previous sections), even if it throws no light on 20th Century, or early 21st Century, economic history.

Elsewhere (see Varoufakis, 2011, 2nd edition 2013), I have sought to provide the kind of answer that Professor Piketty does not. While this is not the place to offer the argument in full, it may be helpful for the reader briefly to sample *one* possible explanation of why the 20th Century was no aberration but, rather, an illustration that, while there is nothing 'natural' or deterministic about the wealth and income distributions that capitalism throws out, nevertheless coherent accounts of the feedback loop between its politics and economics are possible.

In summary, Varoufakis (2011, 2nd edition 2013) hypothesises that, having already run the war economy successfully, the New Dealers feared, with excellent cause, a post-war recession. In charge of the only major surplus economy left after the war had demolished most of Europe, they understood that the sole alternative to a global recession, which might have threatened an already weakened western capitalism, would be to strengthen aggregate demand within the United States by (a) boosting real wages and (b) recycling America's aggregate surpluses to Europe and to Japan so as to create the demand that would keep American factories going. If anything, Bretton Woods was the global framework within which this project was embedded. Its fixed exchange rates, capital controls and an underlying international consensus on labour market policies that would keep the wage share above a certain level, were all aspects of the same struggle to prevent the post-war world from slipping back into depression.

Naturally, the resulting wealth and income dynamics reduced inequality, increased the availability of decent jobs, and produced capitalism's golden age. Was this an aberration? Of course it was not! The Marshall Plan, the Bretton Woods institutions, the strict regulation of banks etc. would not have been politically feasible had capitalism not threatened to commit suicide in the late 1940s, as it does once in a while (the last episode having occurred in 2008). Were these policies and new institutions inevitable? Of course they were not! While the political interventions that had the by-product of reducing income inequality were fully endogenous to the period's capitalist dynamics, the latter are always indeterminate both in terms of the politics that they engender as well as of their economic outcomes.

Alas, Bretton Woods and the institutions the New Dealers had established in the 1940s could not survive the end of the 1960s. Why? Because they were predicated upon the recycling of American surpluses to Europe and to Asia (see above). Once the United States slipped into a deficit position, some time in 1968, this was no longer possible. America would have either to abandon its hegemonic position, together with the dollar's 'exorbitant privilege', or it would have to find another way of remaining at the centre of global surplus recycling. Or, to quote a phrase coined by Paul Volcker, "if we cannot recycle our surpluses, we might as well recycle other people's surpluses".

This is, according to my book's narrative, why the early 1970s, and the end of Bretton Woods, proved so pivotal: The United States, through its twin deficits, began to absorb from the rest of the world both net exports and surplus capital, therefore 'closing' the recycling loop. It provided net exporters (e.g. Germany, Japan and later China) with the aggregate demand they so desperately needed in return for a tsunami of foreign capital (generated in the surplus economies by their net exports to America, and to other economies energised by the United States' trade deficit).

However, for this tsunami to materialise capital controls had to go, wage inflation in the United States had to drop below that of its competitors, incomes policies had to be jettisoned, and financialisation had to be afforded its foothold. From this perspective, inequality's resurgence in the 1970s, the never-ending rise of finance at the expense of industry, and the diminution of collective agency around the world, were all symptoms of the reversal in the direction and nature of global surplus recycling. The manner in which by-product 'inequality' and by-product 'financialisation' coalesced to destabilise capitalism, until it hit the wall in 2008, is a process that several studies have thrown light on in recent times (e.g. see Galbraith, 2012). Professor Piketty's single-minded effort to construct, at any cost, a simple deterministic argument is, unfortunately, not one of them.

7. Conclusion: political repercussions in the struggle for equality and… Europe

Capital in the Twenty-First Century has been hailed as a book to turn the tide of inequality; a treatise that will blow fresh winds into egalitarianism's sails. I very much fear it will do the opposite. For two distinct reasons.

Take a brief look at today's Europe. In its periphery, proud nations are beaten into a pulp, a humanitarian crisis is on the boil and, naturally, inequality is having a field day. Why? Because of the European leaders' denial that this is a systemic crisis in need of systematic treatment and due to their insistence that the crisis was caused by too lax an imposition of the existing rules, as opposed to a faulty economic architecture and rules that were, therefore, impossible to impose once a global financial crisis hit in 2008.

Interestingly, Professor Piketty has recently assembled a group of fifteen French economists (the so-called Piketty Group) that have joined forces with a group of German economists, known as the Glienecker Gruppe, to propose institutional changes that may help resolve the Euro Crisis and return Europe on the path of stability and integration. The parallel with *Capital in the Twenty-First Century* is uncanny. Professor Piketty has a talent for making bold statements replete with good intentions. Just as he presents his *Capital* as a dagger with which to slay the abomination of unbearable inequality, so too his stated intention on Europe is to end the crisis through a recognition that:

> "...Europe's existing institutions are dysfunctional and need to be rebuilt. The central issue is simple: democracy and the public authorities must be enabled to regain control of and effectively regulate 21st century globalised financial capitalism." (Piketty, 2014)

Stirring words! Until, that is, one delves into the actual proposal. Galbraith and Varoufakis (2014), who did precisely that, show that the Piketty proposals for Europe amount to: (a) a fresh spate of universal austerity that will be felt throughout Europe, and (b) a form of political union that, as Varoufakis (2014) argues, can be described better as an 'iron cage' which extinguishes all hope that Europe may move toward a democratic federation.

Similarly with inequality. When it comes to Professor Piketty's policy recommendations for stemming inequality's triumphant march, the new idea on offer is the much-discussed proposal for a global wealth tax.[20] Most commentators have focused on its utopian nature, which is disarmingly

[20] This is not to say that Professor Piketty is renouncing older ideas, like a progressive income tax, inheritance tax etc. However, as his book is meant to be 'groundbreaking' and 'innovative' the reader naturally focuses on the new ideas and policy recommendations on offer.

acknowledged by Professor Piketty himself. I shall not do so. Rather, allow me to assume that it is feasible and that it is agreed to by, say, the G20. Consider what the implementation of this global wealth tax would mean:

Returning to the long-suffering Eurozone, let us pay a visit to one of the thousands of Irish families whose members remain unemployed, or terribly under-paid and under-employed, but whose house has 'managed' to escape the travails of negative equity. According to Professor Piketty, these wretched people should now be paying a new wealth tax on the remaining equity of their homes, in addition to their remaining mortgage repayments. Independently of their income streams!

Taking our leave from these suffering families, whom Professor Piketty's wealth tax would burden further, let us now turn to a Greek industrialist struggling to survive the twin assaults from non-existent demand and from the severe credit crunch. Let us suppose that her capital stock has not lost all of its value yet. Well, soon after Professor Piketty's policy is enacted, it most certainly will, as she must now cough up a wealth tax that is to be paid from a non-existent income stream.

How long will it take, dear reader, before committed libertarians, who believe that wealth and income inequality is not only fine but also an inevitable repercussion of liberty-at-work, latch on to the above repercussions of Professor Piketty's policy proposals? Why would they hesitate before blowing his analysis and recommended policies out of the proverbial water, castigating them as sloppy theorising leading to policies that simultaneously (a) worsen a bad set of socio-economic circumstances and (b) threaten basic liberties and rights? Moreover, is there a greater gift to committed Eurosceptics, bent on demonstrating that the European Union was a step along the road to serfdom, than Professor Piketty's proposals for the Eurozone?

Moving on to the realm of political philosophy, some years back I expressed the view that well-meaning proponents of distributive justice and equality were perhaps egalitarianism's greatest threat. Varoufakis (2002/3) argued that, for too long, western political philosophy was dominated by the clash between:

(a) those who searched ceaselessly for the holy grail of some Optimal Degree of Inequality (ODI), (e.g. Rawls, 1971), *and*
(b) libertarians insisting that there is no such thing as ODI (e.g. Nozick, 1974); that what matters instead is how just the process of wealth and income acquisition is.

Arguing from the perspective of a radical egalitarian, I conceded that the libertarians had the better tunes. That their focus on the justice of the process generating values and what distributes them (i.e. their dedication to procedural theories of justice) was significantly more interesting, useful and, indeed, progressive than the pseudo-egalitarian dedication to end-state, distributive, theories of justice. That the libertarians' readiness to separate 'good' from 'bad' inequality, rather than to treat inequality as a single, uni-dimensional metric, held more promise to those who wished to understand the vagaries, and instability, of capitalism than the social democrats' protestations that income and wealth outcomes were too unequal. That those interested in reinvigorating a pragmatic, radical egalitarianism should abandon static notions, and simple metrics, of equality.

Reading *Capital in the Twenty-First Century* reminded me of how the cause of egalitarianism is often undermined by its most famous, mainstream proponents. John Rawls, despite the elegance and sophistication of his 'veil of ignorance', did untold damage to the egalitarian 'cause' by offering a static theory of justice that crumbled the moment a talented libertarian took a shot at it. Professor Piketty's book will, I am convinced, prove even easier prey for today's, or tomorrow's, equivalent of Robert Nozick. And when this happens, the multitude that are now celebrating *Capital in the Twenty-First Century* as a staunch ally in the war against inequality will run for cover.

References

Akerlof, G and J.Yellen (1986). *Efficiency Wage Models of the Labor Market*, Cambridge: Cambridge University Press

Akerlof, G. (1980). 'A theory of social custom of which unemployment may be one consequence', *Quarterly Journal of Economics*, 94, 749-75.

Akerlof, G. (1982). 'Labor Contracts as Partial Gift Exchange', *Quarterly Journal of Economics*, 96, 543-69.

Akerlof, G. (2007).'The missing motivation of macroeconomics'. *American Economic Review*, 97, 5-36.

Cohen, A.J. and G. C. Harcourt (2003), 'Retrospectives: Whatever Happened to the Cambridge Capital Theory Controversies?', *Journal of Economic Perspectives*, 17, 199–214

Galbraith, J.K. (2000). *Created Unequal: The crisis in American pay*, Chicago: The University of Chicago Press

Galbraith, J.K. (2012). *Inequality and Instability: A study of the world economy just before the great crisis*, Oxford University Press

Galbraith, J. K. (2014). *Kapital* for the Twenty-First Century?, *Dissent*, Spring Issue, http://www.dissentmagazine.org/article/kapital-for-the-twenty-first-century (last accessed 19th September 2014)

Galbraith, J.K. and Y. Varoufakis (2014). 'Whither Europe? The Modest Camp versus the Federal Austerians', *Open Democracy*, 11th June 2014, https://opendemocracy.net/can-europe-make-it/james-galbraith-yanis-varoufakis/whither-europe-modest-camp-vs-federalist-austeri (last accessed 17th September 2014)

Harcourt, G. (1972). *Some Cambridge Controversies in the Theory of Capital.* Cambridge: Cambridge University Press

Klump, R. and H. Preissler (2000). 'CES Production Functions and Growth', *Scandinavian Journal of Economics*, 102, 41-56

Nozick, R. (1974). *Anarchy, State and Utopia*. New York: Basic Books.

Pasinetti, L. (1983). 'The Accumulation of Capital ', *Cambridge Journal of Economics,* 7, 405-11

Passinetti, L. (1977). *Lectures on the Theory of Production*, New York: Columbia University Press

Piketty, T. (2014). *Capital in the Twenty-First Century,* Cambridge, MA: Belknap Press.

Piketty, T. (2014b). 'Our manifesto for Europe', *The Guardian*, 2nd May 2014, http://www.theguardian.com/commentisfree/2014/may/02/manifesto-europe-radical-financial-democratic (Last accessed 17th September 2014)

Rawls, J. (1971). *A Theory of Justice*, Cambridge Mass.: Harvard University Press

Smith, A. (1759,1982). *The Theory of Moral Sentiments,* ed. D.D. Raphael and A.L. Macfie, vol. I of the *Glasgow Edition of the Works and Correspondence of Adam Smith,* Indianapolis: Liberty Fund

Taylor. L. (2014). 'The Triumph of the Rentier? Thomas Piketty versus Luigi Pasinetti and John Maynard Keynes', *mimeo*

Varoufakis, Y. (2002/3). 'Against Equality', *Science and Society*, 4, 448-72

Varoufakis, Y. (2011, 2nd edition 2013). *The Global Minotaur: America, Europe and the Future of the World Economy*, London and New York: Zed Books

Varoufakis, Y. (2013). *Economic Indeterminacy: A personal encounter with the economists' peculiar nemesis*, London and New York: Routledge

Varoufakis, Y. (2014). 'Can Europe escape its crisis without turning into an 'iron cage'?', mimeo, 7th September 2014, http://yanisvaroufakis.eu/2014/09/07/can-europe-escape-its-crisis-without-turning-into-an-iron-cage/ (Last accessed 17th September 2014)

Varoufakis, Y., J. Halevi and N. Theocarakis (2011). *Modern Political Economics: Making sense of the post-2008*

Piketty and the limits of marginal productivity theory

Lars Pålsson Syll [Malmö University, Sweden]

> The outstanding faults of the economic society in which we live are its failure to provide for full employment and its arbitrary and inequitable distribution of wealth and incomes ... I believe that there is social and psychological justification for significant inequalities of income and wealth, but not for such large disparities as exist today (John Maynard Keynes, *General Theory*, 1936).

Introduction

Thomas Piketty's book *Capital in the Twenty-First Century* is in many ways an impressive *magnum opus*. It's a wide-ranging and weighty book, almost 700 pages thick, containing an enormous amount of empirical material on the distribution of income and wealth for almost all developed countries in the world for the last one and a half centuries.

But it does not stop at this massive amount of data. Piketty also theorizes and tries to interpret the trends in the presented historical time series data. One of the more striking – and debated – trends that emerges from the data is a kind of generalized U-shaped Kuznets curve for the shares of the top 10 % and top 1 % of wealth and income, showing extremely high values for the period up to the first world war, and then dropping until the 1970/80s, when they – especially in the top 1% – start to rise sharply.

Contrary to Kuznets's (1955) original hypothesis, there does not seem to be any evidence for the idea that income differences should diminish *pari passu* with economic development. The gains that the increase in productivity has led to, has far from been distributed evenly in society. The optimistic view on there being automatic income and wealth equalizers, commonly held among growth and development economists until a few years ago, has been proven unwarranted.

So, then, why have income differences more or less exploded since the 1980s?

On the illusions of "marginal productivity"

In my own country, Sweden, it is pretty obvious that we need to weigh in institutional, political and social forces to explain the extraordinary increase in the functional income inequality distribution. Not the least changes in the wage negotiation system, weakened trade unions, the new "independent" role of the central bank (Riksbanken) and it's single-mindedly rigid focus on price stability, a new tax-system, globalization, financialization of the economy, neoliberal "Thatcher-Reagan" deregulations of markets, etc., etc., have profoundly influenced wealth and income distribution. What was once an egalitarian Swedish model, has during the last three decades been reduced to something more akin to the rest of continental Europe, with sharply increased income differences (especially incomes from owning capital and trading financial assets). It is difficult to imagine a sustainable explanation for the falling wages share since the 1980s – not only in Sweden, but in virtually all developed countries – that does not to a large part take account of the fight over distribution between classes in an ongoing restructuring of our society and its underlying fundamental socio-economic relationships.

Mainstream economics textbooks – Mankiw and Taylor (2011) is a typical example – usually refer to the interrelationship between technological development and education as the main causal force behind increased inequality. If the educational system (supply) develops at the same pace as technology (demand), there should be no increase, *ceteris paribus*, in the ratio between high-income (highly educated) groups and low-income (low education) groups. In the race between technology and education, the proliferation of skilled-biased technological change has, however, allegedly increased the premium for the highly educated group.

Another prominent explanation is that globalization – in accordance with Ricardo's theory of comparative advantage and the Wicksell-Heckscher-Ohlin-Stolper-Samuelson factor price theory – has benefited capital in the advanced countries and labour in the developing countries. The problem with these theories are *inter alia* that they *explicitly* assume full employment and international immobility of the factors of production. Globalization means more than anything else that capital and labour have to a large extent become mobile over country borders. These mainstream trade theories are *a fortiori* really not applicable in the world of today, and they are certainly not able to explain the international trade pattern that has developed during the last decades. Although it seems as though capital in the developed countries has benefited from globalization, it is difficult to detect a similar positive effect on workers in the developing countries (Altvater and Mahnkopf, 2002).

As Piketty shows, there are, however, also some other quite obvious problems with these kinds of inequality explanations. The impressively vast databank of information on income and inequality that Piketty has created – especially *The World Top Incomes Database* – shows, as noted, that the increase in incomes has been concentrated especially in the top 1%. If education was the main reason behind the increasing income gap, one would expect a much broader group of people in the upper echelons of the distribution taking part of this increase. It is, as recent research has shown (den Haan, 2011), dubious, to say the least, to try to explain, for example, the high wages in the finance sector with a marginal productivity argument. High-end wages seem to be more a result of pure luck or membership of the same "club" as those who decide on the wages and bonuses, than of "marginal productivity".

Mainstream economics, with its technologically determined marginal productivity theory, seems to be difficult to reconcile with reality. But walked-out Harvard economist and George Bush advisor, Greg Mankiw (2011), does not want to give up on his preferred theory that easily:

> Even if the income gains are in the top 1 percent, why does that imply that the right story is not about education?

> If indeed a year of schooling guaranteed you precisely a 10 percent increase in earnings, then there is no way increasing education by a few years could move you from the middle class to the top 1 percent.
>
> But it may be better to think of the return to education as stochastic. Education not only increases the average income a person will earn, but it also changes the entire distribution of possible life outcomes. It does not guarantee that a person will end up in the top 1 percent, but it increases the likelihood. I have not seen any data on this, but I am willing to bet that the top 1 percent are more educated than the average American; while their education did not ensure their economic success, it played a role.

A couple of years later Mankiw (2014) makes a new effort at explaining and defending income inequalities, this time invoking Adam Smith's invisible hand:

> [B]y delivering extraordinary performances in hit films, top stars may do more than entertain millions of moviegoers and make themselves rich in the process. They may also contribute many millions in federal taxes, and other millions in state taxes. And those millions help fund schools, police departments and national defense for the rest of us ...
>
> [T]he richest 1 percent aren't motivated by an altruistic desire to advance the public good. But, in most cases, that is precisely their effect.

Mankiw's card-carrying neoclassical apologetics recalls John Bates Clark's (1899) argument that marginal productivity results in an ethically just distribution. But that is not something – even if it were true – we could confirm empirically, since it is impossible *realiter* to separate out what is the marginal contribution of any factor of production. The hypothetical *ceteris paribus* addition of only one factor in a production process is often heard of in textbooks, but never seen in reality.

When reading Mankiw on the "just desert" of the 0.1 %, one gets a strong feeling that he is ultimately trying to argue that a market economy is some kind of moral free zone where, if left undisturbed, people get what they "deserve". To most social scientists that probably smacks more of being an evasive action trying to explain away a very disturbing structural "regime shift" that has taken place in our societies. A shift that has very little to do with "stochastic returns to education." Those were in place also 30 or 40 years ago. At that time they meant that perhaps a top corporate manager earned 10–20 times more than "ordinary" people earned. Today it means that they earn 100–200 times more than "ordinary" people earn. A question of education? Hardly. It is probably more a question of greed and a lost sense of a common project of building a sustainable society. Or as the always eminently quotable Robert Solow (2014a) puts it:

> Who could be against allowing people their 'just deserts?' But there is that matter of what is 'just.' Most serious ethical thinkers distinguish between deservingness and happenstance. Deservingness has to be rigorously earned. You do not 'deserve' that part of your income that comes from your parents' wealth or connections or, for that matter, their DNA. You may be born just plain gorgeous or smart or tall, and those characteristics add to the market value of your marginal product, but not to your deserts. It may be impractical to separate effort from happenstance numerically, but that is no reason to confound them, especially when you are thinking about taxation and redistribution. That is why we want to temper the wind to the shorn lamb, and let it blow on the sable coat.

Since the race between technology and education does not seem to explain the new growing income gap – and even if technological change has become more and more capital augmenting, it is also quite clear that not only the wages of low-skilled workers have fallen, but also the overall wage share – mainstream economists increasingly refer to "meritocratic extremism," "winners-take-all markets" (Frank and Cook, 1995) and "super star-theories" (Rosen, 1981) for explanation. But this is also – as noted by Piketty (2014, p. 334) – highly questionable:

> The most convincing proof of the failure of corporate governance and of the absence of a rational productivity justification for extremely high executive pay is that when we collect data about individual firms ... it is very difficult to explain the observed variations in terms of firm performance. If we look at various performance indicators, such as sales growth, profits, and so on, we can break down the observed variance as a sum of other variances: variance due to causes external to the firm ... plus other "nonexternal" variances. Only the latter can be significantly affected by the decisions of the firm's managers. If executive pay were determined by marginal productivity, one would expect its variance to have little to do with external variances and to depend solely or primarily on nonexternal variances. In fact, we observe just the opposite.

Fans may want to pay extra to watch top-ranked athletes or movie stars performing on television and film, but corporate managers are hardly the stuff that people's dreams are made of – and they seldom appear on television and in the movie theaters.

Everyone may prefer to employ the best corporate manager there is, but a corporate manager, unlike a movie star, can only provide his services to a limited number of customers. From the perspective of "super-star theories," a good corporate manager should only earn marginally better than an average corporate manager. The average earnings of corporate managers of the 50 biggest Swedish companies today, is equivalent to the wages of 46 blue-collar workers (Bergström and Järliden, 2013, p. 10). Executive pay packages at that outlandish level is, as noted by Solow (2014b, p. 9):

> usually determined in a cozy way by boards of directors and compensation committees made up of people very like the executives they are paying.

It is indeed difficult to see the takeoff of the top executives as anything else but a reward for being a member of the same illustrious club. That they should be equivalent to indispensable and fair productive contributions –

marginal products – is straining credulity too far. That so many corporate managers and top executives make fantastic earnings today, is strong evidence the theory is patently wrong and basically functions as a legitimizing device of indefensible and growing inequalities.

Having read Piketty (2014, p. 332) no one ought to doubt that the idea that capitalism is an expression of impartial market forces of supply and demand, bears but little resemblance to actual reality:

> It is only reasonable to assume that people in a position to set their own salaries have a natural incentive to treat themselves generously, or at the very least to be rather optimistic in gauging their marginal productivity.

But although I agree with Piketty on the obvious – at least to anyone not equipped with ideological blinders – insufficiency and limitation of neoclassical marginal productivity theory to explain the growth of top 1 % incomes, I strongly disagree with his rather unwarranted belief that when it comes to more ordinary wealth and income, the marginal productivity theory somehow should still be considered applicable. It is not.

Wealth and income distribution, both individual and functional, in a market society is to an overwhelmingly high degree influenced by institutionalized political and economic norms and power relations, things that have relatively little to do with marginal productivity in complete and profit-maximizing competitive market models – not to mention how extremely difficult, if not outright impossible it is to *empirically* disentangle and measure different individuals' contributions in the typical team work production that characterize modern societies; or, especially when it comes to "capital," what it is supposed to mean and how to measure it. Remunerations, *a fortiori*, do not necessarily correspond to any marginal product of different factors of production – or to "compensating differentials" due to non-monetary characteristics of different jobs, natural ability, effort or chance). As Amartya Sen (1982) writes:

> The personal production view is difficult to sustain in cases of interdependent production ... i.e., in almost all the usual

> cases ... A common method of attribution is according to "marginal product" ... This method of accounting is internally consistent only under some special assumptions, and the actual earning rates of resource owners will equal the corresponding "marginal products" only under some further special assumptions. But even when all these assumptions have been made ... marginal product accounting, when consistent, is useful for deciding how to use additional resources ... but it does not "show" which resource has "produced" how much ... The alleged fact is, thus, a fiction, and while it might appear to be a convenient fiction, it is more convenient for some than for others ...
>
> The personal production view ... confounds the marginal impact with total contribution, glosses over the issues of relative prices, and equates "being more productive" with "owning more productive resources" ... An Indian barber or circus performer may not be producing any less than a British barber or circus performer — just the opposite if I am any judge — but will certainly earn a great deal less ...

Put simply – highly paid workers and corporate managers are not always highly productive workers and corporate managers, and less highly paid workers and corporate managers are not always less productive. History has over and over again disconfirmed the close connection between productivity and remuneration postulated in mainstream income distribution theory.

Neoclassical marginal productivity theory is a collapsed theory from a both historical and – as shown already by Sraffa in the 1920s, and in the Cambridge capital controversy in the 1960s and 1970s – theoretical point of view. But, unfortunately, Piketty trivializes the concept of capital and the Cambridge controversy over it. As in every mainstream textbook on growth theory and as with most neoclassical economists, Piketty just chooses to turn a blind eye to it and pretend it is much fuss about nothing. But they are wrong.

As Joan Robinson (1953, p. 81) writes:

> The production function has been a powerful instrument of miseducation. The student of economic theory is taught to write Q = f (L, K) where L is a quantity of labor, K a quantity of capital and Q a rate of output of commodities. He is instructed to assume all workers alike, and to measure L in man-hours of labor; he is told something about the index-number problem in choosing a unit of output; and then he is hurried on to the next question, in the hope that he will forget to ask in what units K is measured. Before he ever does ask, he has become a professor, and so sloppy habits of thought are handed on from one generation to the next.

And as Edwin Burmeister (2000, p. 312) admitted already fifteen years ago:

> It is important, for the record, to recognize that key participants in the debate openly admitted their mistakes. Samuelson's seventh edition of Economics was purged of errors. Levhari and Samuelson published a paper which began, 'We wish to make it clear for the record that the nonreswitching theorem associated with us is definitely false' ... Leland Yeager and I jointly published a note acknowledging his earlier error and attempting to resolve the conflict between our theoretical perspectives ... However, the damage had been done, and Cambridge, UK, 'declared victory': Levhari was wrong, Samuelson was wrong, Solow was wrong, MIT was wrong and therefore neoclassical economics was wrong. As a result there are some groups of economists who have abandoned neoclassical economics for their own refinements of classical economics. In the United States, on the other hand, mainstream economics goes on as if the controversy had never occurred. Macroeconomics textbooks discuss 'capital' as if it were a well-defined concept — which it is not, except in a very special one-capital-good world (or under other unrealistically restrictive conditions). The problems of heterogeneous

> capital goods have also been ignored in the 'rational expectations revolution' and in virtually all econometric work.

In a way these deficiencies are typical of Piketty's book – while presenting and analyzing an impressive amount of empirical data, the theory upon which he ultimately grounds his analysis, does not live up to the high standard set by the empirical material.

Piketty (2014, p. 333) is obviously, at least when discussing the remuneration of the top 1 %, aware of some of the limitations of neoclassical marginal productivity theory, but nonetheless, rather unwarranted and without much argumentation, holds it to be applicable to the more ordinary levels of wages and incomes:

> To be clear, I am not claiming that all wage inequality is determined by social norms of fair remuneration. As noted, the theory of marginal productivity and of the race between technology and education offers a plausible explanation of the long-run evolution of the wage distribution, at least up to a certain level of pay and within a certain degree of precision. Technology and skills set limits within which most wages must be fixed.

But, of course, once admitting that the top 1% can side-step marginal productivity concerns, the theory is seriously undermined since there is no consistent reason presented to exclude other segments of income earners from having the same degree of freedom. And as Hicks (1932) has already pointed out – as long as we only have rather uncertain measures of the elasticity of demand, the marginal productivity theory cannot, anyway, say how the relative shares of incomes will develop.

Conclusion

In an ongoing trend towards increasing inequality in both developing and emerging countries all over the world, wage shares have fallen substantially

– and the growth in real wages has lagged far behind the growth in productivity – over the past three decades.

As already argued by Karl Marx 150 years ago, the division between profits and wages is ultimately determined by the struggle between classes – something fundamentally different to hypothesized "marginal products" in neoclassical Cobb-Douglas or CES varieties of neoclassical production functions.

Compared to Marx's *Capital*, the one written by Piketty has a much more fragile foundation when it comes to theory. Where Piketty is concentrating on classifying different income and wealth categories, Marx was focusing on the facedown between different classes, struggling to appropriate as large a portion of the societal net product as possible.

Piketty's painstaking empirical research is, doubtless, very impressive, but his theorizing – although occasionally critical of orthodox economics and giving a rather dismal view of present-day and future capitalism as a rich-get-richer inequality society – is to a large extent shackled by neoclassical economic theory, something that unfortunately makes some of his more central theoretical analyses rather unfruitful from the perspective of realism and relevance.

A society where we allow the inequality of incomes and wealth to increase without bounds, sooner or later implodes. A society that promotes unfettered selfishness as the one and only virtue, erodes the cement that keeps us together, and in the end we are only left with people dipped in the ice cold water of egoism and greed.

If reading Piketty's *magnum opus* get people thinking about these dangerous trends in modern capitalism, it may – in spite of its theoretical limitations – have a huge positive political impact. And that is not so bad. For, as the author of the original *Capital* once famously wrote:

> The philosophers have only interpreted the world, in various ways. The point, however, is to change it.

References

Altvater, Elmar & Mahnkopf, Birgit (2002). *Grenzen der Globalisierung*. Münster: Westfälisches Dampfboot.

Bergström, Jeanette & Järliden Bergström, Åsa-Pia (2013). *Makteliten: klyftorna består*. Stockholm: LO.

Burmeister, Edwin (2000). "The capital theory controversy," pp. 305-314 in Kurz, Heinz-Dieter (ed.) *Critical essays on Piero Sraffa's legacy in economics*. New York: Cambridge University Press.

Clark, John Bates (1899). *The distribution of wealth: a theory of wages, interest and profits*. New York: Macmillan.

den Haan, Wouter (2011). "Why Do We Need a Financial Sector?" *Vox* October 24.

Frank, Robert & Cook, Philip (1995). *The Winner-Take-All Society*. New York: The Free Press.

Hicks, John (1932). *The theory of wages*. London: Macmillan.

Kuznets, Simon (1955). "Economic Growth and Income Inequality." *American Economic Review*, pp. 1-28.

Mankiw, Gregory (2011). "Educating Oligarchs." *Greg Mankiw's blog*, November 5.

Mankiw, Gregory (2014). "Yes, the Wealthy Can Be Deserving," *New York Times*, February 15.

Mankiw, Gregory & Taylor, Mark (2011). *Economics*. Andover: South-Western Cengage Learning.

Piketty, Thomas (2014). *Capital in the Twenty-First Century*. Cambridge, Mass.: Belknap Press of Harvard University Press.

Robinson, Joan (1953). "The Production Function and the Theory of Capital", *Review of Economic Studies*, pp. 81-106.

Rosen, Sherwin (1981). "The Economics of Superstars." *American Economic Review*, pp. 845-858.

Sen, Amartya (1982). "Just deserts." *New York Review of Books*, March 4.

Solow, Robert (2014a). "Correspondence: The One Percent." *Journal of Economic Perspectives*, pp.

Solow, Robert (2014b). "Thomas Piketty Is Right." *New Republic* April 22.

Piketty's determinism?

Ann Pettifor and Geoff Tily [PRIME (Policy Research in Economics) UK / UK Trade Union Congress]

There can be no doubt that Thomas Piketty's book *Capital in the Twenty-First Century* has helped catapult inequality to the top of the global agenda, particularly in the United States. So concerned is the global elite, that the World Economic Forum is in the process of "overhauling how the institute examines growth", and has a WEF economist Jennifer Blanke declaring that "it is extremely important to include the issue of income inequality in how we assess countries".[1] The book has rattled the American Right and placed it on the defensive. The *Wall St Journal* has had to resort to rhetoric about a "neo-Marxist polemic".[2] The book is also a publishing sensation, one overlooked by the world's biggest conglomerates, and published instead by the Belknapp Press at Harvard University Press.

These are all considerable achievements for its author. We are therefore uneasy contesting a progressive work that has done much to raise issues of equity. Nevertheless we find, as many others do, that the work remains in the mainstream tradition that for many has been proven flawed. In this contribution we address specifically TP's determinism, exemplified as we see it by his two millennia time series history of interest rates and growth. He shows these on Figures 10.9 and 10.10; the first is reproduced below.

The discussion here proceeds by deconstructing each variable (sections 1 & 2), addressing interactions (3), and concludes with policy (4). We include some discussion of sources, for it is striking that these central explanatory

---

[1] In 'An unequal world is an uncharted economic threat' by Gillian Tett, *Financial Times*, September 4, 2014. http://www.ft.com/cms/s/0/f0a593b2-3413-11e4-b81c-00144feabdc0.html?siteedition=uk#axzz3CYIfaRmR

[2] '*Money*' by Steve Forbes and Elizabeth Ames, reviewed by George Melloan, WSJ, July 24, 2014. http://online.wsj.com/articles/book-review-money-by-steve-forbes-and-elizabeth-ames-1406243735?KEYWORDS=Forbes

variables of his analysis are considerably less firmly-based than those related to outcomes.[3]

While it is encouraging to see interest rates reverting to a central position in such a high-profile piece of economic analysis, the manner of both his theoretical and empirical interpretation must be contested. Our own work on the role of interest rates in economic outcomes, leads to very different theoretical and practical conclusions (eg Pettifor, 2014 and Tily, 2010).

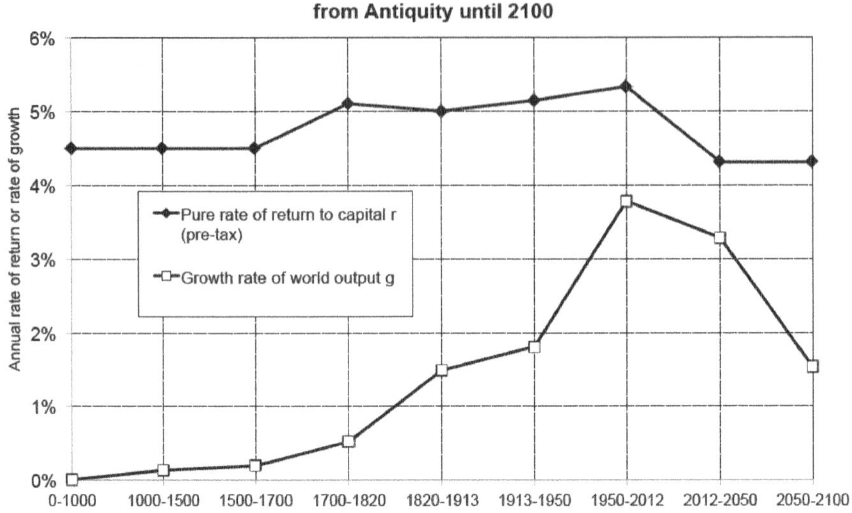

1. Growth

TP appears to consider that the extent of economic activity (as opposed to its distribution) through history is reasonably and sufficiently represented as a series of output growth. Moreover it is not implausible to project this measure one century into the future.

---

[3] Though exactly how these figures are derived, and whether they are independent of earlier assessments of α and β, we cannot say for sure and would welcome clarification on these matters. After such a massive read, this lack of clarity is troubling.

This historic record of growth owes everything to Maddison's dataset,[4] beyond an update in the more recent years. These figures are surely very far from a matter-of-fact, notwithstanding any associated painstaking research. Presumably this worldview must have been contested, but any scepticism must be reiterated: is it plausible to portray the dynamic of world history as a relatively smooth function of this kind? An alternative interpretation would regard history as non-linear and discontinuous, and not so obviously represented in growth space. Plainly any such assessment on our part must be subjective, and certainly no matter for economists alone. But our crude reading of history suggests that ancient Mesopotamia gave way to Egypt and then to Greece, and, after a Roman interval, to Byzantium. The medieval glories of Venice and Northern / Norman Europe, after darker ages, led to the Renaissance, Reformation and Enlightenment. An Imperial age finally gave way, after the Great Depression and Second World War, to a golden age of more progressive, equitable and democratic nature; and this was then gradually undone. Whether it is meaningful to make assessments of growth both within or between all these civilisations is surely highly contentious.

For GDP is a measure devised in the 1930s and 1940s, that evolved into an ideology and rationale for progress that has existed for only a little more than half a century. The imposition of this – ultimately technocentric – view on history is far from unquestionably legitimate. It is only on this basis that TP can assert that there is "no doubt whatsoever" (p. 74) that the pace of growth was quite slow from antiquity to the industrial revolution. Such a perspective presumably explains why there is very little discussion of the trajectory of growth: it follows naturally from technology and invention leading matters, and common sense apparently tells us the trajectory of invention. While TP appears fairly well disposed towards the state on distributional grounds, his description of the golden age still has supply in the driving seat in terms of aggregate activity: "the very rapid expansion of the role of government in the three decades after World War II was greatly facilitated and accelerated by exceptionally rapid economic growth" (p. 481).

---

[4] Technical appendix to Chapter 1.

2. Rate of interest

Others have contested TP's approach of conflating industrial and other non-financial capital with financial capital,[5] and emphasised the fundamentally neo-classical approach to interest as the marginal product of capital. But 'the' rate of interest (as Keynes saw it) requires careful consideration, in a way that has not been the case for some time, in both convention and mainstream literature.

Piketty's definitional confusions are perhaps symptomatic of this state of affairs. His emphasis on wealth, leads to a view of interest as a return on the part of wealth holders. This follows from his definition of 'capital', derived deliberately from the French 'patrimoine' and not from the more common 'richesse'. (The French language title to Adam Smith's *Wealth of Nations* is *la Richesse des Nations*). 'Patrimoine' is translated almost everywhere in the English edition of Piketty's book, as 'wealth'. But the primary sense of 'patrimoine' in French is not just 'wealth' as a snapshot of a person's current property of all kinds, or as an additive list of property at a given moment, but rather as a 'heritage', or an 'estate'. That said, developments since the financial liberalisation process that began in the 1970s mean that his main thesis is right. Wealth is begetting obscene wealth, which is not taxed or otherwise impeded in its mobility or accumulation, and today faces few barriers in its transmission from generation unto generation. It is a bleak picture.[6]

On a theoretical basis, it was Keynes's insight that any such return to which the rentier was accustomed and would subsequently demand could be very different to any likely return on physical capital investment. Similarly TP sees that his empirical assessment of interest rates is problematic from the

[5] From the national accounts perspective, the share of gross operating surplus in the income measure of GDP does not correspond to any such return on capital. Yet this flow estimated at 30 per cent is compared with wealth as a share of income at 600 per cent as one way of deriving an interest rate at 5 per cent.

[6] And yet, maybe the picture he paints is not bleak enough. For his definition of "capital" is in essence a financial calculation of owned assets minus liabilities. Leaving aside other definitional issues, what is missing, or not pursued, is the power that great wealth gives itself not only to further accumulate rapidly – but also the power gained through access to credit and other forms of financial manipulation to debt-finance gains.

point of view of neo-classical theory. As Kapeller (2014) observes, sustained high returns are not consistent with diminishing returns to capital. TP effectively amends mainstream doctrine:

> Technological development has brought along highly differentiated and multilayered means of investment, which devaluate the old principle "too much capital kills the return on capital". "This is perhaps the most important lesson of this study thus far: [...] because capital has many uses one can accumulate enormous amounts of it without reducing its return to zero" (TP in Kapeller, p. 4).

Equally, the methodological approach underpinning TP's empirical assessment on Figure 10.9 seems highly contentious. The historical series appears to rest on his observation that:

> I write on p.207 that the interest rate on the public debt is typically around 4%-5% per year during the 18th and 19th centuries. One of the most documented cases is the United Kingdom, where we have quite complete annual series started at the end of the 17th century and the beginning of the 18th century. We notice that returns often reached 5%-6% in the 18th century, or even 6%-7% at the end of this century and at the beginning of the 19th century (and during the Napoleonic wars; see appendix to chapter 3), then progressively decreased again during the 19th, to eventually be barely 3%-4% at the end of the century (or even less than 3%, while in a deflationist context, so that the real returns were in fact significantly higher). See series gathered in *Capital is Back...*, 2013 (in particular Table DataUK4). The series that are available for other countries, specially France and the United States, are less systematic but show the same kind of evolutions and fluctuations around an historical mean about 4%-5% in the 18th and 19th century (Technical appendix, pp. 36-7).

These observations on nominal government rates for three countries across three centuries, seem to be the foundation for two millennia of global figures. Surely this cannot possibly capture a dynamic that Homer and Sylla (2005) – authors of the monumental *A History of Interest Rates*[7] – depict in these terms:

> Students of history may see mirrored in the charts and tables of interest rates over long periods the rise and fall of nations and civilisations, the exertions and the tragedies of war, and the enjoyments and the abuses of peace. They may be able to trace in these fluctuations the progress of knowledge and of technology, the successes or failures of political forms, the long, hard, and never-ending struggle of democracy with the rule of the elite, the difference between law imposed and law accepted (p. 3).

Interest and money have been the dominant preoccupation of political, academic and religious classes since the dawn of civilisation. Correspondingly, it has been a central preoccupation of certain progressive authorities to facilitate reductions in interest. In his time series, TP may betray a wider lack of interest or even ignorance on the part of recent academic and policy discourse to the great part of academic history (beyond narrower questions primarily concerning discount rates).

The rates on the British government bonds – consols – that are so valuable to TP's assessment were the outcome of hard fought institutional developments, not least the instigation of the Bank of England under William of Orange and Robert Walpole's great advances in the management of the public finances. Half a century before, in his *Brief Observations Concerning Trade and the Interest of Money*, Sir Josiah Child (1630-1699)[8] looked to the prosperous and financially advanced Netherlands:

> Their use of BANKS, which are of so immense advantage to them, that some not without good grounds have estimated the profit of them to the Publick to amount to at least one

[7] Cited only incidentally and on a technicality by TP: n. 16 to Chapter 10.
[8] Merchant, economist, politician and governor of the East India Company.

> million of pounds sterling per annum.... [However, discussion focuses on] The Profit That People have received, and any other may receive, by reducing the Interest of Money to a very Low Rate. This in my poor opinion, is the CAUSA CAUSANS of all the other causes of the Riches of that people; and that if Interest of Money were with us reduced to the same rate it is with them, it would in a short time render us as Rich and Considerable in Trade as they are now (Child, 1668).

Moreover, while Bank rate was set at 5 per cent for over a century, Consols were most famously established at 3 per cent.

More recently in 1945, after the National Debt Enquiry (see Tily, 2010, appendix to chapter 3), HM Treasury set out the framework for post-war debt management policy that would be adopted by the first majority Labour Government in history:

> 6. *General desirability of low rates*. There is a wide measure of agreement, though not complete unanimity, in the present Committee in the view that on the whole, subject to the qualification dealt with in paragraphs 11 to 15 below, the desirable ideal for this country for a long time to come is not merely the continuance but even the reduction of the existing relatively low levels of interest rates both for long term and for short.

The lower rates achieved were a feature of the golden age across the world. Fundamentally they were the outcome of *deliberate* monetary action. Keynes's notion that the rentier could become accustomed to a lower rate of return was vindicated.

In TP, this reduction in rates is seen on his Figure 10.10 where an adjustment for tax and capital losses leads to the rate of return falling to 1 per cent over 1913-50, and staying close to 3 per cent over 1950-2012. It is the only movement of any note in history, and is explained as a result of the expanding role of the state and introduction of progressive income taxation motivated by the Great Depression and World Wars. Matters revert to normal with "the political shifts of the past several decades, especially in regard to taxation and finance" (p. 20). We agree that over this period (real) interest rates reverted to historic highs, but would place all emphasis on institutional developments leading to the liberalisation of finance.

The rentier did not tolerate low rates indefinitely.

3. Interest, output and distribution

As all his readers know, for TP the distribution of income and wealth depends on the relation between interest and growth. According to the preceding discussion the lines are interdependent, to the extent that a high marginal product drives high growth. But it is not clear how important this is for TP. His main emphasis is on the specific episode of the golden age/*trente glorieuses*, when the post-tax rate of interest falls below growth (r<g) and the great narrowing in distribution of the twentieth century began. Moreover this is the only more equitable episode in history. For the rest of history his empirics imply that the wealth distribution has only widened. We are sceptical of both his theoretical reasoning and empirical judgements.

Issues of causality as well as interdependence are opaque, but plainly for TP matters are determined on the real side, primarily as a consequence of technological advance. But the actions of the financial authorities over history are inconsistent with this reasoning. While Homer and Sylla carefully avoid generalisations on cause and effect, their analysis shows great ages of civilisation accompanied by material and sustained reductions in interest, and conversely darker ages by severely elevated rates. Josiah Child got the low rates of interest he sought, and the financial environment permitted Britain her economic and political pre-eminence on the global stage for over a century. The National Debt Enquiry likewise, and the golden age ensued. In the *General Theory*, Keynes was clear that causality was from the rate of interest to aggregate activity. So any relation between interest and growth is far more complex than TP implies, and fundamentally contingent on human initiative.

Distributional considerations were not his central concern, but Keynes's perspective likely arrives at the same place as TP with regard to a narrowing of the income and wealth distribution in the Golden Age. With the interests of the wealthy no longer paramount, he rejected conventional arguments against income and inheritance taxes. Lower returns on capital were inherent to a cheap money policy, obviously. Moreover lower unemployment plainly advantages labour.

That said, looking further back into history it seems unlikely that other civilisations saw only regressive times, and it is far too crude to see only continuously increasing inequality on any global basis. Our empirical judgements suggest a far more complex trajectory through history for interest and growth (or the level of activity), and our theoretical reasoning leads us to reject such a straightforward relation between interest, growth and the income distribution.

Nonetheless we are in full agreement that developments since financial liberalisation over the 1970s have tended to a severe inequality of income and wealth. TP argues too that inequality is set to continue to rise indefinitely on the basis of the ongoing reversion of growth back below and interest (with slower population growth playing a part). Again we agree, though we reach this conclusion as representing a consequence of the reversal of Keynes's approach set out above, given lower taxes, higher returns to the wealthy and higher unemployment of the liberalised age. But the fundamental point is that it doesn't have to be this way.

4. Policy

TP rescues himself from a deterministic straitjacket and from an economic history that is pre-ordained through his emphasis on distributional and associated policies; though his regarding the recommended policies as implausible in practice must be problematic. In the meantime attention is diverted from more fundamental matters of monetary architecture, economic and financial stability, and unemployment. Income distribution is only one of a number of symptoms of a liberalised system that has failed in a spectacular way. The global financial crisis which has gravely exacerbated an already severe failure to deliver work – and decent work – to the vast majority of the population must be our paramount concern. (The word unemployment does not feature in the index of the English edition.)

On our worldview, substantial and sustained interest rate changes follow from progressive governments taking control of money. The level of output and employment is then a function of interest so obtained. So the golden age *was* because of low interest, but it was not a happy coincidence of exogenously driven growth coupled with progressive taxation policies. In a fleeting recognition that such a worldview might exist, TP has a cursory look at usury laws (p. 531), and dismisses them as initially wrongheaded and finally conflates such initiatives with those he regards as ending in the Soviet Union.[9] This is very disappointing in a work that purports to be progressive.

References

Homer, Sidney and Sylla, Richard (2005 [1963]) *A History of Interest Rates*, 4th edition, John Wiley & Sons Inc: Hoboken New Jersey.

Kapeller, Jacob (2014) 'The return of the rentier', review of Piketty, *ICAE Working Paper Series*, 26, July.

Pettifor, Ann (2014) *Just Money*: Commonwealth Publishing.

Piketty, Thomas (2014) *Capital in the Twenty-First Century*, trans. by A.Goldhammer, Cambridge, MA: The Belknap Press (of Harvard University Press).

Tily, Geoff (2010 [2007]) *Keynes Betrayed: The* General Theory*, the Rate of Interest and 'Keynesian' Economics*, Basingstoke: Palgrave Macmillan.

[9] Though his rhetoric is occasionally more ambiguous. He concedes China is doing well without international finance (funding all from savings, p. 71), but finance is "not all …bad … to some extent natural and desirable" (p. 42).

Piketty's global tax on capital: a useful utopia or a realistic alternative to a global disaster?

Heikki Patomäki [University of Helsinki, Finland]

One of the key claims of Thomas Piketty's *Capital* is that there is a tendency for r > g, where r is the average annual rate of return on capital and g is annual economic growth. This is especially likely for regimes of slow growth. Past wealth becomes increasingly important and inherited wealth grows faster than output and income. If this is combined with the inequality of returns on capital as a function of initial wealth, the result is an increasing concentration of capital (p. 443).

Piketty argues new solutions are required in our globalising world and that a global tax on capital is the most appropriate response to this fundamental tendency in capitalist market economy towards divergence (p. 532). As such he considers it a utopian idea, but possibly realisable on a regional basis, perhaps even in a relatively short run. Thus the proposal for a global tax on wealth plays a critical role in Piketty's overall argument. It is the chief normative conclusion from his analysis of the causes of the concentration of wealth that the world has experienced since the 1970s.

I agree with Piketty that new tools are required to regain democratic control over the globalized financial capitalism, and that a global tax on capital is a promising idea. In this paper, I make three points. First, tax reforms are not only made possible or at least easier by major wars, as Piketty maintains; arguably it is also true that concentration of capital makes major wars more likely. This strengthens Piketty's argument and underlines the urgency of reforms.

Second, on a more critical note, the choice between a utopian global approach and a more feasible regional approach to the tax is somewhat misleading. There are easier ways to realise a global tax. Third, while Piketty's exclusive focus on wealth distribution may make it plausible to assume that a single global tax would suffice to reverse the trends of the past decades, in reality economic policy involves many issues and concerns a number of other processes as well. A global tax on capital would have to be accompanied by a more general shift towards global Keynesian economic policies. This would not make changes necessarily more difficult.

Large-scale wars and tax reforms

The world wars of the 20th century constituted major economic and political shocks. Piketty goes so far as to argue that "we can now see those shocks as the *only* forces since the Industrial Revolution powerful enough to reduce inequality" (p. 8; italics HP). This is a point he repeats several times in the book; he also gives ample statistical evidence on the impact of the world wars on the level of taxation and inequalities (for instance pp. 18-20, p. 41, p. 141, p. 287, p. 471, pp. 498-500).

Piketty, however, is not fully consistent in formulating this point. Counterfactual developments are uncertain. Without the shock of World War I, "the move toward a more progressive tax system would at the very least have been much slower, and top rates might have never risen as high as they did" (p. 500). The war facilitated and speeded up change, but it was not a necessary condition for it. The weakest formulation is this: "[P]rogressive taxation was as much a product of two world wars as it was of democracy" (p. 498). Thus democratization too seems to have played a facilitating role. A problem is, however, that democracy cannot explain the decline of progressive taxation and the re-rise of widening inequalities since the 1970s.

Piketty turns his world-historical insight – that there is a close relationship between major modern wars and reduction of inequalities – into a question about possible futures. Must we wait for the next major crisis or war, this time truly global? Or are peaceful and lasting changes possible? (p. 471) For instance, the global financial crisis 2008-9 was not compelling enough to make any major difference in terms of the underlying structural problems, including the lack of financial transparency and the rise of inequality. A much more devastating economic and political shock seems to be required for any real changes to become possible.

This is an important problematic. Here I would like to reverse the question, however. What will the concentration of capital and the rising importance of past and inherited wealth mean to the likelihood of a major economic and political disaster? Piketty maintains that the developments we are now observing are likely to erode democracy. The concentration of capital can reach very high levels – "levels potentially incompatible with the meritocratic values and principles of social justice fundamental to modern democratic societies" (p. 26). Are these high levels also incompatible with democracy *per se*? What are the consequences of de-democratisation?

John Rawls (1973) warned about the consequences of the accumulation of privileges in his *A Theory of Justice*. Wealth can be translated into political influence also in liberal democracies. The rules restricting this influence can be changed:

> The liberties protected by the principle of participation lose much of their value whenever those who have greater private means are permitted to use their advantages to control the course of public debate. For eventually these inequalities will enable those better situated to exercise a larger influence over the development of legislation. In due time they are likely to acquire a preponderant weight in settling social questions, at least in regard to those matters upon which they normally agree, which is to say in regard to those things that support their favored circumstances (ibid., p. 225).

We should be able to observe these developments especially in the US, which in the last few decades has become noticeably more inegalitarian than most European countries, even though the latter have experienced increasing inequalities as well. For instance, the Task Force on Inequality and American Democracy (APSA, 2004) formed under the auspices of the 14,000-member American Political Science Association concluded "that Progress toward realizing American ideals of democracy may have stalled, and in some arenas reversed". The US political system is now much more responsive to the needs and wishes of the privileged than those of the ordinary American citizens. A further problem is that this process tends to become self-reinforcing. Logically, in the absence of powerful countertendencies, it follows that over time democracy must be getting thinner and thinner. Real power relations are turning steeply asymmetric, reflecting the hierarchies of the inegalitarian society in which capital is increasingly concentrated in the hands of relatively few people.

The concentration of capital shapes also the production and distribution of knowledge in society. Humans tend to incorporate confirming evidence, while disconfirming evidence is often filtered out (e.g. Gilovich, 1993). This tendency is liable to becoming stronger in a context which is developing into an increasingly homogenised direction, also through organizational changes (such as funding, ownership and power relations in education and research, media etc). When the point is reached that a particular interpretation and related expectations in various positioned practices turn into mutually self-fulfilling prophecies also the cognitive process becomes self-reinforcing. In other words, actors act on the basis of shared expectations, and this tends to reproduce a sufficient number of those expectations, thus giving evidence for a generalised world view and reinforcing it.

In this process, actors tend to lock themselves in particular and increasingly narrow epistemic positions, which then become constitutive of their mode of being and agency, as well as their ethical and political identities. Under these circumstances, anything perceived as threatening to the basic values, as seen from this vantage point, may be securitised; and anyone disagreeing with the direction, may be constructed as a potential or actual enemy. (See Patomäki, 2008, 26-31, 128-30) The logic of securitisation in this sense boosts tendencies towards "inverted totalitarianism". According to a American political theorist Sheldon Wolin (2010), who has coined the term, this is what has already, to a large degree, happened in the US.

These developments will not stay at home but spread across the across the globalising world, also through international law. New constitutionalism (Gill, 1992, 2008) is a political and legal strategy that has been actively pushed by the US and EU to disconnect economic policies from democratic accountability and will-formation by means international treaties and institutions, often framed in terms of "free trade". Many international treaties and institutions are more difficult to revise than typical national constitutions, thus providing protection against political changes.

There are two main reasons why these developments would increase the likelihood of major economic and political shocks. First, they strengthen the relative power of those actors who are predisposed to disregarding those rational economic policies needed to ensure full employment and steady economic developments. Michał Kalecki (1943) famously argued that the business leaders and capitalists wish to create circumstances in which policies depend on their confidence; the scope of free markets are maximised; and hierarchical power-relations in the workplace are ensured. If and when they get their will through, we should expect a slackening growth-trend; and within it unequal growth, concentration of capital and resources, oligopolization or monopolization of world markets, and increasingly large oscillations with perhaps increasing amplitude, not least in finance. Thereby the likelihood of major *economic* crises and shocks must increase.

Second, de-democratisation, securitisation, enemy-construction and inverted totalitarianism are likely to generate and aggravate antagonistic relations with different others. For instance, the "what is good for us must be good for you" attitude can mean imperial involvement in the developments of those regions that are lagging or falling behind or actively resisting the prevailing direction. However, as Piketty stresses, when countries face the increasingly adverse consequences of free-market globalisation, some of them can also respond by turning to nationalism and protectionism – and to measures which are unacceptable for those who defend free market globalisation and its quasi-constitutional guarantees. These kinds of juxtapositions can all too easily pave way for the escalation of conflicts, thus increasing the likelihood of major *political* shocks, even a new world war.

Global capital tax: from utopia to a feasible strategy of peaceful changes

If Piketty's detailed diagnosis and my sketchy analysis of the prevailing trends is even roughly on the mark, the world seems to be heading towards a global disaster. From this perspective it may seem slightly worrying that Piketty presents his main cure, a global capital tax, as "utopian". Does this mean that there is no feasible alternative at this point, that the best we can do is to hope that we will survive the inevitable global disaster, and that in its aftermath we will see, once again, a jump to a more egalitarian society? What then? Will the cycle continue also after this round?

Piketty himself is far from hopeless, although he repeatedly warns about the likely dire consequences of the on-going developments:

> Admittedly, a global tax on capital would require a very high and no doubt unrealistic level of international cooperation. But countries wishing to move in this direction could very well do so incrementally, starting with at the regional level (in Europe, for instance). Unless something like this happens, a defensive reaction of a nationalist stripe would very likely occur. (pp. 515-6)

Rather optimistically, Piketty praises the recent progress of the proposed financial transaction tax (FTT) in Europe, arguing that "it could become one of the first truly European taxes" (p. 562). Unfortunately the situation is not this simple. During the global financial crisis, the EU leaders tried to push the financial transaction tax onto the G20 agenda. At the G20 summit in Cannes in November 2011 several countries joined with the United States in opposing the idea. In September 2011, the Commission made a proposal that such a tax should be realised in the EU, that such a tax is necessary both from an economic perspective and in the interests of fairness.

The September 2011 proposal by the Commission comes close to Piketty's idea of "one of the first truly European taxes" (although falling short of the global idealism of the so called Tobin tax movement). However, as the UK and even some Eurozone countries have continued to reject the FTT, a part of the Eurozone has decided to take the lead as an area of enhanced cooperation. This is a procedure where at last nine member states can agree on some measures to further integration.

In June 2012, it was concluded that the proposal for a Financial Transaction Tax will not be adopted by the Council within a reasonable period, and that enhanced cooperation is the only way to proceed. The UK challenged even this idea in the European Court of Justice. Although the ECJ dismissed the United Kingdom's action against the authorization of the use of enhanced cooperation in April 2014, the current proposal seems more like an agreement to jointly implement national taxes than a European tax. The way it will be implemented remains to be seen.

As Piketty says, the FTT is far less significant than a tax on capital or corporate profits (p. 562). The fate of Commission's FTT scheme is thus not very promising in view of Piketty's more ambitious proposals. The most feasible path may not be to start with separate regional taxes, however. The first problem with this approach is that a realistic analysis of power-relations and the state of democracy in the EU indicates that the 'wishes' of business leaders and capitalists in the Kaleckian sense have become entrenched also in the prevailing EU culture, vested interests and institutional arrangements, thus making changes difficult. Even if some of the member-states may conclude that progressive changes are needed, and even when some rethinking and learning occurs within Commission, the cumbersome structure of the Union makes it exceedingly difficult to implement new ideas. (Patomäki, forthcoming)

The second problem is that the EU is for many purposes comparable to some of the largest states in the world economy. As much as a EU-wide capital tax could do in Europe, from a global perspective it would be no more than a "national" solution –potentially vulnerable to the exit options provided by economic globalisation.

There is a better way, however. The enhanced cooperation procedure can be globalised. Any coalition of willing countries can start of a system of global taxation by negotiating a treaty, which establishes a system of taxation and a new organisation to govern the tax and some of its revenues. The system can be designed in such a way as to encourage outsiders to join it. If the idea is to regain democratic control over the globalized financial capitalism, the tax system has to be democratic. A global tax organisation could combine, in a novel way, principles of inter-state democracy (council of ministers), representative democracy (representatives of national parliaments in its democratic assembly) and participatory democracy (civil society representatives in its democratic assembly). This would make it open to different points of view; capable of reacting rapidly to unexpected changes; and qualified to assume new tasks if needed. Alternatively, a directly elected body is possible as well.

Towards global Keynesian economic policies

Is it really true that a single global tax would suffice to cure the ills of capitalist market economy? In chapter sixteen, "The Question of Public Debt" (pp. 540-70), Piketty discusses various questions of European and world economic policy, such as what the role of the central bank should be; whether inflation could be a solution to public debt and the need for redistribution; what kind of common European budget is needed and how it should organised democratically; and what should we do to control climate change. None of these questions can be reduced to mere income or wealth redistribution. Piketty, too, seems to agree that more is needed than a mere tax.

Nonetheless, Piketty's overall argument is geared towards the promise that once wealth is redistributed through the global tax on capital, and via institutions of the social state, the capitalist market economy should work just fine. This excludes for instance questions related to Keynesian demand management. Piketty appears to explain the rate of growth, and especially the current slow growth period in Europe and elsewhere in the OECD world, in terms of (i) normal rate of growth and (ii) a global convergence process in which emerging countries are catching up (pp. 72-109). "The history of the past two centuries makes it highly unlikely that per capita output in the advanced countries will grow at the rate above 1.5 percent" (p. 95). Piketty also hints at the possibility that the most recent waves of innovation may have a much lower growth potential than earlier waves (p. 94); and notes that while in the service sector productivity growth has been slow or non-existent, nowadays some 70-80% of the workforce in the developed world works in this sector (p. 90).

These are all plausible hypotheses and possible partial explanations, but they exclude Keynesian concerns about aggregate efficient demand, nationally, regionally and globally. The lack of efficient demand is the source of many contradictions in global political economy. For instance, states may be committed to improving their current account balance by enhancing their "competitiveness". The problem is that current account deficits and surpluses cancel out and, moreover, attempts to increase cost competitiveness through internal devaluation tend to prove contradictory due to decreasing effective demand. Moreover, in contrast to a positive catch-up processes that almost automatically even out developments across the planet, post-Keynesian economists have stressed the equal importance of self-reinforcing tendencies towards uneven and contradictory trajectories of developments (e.g. Kaldor, 1972, 1996).

These and other global political economy contradictions can be resolved by means of collective actions and by building more adequate common institutions (Patomäki, 2013, pp. 164-93). For instance, it is possible to build a mechanism by means of which world trade surpluses and deficits are automatically balanced through tax-and-transfer along the lines of the Keynes-Davidson plan and a global central bank that can issue reserve money.

These kinds of institutions can be characterised as global Keynesian, framing questions of public economic policy and politics on the world economic scale. Global Keynesianism aims to regulate global interdependencies to produce stable and high levels of growth, employment, and welfare for everyone and everywhere, simultaneously. To put it in Pikettian terms, a well-working global Keynesian system could make a big difference in terms of whether $r > g$ or $g > r$.

A well-working global Keynesian system would require several new institutions. Reforms and evolutionary changes may be piecemeal, and proceed through coalitions of the willing, but they are not necessarily separate. Processes are connected and interwoven in various ways. Hence, it may become increasingly evident to many that global warming requires global Keynesian responses, such as a democratically organised global greenhouse gas tax and world public investments, rather than a cap-and-trade system premised on the market. Accumulation of relatively small changes in specific areas may lead to ruptures and sudden transformations in others, as issues and processes are often linked.

Using this insight, a series of feasible political economy reforms can also be forged into a strategy of a democratic global Keynesian transformation. After a critical point, changes towards a particular direction can become mutually reinforcing and this may also be their deliberate purpose. Thereby, in the best-case scenario, one world-historical developmental path would come to be replaced by another.

References

APSA Task Force on Inequality and American Democracy (2004) 'American Democracy in an Age of Rising Inequality', The American Political Science Association, 26 July 2004. Available HTTP: http://www.apsanet.org/imgtest/taskforcereport.pdf (accessed 10 Sept 2014).

Gill, Stephen (1992) "The Emerging World Order and European Change", in R. Miliband and L. Panitch (eds) *The Socialist Register*, London: Merlin Press.

Gill, Stephen (2008) *Power and Resistance in the New World Order*, 2nd Edition, Houndmills, Basingstoke: Palgrave Macmillan.

Gilovich, Thomas (1993) *How We Know What Isn't So: Fallibility of Human Reason in Everyday Life*, New York: The Free Press.

Kaldor, Nicholas (1972) "The Irrelevance of Equilibrium Economics", *Economic Journal*, (82):328, pp.1237-55.

Kaldor, Nicholas (1996) *Causes of Growth and Stagnation in the World Economy*, Cambridge: Cambridge University Press.

Kalecki, Michał (1943) "Political Aspects of Full Employment." *Political Quarterly*, (14):4, pp. 322-31.

Patomäki, Heikki (2008) *The Political Economy of Global Security. War, Future Crises and Changes in Global Governance*, London: Routledge.

Patomäki, Heikki (2013) *The Great Eurozone Disaster. From Crisis to Global New Deal*, London: Zed Books.

Patomäki, Heikki (forthcoming) "Can the EU Be Democratised? A Political Economy Analysis", in R.Fiorentini & G.Montani (eds.) *The European Union and Supranational Political Economy*, London: Routledge.

Piketty, Thomas (2014) *Capital in the Twenty-First Century*, trans. by A.Goldhammer, Cambridge, MA: The Belknap Press (of Harvard University Press).

Rawls, John (1973) *A Theory of Justice*, Oxford: Oxford University Press.

Wolin, Sheldon S. (2010) *Democracy Incorporated: Managed Democracy and the Specter of Inverted Totalitarianism*, Princeton: Princeton University Press.

Reading Piketty in Athens

Richard Parker [Harvard University, USA]

> When the accumulation of wealth is no longer of high social importance, there will be great changes in the code of morals. We shall be able to rid ourselves of many of the pseudo-moral principles which have hag-ridden us for two hundred years, by which we have exalted some of the most distasteful of human qualities into the position of the highest virtues (John Maynard Keynes).

I have been reading Thomas Piketty this past week in Athens, where I came back to assess how Greece is faring half a decade after its economy imploded, initially as a consequence of its own ills and then – in an act of monumental malpractice by Germany, the ECB, and the IMF – the cure imposed.[1]

Signs of recovery are few.

It is hot here, as Mediterranean summers always are – but as thick as the heat is, an air of solemnity and defeat lies far more thickly over this concrete-gray capital and its now concrete-gray people, for whom what we know as the Great Recession has been their Great Depression, where the GDP has contracted 40% in five years and more than a quarter of its workforce can find no paid employment.

Four years ago, tens of thousands of Greeks would turn up regularly, week after week, at Syntagma Square in the heart of Athens to protest, again and again, the terms of the European-and-IMF-designed austerity regime that was the price Greece was being made to pay for loans meant to keep its government and economy afloat.

The streets lack protestors now, filled instead by tourists (more than 20 million visitors are expected this year, nearly two tourists for every Greek

---

[1] I served as an economic advisor to Prime Minister Papandreou, 2009-2012.

citizen) but also with drunks, junkies, and beggars out in alarming numbers of their own. Syntagma Square – jammed when I was here in 2011 with the tents and makeshift lean-tos of young protestors – has been scrubbed clean, the grass and flowers replanted, and new marble steps and benches replacing the stonework that had been chipped and broken to provide rocks to hurl at riot police.[2]

But cross the street from Syntagma Square and walk into the five-star Hotel Grande Bretagne and you suddenly encounter the tangible meaning of "unequal privilege" and what the incomes of the One Percent buy today – the quiet, the coolness, the sheen and rich color of the marbled floors and brocaded chairs and banquettes, the glistening reflection of silver tableware and brass sconces, the comforting thickness of the imported carpets, the watchful eye of both waiters and security guards – all take on a jarring immediacy that is, for me, sensory and ethical at once.

In Athens today, because you can in 30 seconds walk out of a world of beggars and into that of bankers, you can't help but reflect on how vividly Piketty's dry-as-bone wealth and income tables and graphs can translate into human experience. This makes reading *Capital in the Twenty-First Century* in Athens profoundly immediate and unsettling.

Yet simultaneously the various aspects of deep inequality in Athens – of wealth, of income, of opportunity, of hope, of trust – everywhere underscore the oddly-disconnected (even sometimes ethereal) feeling *Capital* conveys, although Piketty goes to great length to emphasize his own connectedness to human life through his empiricism, both in terms of the data he's assembled and in its rootedness in a historian's vivid chronology of politics and societal change rather than an economist's usual ordered placement of such data in the sterile ahistoricity of time series.

The fundamental genius of *Capital in the Twenty-First Century*, though, lies in its mapping and detailed decomposition of the great U-curve track income

[2] A wealthy Greek banker told me that the owner of the Grande Bretagne, Athens' most famous luxury hotel, and which sits on one edge of Syntagma Square, had paid more than 2 million Euros to repair the park because neither the city nor the national government had funds to do so.

and wealth distribution have followed over the 20th century – first, sharply declining inequality, especially during the thirty or so years from World War II's end up to the mid-1970s (what the French, Piketty reminds us, nostalgically still call "les trentes glorieuses"), then inequality's equally-sharp rise from the 1970s to today. It's what gives the book a monumental facticity of unusual scale and scope that, in no small part, explains the attention Piketty's work has garnered these past few months.

Yet that attention is also thanks to the moment in which the book has appeared. Just as Keynes's *General Theory* struck with such force because it was published in 1936 – and not 1926 or 1916 – so Piketty's *Capital*, by appearing (in English translation) in 2014 – and not 2004 or 1994, has arrived at a pitch-perfect message to be heard.

Capital's prominence

In truth, *Capital* is not quite as path-breaking as many believe. A fair-sized body of work on rising inequality – much of it quite good – had already been generated by other economists during the past 40 years.[3] But most of that work went to press without an economics mainstream (let alone a ready public audience) able to see its importance thanks in no small part to the profession's monocular preoccupations with "growth" in aggregate, shorthanded in the annual performance of GDP.

Not so long ago, the idea that aggregate national economic growth – denominated by GDP and the percentage changes of it – represented *the* 20th century's solution to elemental human tensions of class, interest group, and nation reigned, in imaginative terms, with the thoroughness equal to that which Roman Catholicism exercised in medieval Europe. Indeed, for the first 25 years after World War II, the conjunction of growth with clearly-declining inequality served as unalloyed reason to celebrate the ever-rising GDP – it was, quite simply, in fact a tide that was lifting (almost) all boats.

---

[3] I'm thinking, for example, of work by James Galbraith, Robert Kuttner, the Economic Policy Institute, Edward Wolff, et al. Gabriel Kolko, *Wealth and Power in America,* is among the very earliest, published in 1962.

But in the 1970s, as growth faltered across the developed world – and with it, the Keynesian consensus – the new demands to restore growth through pre-Keynesian means subordinated any serious reconsiderations of inequality's unique importance or relations to not only the market's growth but democracy's health to the "larger" imperative of GDP's restoration. Keynesianism, its many conservative critics insisted, had clearly shown it wasn't really the means to, but the enemy of, growth – and that only by extensive deregulation of markets and deep cuts in taxation (especially of capital and the incomes it generated) could we restore what had been lost.[4]

Ronald Reagan famously encapsulated the new consensus in a sentence: "Government is not the solution to our problem; government is the problem." Faced with humiliating confusions and ferocious accusations, some shaken Keynesians themselves now even postulated an inverse growth-equality relationship – "equity vs. efficiency" – as the trade-off needed to recover GDP health.[5]

GDP growth, more importantly, for much of the Cold War was frequently cast not just as a desideratum in terms of our economic well-being but a necessity in terms of our survival. In the 1950s and 1960s, the CIA had repeatedly warned that the Soviets and Chinese seemed capable (perhaps even on the verge) of "burying" capitalist democracies thanks to Moscow's and Beijing's superiority at solving growth equations for their military-industrial economies. Inevitably the CIA's assessments leaked, stirring great public alarm – and, not unexpectedly, produced expanded American defense budgets.[6]

---

[4] In Robert Lucas's famous phrase, Keynesians by the late 1970s were worse than defeated; they were laughing stock. "At research seminars," he said, "people don't take Keynesian theorizing seriously anymore; the audience starts to whisper and giggle to one another." His Chicago colleague John Cochrane generously explained that Keynesian ideas were "fairy tales that have been proved false. It is very comforting in times of stress to go back to the fairy tales we heard as children, but it doesn't make them less false."

[5] Robert Collins, *More: The Politics of Growth in Postwar America* (Oxford, 2002).

[6] Liberal Keynesians, nostalgic for the long era of growth-with-equality, often overlook or elide acknowledgement that for most of those first 30 years after World War II, the Pentagon consumed half of the federal budget.

All that, of course, changed in the late 1980s when the Berlin Wall fell, leaving capitalism the seeming sole inheritor of the earth. After Lehman fell in 2008, however, the West's questions (and doubts and angers) about growth all of a sudden sprang not from a fear of communism but a new-found fear of capitalism. The Great Recession – in sum, not just Lehman's collapse, but the Occupy movement in America, Europe's frightening swoon after Greece's collapse, the need for multi-trillion-dollar rescue of markets by states, capped by the ongoing worldwide failure of GDP to recover meaningfully or unemployment to recede significantly, plus the failure to craft a strong architecture of remedy or prevention for Wall Street's inevitable future excesses, and beneath all of that, the ongoing profound absence of confidence about the future after the greatest global contraction since the 1930s – has delegitimized for millions the fundamental "growth" consensus that had reigned since World War II.

What if anything will replace that consensus, when and how, is not at all apparent, of course – and not least explains the excited reception given to *Capital in the Twenty-First Century.* Some have been so excited that they've even compared *Capital* to *The General Theory*, and Piketty to Keynes, in terms of its insights and influence – claims that to me seem premature, though in some attenuated way possible.[7]

It's clear that Piketty has done two *very important things*: first, *he has forced us to look anew at income and wealth distribution by drawing our attention away from GDP growth as such*; second, he has refocused us away from just the recent past toward *la longue duree* that simultaneously points to a long, rather than near, future. In so doing, he has leapfrogged – at least for his admirers – the staleness of both America's gridlocked politics and Europe's policymaking briar patch, and pointed us toward an authentically-fresh research as well as a fresh policy and political agenda that must

[7] If precedents to *Capital* are needed, I'd sooner point to Milton Friedman and Anna Schwartz's *A Monetary History of the United States, 1867-1960.* Both works are densely empirical and historically grounded (which *The General Theory* was not), with extensive tabular and graphic presentations, and the authors' conclusions about the economic patterns they observe are generalized into focused economic rules – in Friedman's case, the crucial role of monetary policy (rather than Keynesian fiscal policy), in Piketty's, that of income and wealth distribution (compared to aggregated GDP), for determining what each considers optimal growth paths.

henceforth focus binocularly on growth and inequality. In this, his admirers can fairly draw comparisons to Keynes's impact because he has hinged *Capital in the Twenty-First Century* to wealth and income distribution as surely as *The General Theory* was hinged to aggregate demand.

Rather than rehashing the endless debates of the past 30 years about the relative merits of markets and states, Piketty in short shows us how to see the fluctuations (and constancies) of inequality over the past two centuries – and suggests what we might anticipate about its future. He reminds us that, as Old Europe's monarchies and empires gave way after World War I, the rise of Bolshevism, Fascism, and Nazism overturned long-established patterns of social, political, and economic order and organization – not least, as he is at pains to point out, patterns and sources of wealth and income inequality that made the 19th century different from the emerging 20th.

But because the Great War's great *boulversements* led from shattered empires to violent revolutions (and equally-violent ultramontane reactions), and then soon enough to the Great Depression and a second world war – the century's "great levy" of blood, fortune, power, and rank – by 1945 meant that the West was brought to a singular juncture.

Right after the end of World War II, relying on the still-powerful capacities of industrial capitalism, and counter-posing the threat of Stalinist expansion to the promise of democratic affluence for most (if not all), elites in the West, with American elites in the lead, during an extraordinary few years re-patterned the course of our history. We today are still living out the disrupted final stages of the new age they created as the world prepares to enter a subsequent age led by new hegemonic powers and alliances.

Piketty is keen to reframe that re-patterning in terms of a V-shaped turn of income and wealth distribution rather than simply the rising tide of postwar GDP – and rightly so, given all the benefits early growth-with-redistribution brought. (In the US at least, initially these gains came about through the legacy of wartime "wage compression" policies, then after the legendary Treaty of Detroit in 1950, the Big Business-Big Labor concordat that shared productivity gains in exchange for labor peace, and vast expansion of federal spending, first on the military, then finally after the JFK-LBJ years expanded social welfare, increasingly through public transfers rather than market-based allocations.)

For the first time in history, at least in North America and Western Europe[8], the majority was now living a life of relative plenty and security, with its continuance seemingly insured and its constant improvement promised – the new world John Kenneth Galbraith legendarily named "The Affluent Society". The old apocalyptic threats to humankind of famine, civil war, disease, gross injustice at the hands of authorities and one's "betters" (and, of course, poverty) receded after World War II from the experience – even the memories – of several hundred million fortunate North Americans and Western Europeans.

Operationalizing an inequality focus

But that's to look backward – when the more important challenge Piketty poses, it seems to me, is to look forward. He himself famously does so in two ways in *Capital:* first, by postulating r>g as a new economic "law" to explain why returns to capital will continue indefinitely to exceed GDP growth rates, and then by suggesting a global wealth tax as partial remedy for the alleged invariability of r>g. Each of these has attracted much comment from reviewers as well as controversy – r>g for its claim to being a "law," the global wealth tax for what many take to be its utopianism.

Resolving whether r>g is in fact a new economic law or an empirical pattern based on trend lines that are capable of shifting or even reversing – just as inequality trends first declined, then reversed, after World War II – remains, in some sense, for the future rather than blackboard modeling to tell. (Older economists may want to reflect here on the claims to law-like status accorded the Phillips Curve in the 1960s or Supply Side's bell curve in the 1980s.) Implementation of an effective global wealth tax meanwhile, as Piketty fully understands, is not even a matter for economic modeling but of making rather heroic assumptions about earnest economists' policy

[8] A few Western-settled outposts such as Australia and New Zealand and white South Africa can be appended to this short list.

persuasiveness and enormous changes in the likely political/ideological landscapes of the decades ahead.

Without solving either of these Pikettyan meta-issues, the question arises: Are there other things we as economists can do if, like Piketty, we're concerned (alarmed? appalled?) about current levels and trends of inequality? How – absent meta-solutions – should we or could we move an inequality-reduction agenda forward? What issues or strategies or agendas might help advance absorption of Piketty's focus on distribution and reframe a mainstream professional and public discourse still fixed almost monocularly on aggregated, rather than a distributionally-differentiated, GDP?

As I contemplated that question in Athens this summer, several possible projects occurred to me as worth at least consideration and debate. Some readers will no doubt find these suggestions too small, too pallid, too technical, or too bureaucratic, but I'm motivated to raise them – rather than more sweeping or heroic responses to *Capital* – in part by my reading of the ways *The General Theory's* lessons were absorbed, initially by academics, then policymakers, and then by elements of the press and wider public, during the first 25 years or so after its publication (about which more shortly). What academic, government, and policy NGO economists could, in my opinion, usefully do or call for over the next several years includes, at very least, the following:

1) Academic economists could begin teaching macro courses (undergraduate and graduate) as well as a research and publishing program focused on the big distributional questions, or at least the old growth questions reframed and disaggregated by distributional ones, in order to ground our students and our colleagues in the relationships between growth and inequality.

2) Behavioral economists in particular could expand their own teaching and research on, for example, the field's early findings about the effects of positional goods and relative incomes. As one example, David Moss at

Harvard Business School and the Tobin Project are here already doing some pioneering work.[9]

3) Cross-disciplinary teaching and research – in cooperation with political scientists, sociologists, social psychologists, historians, and moral philosophers – present a fertile range of opportunities for teaching and research. I've participated for several years, for example, in the multi-disciplinary Harvard Inequality and Social Policy program, just one model of how this could be done or approached.[10]

4) Academic and policy NGO economists could start calling on government colleagues and statistical agencies to do (including spending) more to improve their collection and processing of income and wealth distribution data worldwide, given the myriad inherent limits of tax returns, social security files, and household survey data now in use. As we enter the era of Big Data – for better or worse – the sheer quantity of information available that could vastly supplement and enrich our attempts to measure and answer distributional questions – as well as the graphical means to make our findings more easily understood to audiences outside our profession – seem untapped.

5) Organized calls from economists and other social scientists could press the IMF, OECD, Eurostat, the UN and the like to prioritize greater harmonization of the definitions and indices of inequality, to allow more meticulous comparison internationally. Mme. Lagarde has already publicly said that the IMF must "do more" about inequality (though without much precision about what it might do)[11]; one precedent here is the pioneering role the UN and IMF played in spreading national income accounting around the globe in the early 1950s.

---

[9] On Moss and the Tobin Project, see "How Income Inequality Shapes Behavior" at http://hbswk.hbs.edu/item/7283.html

[10] On the Harvard Inequality and Social Policy, see http://www.hks.harvard.edu/inequality/index.htm

[11] See Lagarde, "Economic Inclusion and Financial Integrity – an Address to the Conference on Inclusive Capitalism", at https://www.imf.org/external/np/speeches/2014/052714.htm

6) It seems important to me to find ways to elevate and "normalize" public reporting of the distribution issue in a super-condensed headline form, aimed not at economists but at the press, politicians, and the public. Let me call this simply the need, for want of a more elegant formulation, for "*GDP-plus-Gini*" – in lieu of GDP alone as *the* single-number metric of a nation's economic performance.

The Gini coefficient has numerous problems of which we're all aware, of course, though in this it is no different than GDP. Its advantage lies, I would argue, in the power of that one number's ability to reach a wider public and to shape policy and politics beyond our own limited world of classroom and peer journals. No president or prime minister runs on a platform promising to lower or even maintain current GDP.

How might we best get a one-number summary of inequality before the public as GDP has done for aggregate growth? The World Bank, among others, already regularly ranks countries by their Gini coefficients – and its website allows users an easy choice of display as table, graph, or map.[12] There, one can quickly learn that the Bank ranks Sweden at 0.25 as the world's most egalitarian nation, South Africa at 0.63, the most inegalitarian.[13] The United States, at 0.41, hunkers down among a host of developing economies such as Turkey, China, and several West African states – and, needless to say, far behind every other high-income developed country (Germany is at 0.28, France and Canada both at 0.33, the European Union as a whole, at 0.31).

The merit of such rankings – if they were presented annually by national statistical authorities alongside GDP performance – is the way Gini's simple single number translates rankings into performance that can, alongside traditional GDP, be reported on the evening news or Internet or debated in the halls of Congress. (Piketty himself has casually noted his own preference for calculation of two separate Gini coefficients – one based on labor income, one on capital income; on this, I'm for now agnostic though I take his important point.)

---

[12] World Bank Gini rankings at http://data.worldbank.org/indicator/SI.POV.GINI/countries/all?display=graph

[13] I omit here a number of micro-states.

A graphic supplement to such Gini ranking would be to disaggregate annual income and wealth changes by quintile or decile (with special attention to the top 1% and 0.1%, a la Piketty). There are already many variants of such presentations (see below); the point would be to elevate them to the prominence that reporting of GDP itself enjoys today.

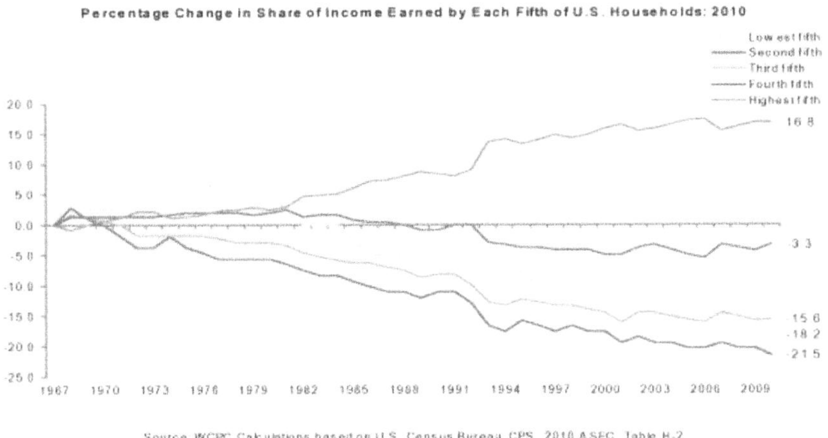

7) Far more research and debate on the intersections of growth and equality is capable of leading in turn to our clearer understanding of what a band of "democratic growth" or "egalitarian growth" paths among the variety of growth paths might look like, calculated both in terms of private income and wealth distribution and the divide between public and private income and spending. Jonathan Ostrey and colleagues, to cite one example, have already published three quite solid IMF papers ("Redistribution, Inequality, and Growth", "Inequality and Unsustainable Growth," and "Efficiency and Equity") that have begun opening up this sort of research, in a rich but preliminary way, to serious academics and policymakers. (I mention only these because fully enumerating the various strategies and sub-topics in this field would require its own separate paper.)

Lessons from early Keynesianism

Why should such seemingly prosaic and rather bureaucratic efforts to change economic teaching, government statistics, and research agendas matter? History offers a clue. Young economists tend to know very little about how early Keynesian thought evolved and took hold in both mainstream economics and public policy – or how hotly contested the process was – in the first decades after *The General Theory*'s publication and then after Keynes' death in 1946.

It was a process not dissimilar to the agenda steps I've described, of what in many cases seemed rather small contributions by academic and government economists and policymakers – of courses offered, textbooks written, and articles published, that were then over time noticed by more senior policy figures in Washington, then some in the press, then slowly and unevenly by politicians, business, and labor leaders, and only much later by the informed public.

In the late 1930s, the initial US shift toward Keynesian thinking gestated in a handful of university economics departments – with Harvard and Alvin Hansen in leading roles – and among a tiny but strategically-placed group of young Washington economists, mainly in Treasury, Commerce, and the Bureau of the Budget, who were loosely connected (and sometimes had been recruited) by Lauchlin Currie. Currie himself had been pushed out of Harvard for his proto-Keynesian views in the early 1930s but by 1938 had become FDR's chief economic advisor (this nearly a decade before the Council of Economic Advisors was created).[14]

It then gathered momentum as a few journalists at influential papers and magazines began to take note (Henry Luce, through *Time*, *Life*, and *Fortune*,

---

[14] See John Kenneth Galbraith, "How Keynes Came to America" (Boston, 1965), for a condensed – and entertaining – version of Keynesianism's early US advances; see Albert Hirschman, "How Keynes Was Spread From America," *Challenge*, November 1988, and for greater detail, Peter Hall, *The Political Power of Economic Ideas: Keynesianism Across Nations* for a broader multinational survey.

perhaps the most influential).[15] Small conferences were convened by interested institutes or foundations (such as the Council on Foreign Relations, Committee on Economic Development, and Twentieth Century Fund), and then in some ways most importantly, as wartime attempts to use GDP estimates to calculate the size and shape of the post-war economy drew the attention of business, labor, and politicians to the new way of thinking.

After the war, the creation of the Council of Economic Advisors – and the early chairmanship of Leon Keyserling – planted Keynesian approaches in Washington, albeit through the new role federal macro-management and growth stimulation would play with the sudden emergence of the Cold War. America's Military-Industrial Complex would now justify previously-elusive bipartisan support for the federal government's rapid expansion and economic interventions. (One can only guess at what Keynes would have thought of this guns-make-butter use of his thought; what it did do, for different reasons, was make both liberal Keynesians and traditional market conservatives deeply apprehensive. Liberals hated what the money was spent on but loved the jobs federal spending and policies generated, while conservatives embraced America's new military power even as they feared the amounts spent, with their attendant risks of inflation and deficits.) Military Keynesianism – a concept never proposed or even imagined by Keynes – became, it's often forgotten, the means by which Keynesianism moved into the Western mainstream of thought and public policy. (An Oxford tutor of mine long ago slyly remarked that Stalin had done for early Keynesianism what Constantine did for early Christianity.)[16]

---

[15] Luce, a deeply Republican figure, nonetheless in 1943 hired a young John Kenneth Galbraith as economics editor of *Fortune* in order to familiarize – and win over – its powerful audience of business leaders to the heresy of postwar US government macro-management of the American (and in several ways the world) economy. On the crucial but barely-known role of American big business in promulgating Keynesianism – and the reasons, see Robert Collins, *The Business Response to Keynes, 1929-1964*.

[16] He'd then added, with a touch of English wistfulness, that as Keynesianism in Neoclassical Synthesis form replaced early Keynes, "power in postwar economics shifted in the 1950s from the Jerusalem of England's Cambridge to the Rome of America's Cambridge, with the Master's teachings now filtered and interpreted through the teaching of St. Paul".

Whether China's ascendency to world's largest economy and its emerging role as the West's new "frenemy" – or the likely ongoing[17] costs of combatting political Islam – might at some point play a role in generating a new era of redistributive politics in the West is an intriguing question. Both the Chinese and political Islamic challenges emerged during the West's post-1970s decades of rising inequality(with China's low-wage exports arguably exacerbating Western inequalities), and in America's case since the first Gulf War a quarter-century ago, of ever-rising military expenditures – now in the trillions of dollars – that might otherwise have been funds diverted to other, better ends than war.

The point here is two-fold: first, that the early efforts to install and expand Keynesian thinking were in many ways mundane and routine, concerned with the "bureaucratization" of this new economic policy strategy, the deepening of its research foundations, and the spread of its applications. Then suddenly events and shifting views arising in the political world created the opportunity to "operationalize" Keynesian precepts through the new bureaucratic tools and communities that the earlier efforts had fostered.

One can't with any certainty say what "events and shifting views" in the 21st century might operationalize Pikettyan views on how to lessen income and wealth inequality. But without the bureaucratic and academic substructures in place beforehand, there will be little likelihood that in the political world, where operationalization will necessarily take place – through tax policy changes, for example, or new rules on financial systems, or cross-border agreements on tax havens, or changes in rules governing executive compensation on one end or minimum wages on the other – far less will happen than we might desire.[18]

---

[17] Small digression: It strikes me that one here could argue for the observed existence of a Piketty-like law – call it M>g – to denote the V-shaped curve of once-declining but now rapidly-rising American military costs at rates that are steadily exceeding GDP growth.

[18] I would offer one warning to future Pikettyans: pay attention to the moment when your success in establishing Pikettyanism seems to be finally embraced at the heights of power. The first American president to publicly declare "I am a Keynesian" was Richard Nixon, thirty-five years after *The General Theory* first appeared. Disappointments followed.

Capital in context: perceptions and data

It's easy for Piketty enthusiasts – given the enormous attention and praise *Capital* has garnered to imagine either that "everyone" now grasps the outlines of his data and conclusions, or that it is only a matter of time before they do. That seems to me implausible.

For one, although *Capital* may be an easy read for economists, it has turned out, by one analysis, to be "the most unread best-seller of 2014".[19] Even among well-educated Americans, the grasp of Piketty's data is weak at best. In my Harvard economics policy course, when I turn to wealth and income distribution, I like to show students the chart below, which distinguishes what *US wealth distribution actually is*, what Americans *estimate it to be*, and finally *what they think it ought to be* – just to underscore for them that the public's estimates and Piketty's findings vary enormously (and yet how both favor an "ideal distribution" of much greater equality):

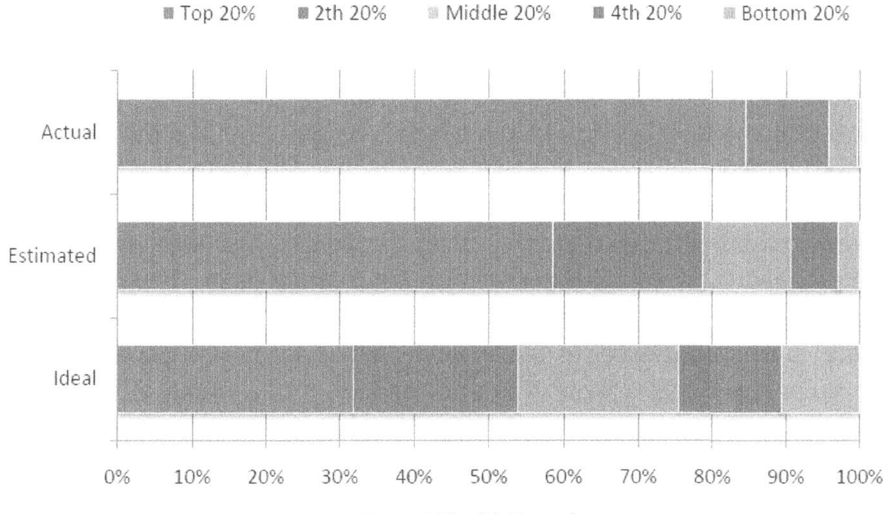

[19] See Emily Cohn, "Not Many People Got Past Page 26 Of Piketty's Book", at http://www.huffingtonpost.com/2014/07/07/piketty-book-no-one-read_n_5563629.html

There are many reasons why such gaps between understanding and ideal norms abound, not least the under-reporting for so long of distributional data as far as the public is concerned. But even economists versed in reading quantitative presentations display surprising limits to their familiarity with the data.

One factor is, as I've noted, the longstanding monocular focus of the profession on GDP growth as such, understandable in the first decades after World War II because greater equality seemed a byproduct of Keynesian-led growth strategies. Even though the 1960s' "rediscovery" of poverty in America meant acknowledging that growth's impact on inequality had been real and extensive but far from universal, the mainstream profession's response was to intensify Keynesian claims to solve the problem through targeted programs (the War on Poverty) alongside intensified economy-wide efforts to reach near-full employment (the Kennedy-Johnson tax cut). If growth's results crimped the decade's confidence in rising tides lifting all boats, to the shipwright-economists of the Neoclassical Synthesis-era, solutions seemed within their command.

By the late 1970s, the Keynesians were being driven from the boatyards of policy, supplanted by supply-siders, tax-cutters, and deregulators who looked on the Keynesians with the arrogance new steamship builders once looked on the old makers of sails. When by the late 1980s, the process of globalization seemed somehow connected to falling wages and collapsing firms across the nation's broad industrial heartland, and the new world of deregulated finance began throwing up fortunes not seen since the Gilded Age, questions of inequality started surfacing only to be met with claims either to their transience (as the economy "adjusted" to new global realities) or necessary ("getting incentives and rewards right"). Remedy lay, it was claimed, in re-education and intensified competition, not downward redistribution of the new distributional realities.

And there the debate remained – until the Great Recession. In the six years since, there has been a sudden new interest in inequality, though much of it has been surprisingly inconclusive or contradictory in analysis and (where offered) prescription. Thrust into that welter (quite similar in many ways to the New Deal's own often-confused and contradictory debates and policies before *The General Theory*), the arrival of *Capital in the Twenty-First Century*, with its singular scale and scope, has forced a new framework onto the debates, its monumentality alone reason it can't be ignored.

Yet even so, in our era of headlong globalization, Piketty's cross-national data is striking for how few countries they cover (basically France, Great Britain, and the United States), how limited the sets are in duration, how variable in collection quality and depth, how dependent the data are on the means of collection (mainly tax returns and/or household surveys, with all their own attendant methodological problems), and how infrequently distribution issues have been linked to growth paradigms. This, one hastens to add, is not for lack of effort by Piketty and his colleagues, but measure of how little serious attention has historically been paid to collection, let alone, analysis of the necessary data.

There are, of course, other data sets besides Piketty's – the Luxembourg Income Study perhaps the best known to economists (though unknown to the general public) – that cover more countries than Piketty's, but the number of countries covered is still small, less than 30 in a world of nearly 200 independent nations. However, the LIS lacks the historical depth that Piketty uses to such advantage with the US, UK, and France.

The United Nations University's WIDER project collects data through its World Income Inequality Database (WIID) from substantially more countries that the LIS, especially developing and transitional states. James Galbraith and his coworkers have for more than a decade also been analyzing, with great success, global income distribution patterns in the University of Texas Inequality Project.

The World Bank's work on inequality, much of it done by Branko Milanovic and colleagues between 1990 and 2010,[20] has so far been the most extensive in its country coverage – 119 at last count, containing over 80% of the world's populace and 95% of global GDP.[21] Milanovic, however, has been frank about the quality and consistency limits of the national surveys

---

[20] Milanovic has left the Bank, and now teaches at the City University of New York

[21] Milanovic and Yitzhaki, "Decomposing World Income Distribution: Does the World Have a Middle Class?"

he's collected – some measure income, others expenditure, some are calculated by individual, some by household, some by family. He's quite clear also that little can be said reliably about global income distribution before the late 1980s, given the lack, or highly uneven quality, of data before then.[22]

What all this work underscores is not just that better, more systematic, and richer data is needed to carry forward Piketty's focus, and why better standardization of definitions and metrics is needed as well.[23] In the late 1940s and early 1950s, the GDP concept gained crucial traction in terms of its adoption worldwide first through the UN's income- accounting standards-setting in 1947 followed by the IMF's own standardization measures in 1951 and thereafter. Refining cross-national standardization for collection and measurement of income and wealth distribution should be made a priority for both agencies over the next few years.

Apart from improving accuracy of measurements, we will also need greater accuracy and agreement about what it is we want to measure. When Piketty visited Harvard last spring, I asked him at the end of his talk why he'd analyzed only pre-tax, pre-transfer "market income" in *Capital.* He replied, with a Gallic shrug, that "measuring the distribution of tax and transfer consequences is very difficult" – and then encouraged me and others to take up the challenge. But others have already: conservatives in particular have made much of the significant impact government transfers of all kinds have on mitigating Piketty's finding of rising inequality of pre-tax, pre-transfer income.[24]

---

[22] "Sources of data" in Milanovic and Yitzhaki, "Decomposing World Income Database"; Milanovic, "Global Inequality in Numbers: In History and Now," *Global Policy*, May 2013, gives narrative overview of measurement issues.

[23] The many problems of incompatible definitions and metrics is, I must stress, exist not just in cross-national comparisons but in national analyses. For an introduction to several large problems in US income distribution measurement, from tax units versus households, pre- and post-tax-and-transfer income, household size, tax filers and non-filers, see Burkhauser et al., "A 'Second Opinion' on the Economic Health of the American Middle Class," at http://www.nber.org/papers/w17164

[24] For example, Alan Reynolds, "The Misuse of Top 1 Percent Income Shares as a Measure of Inequality", at www.cato.org/workingpapers

There is no doubt that government social welfare programs of all kinds have grown since the 1920s to have a significant distributional effect on final household incomes, as this chart, for example, shows for the US:

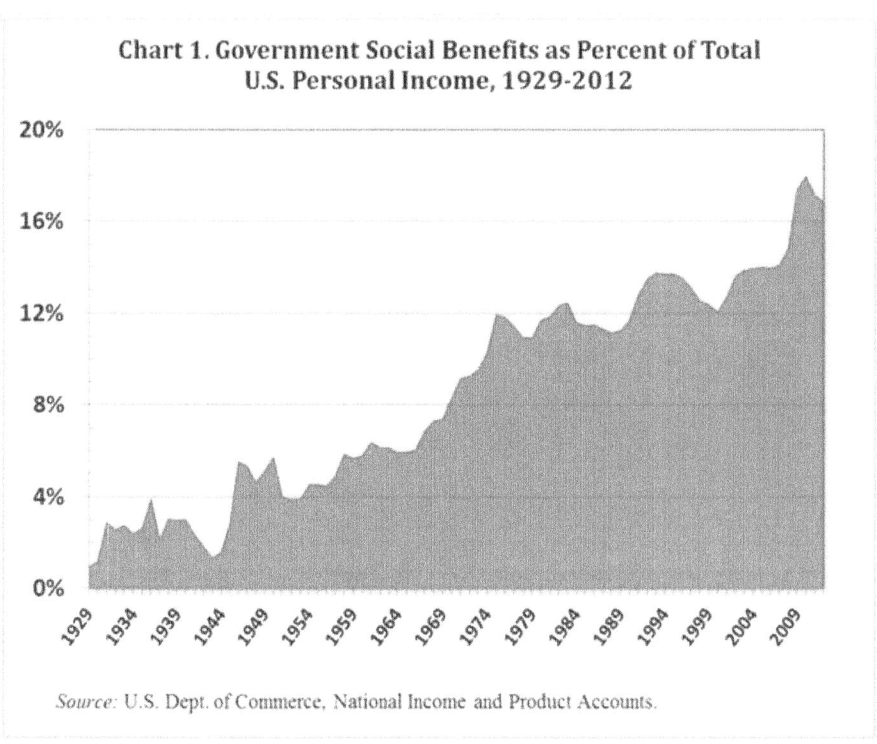

Conservatives aren't, however, the only ones pointing to governments' already significant redistributive impact – and on the significance of Piketty's focus on pre-tax-and-transfer income. Gary Burtless of the Brookings Institution has cited Congressional Budget Office studies, for example, showing that the bottom US income quintile, measured (as Piketty does) by pre-tax "market" income, receive three-quarters of its total post-tax-and-transfer income from the government rather than the market. Even for the middle quintile, the post-tax-and-transfer income is one-sixth of total income, as this table shows:[25]

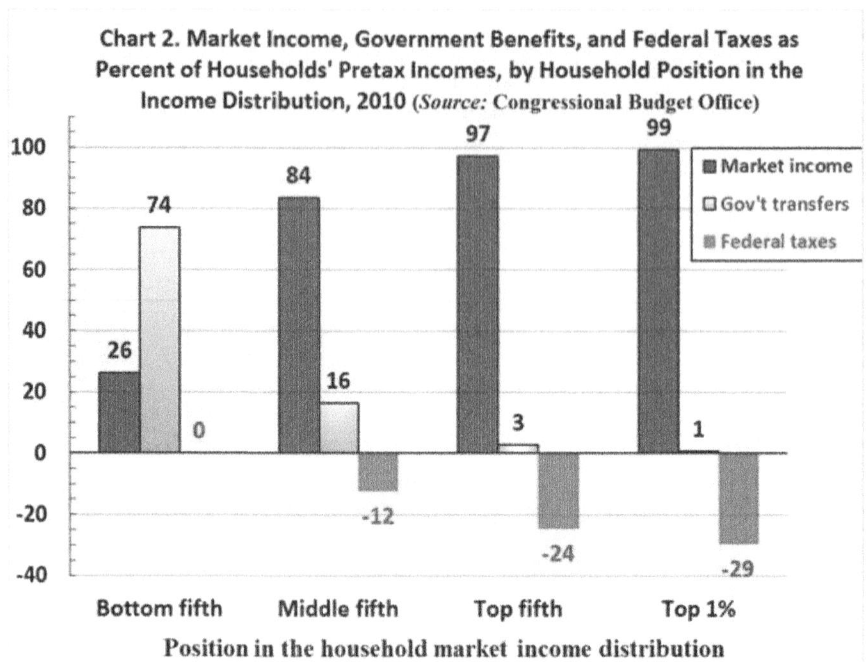

Measurement of tax and transfer is inordinately difficult – but inescapably important in the 21st century,[26] especially (but not only) in OECD countries where non-means-tested transfers for health, education, and retirement

[25] See Gary Burtless, "Has Rising Inequality Brought Us Back to the 1920s? It Depends on How We Measure Income", at http://www.brookings.edu/blogs/up-front/posts/2014/05/20-rising-inequality-1920s-measuring-income-burtless

[26] NYU economist Edward Wolff and colleagues are among those who are working to measure income and wealth more comprehensively, including tax and transfer impacts, through the Levy Institute Measurement of Economic Well-Being program. See http://www.levyinstitute.org/pubs/lmw_feb_09.pdf for both an introduction to their conceptual framework and its application to US income distribution n, 1959-2004. For a full range of Wolff's papers in the Levy program, see http://www.levyinstitute.org/publications/edward-n-wolff.

account for over 20%, sometimes as much as 30%, of GDP – compared to, at most, 2-5% a century ago.[27]

Wealth analysis – a subject that Piketty has rightfully elevated to attention after years of neglect by economists – is equally complicated by government transfers. *Capital*, for example, doesn't incorporate the value of government-provided retirement income and health care, which are of course distributed across all classes in the OECD countries, and which ought to be counted, however calculated, as assets. (Because of complex variations in tax-advantaged personal retirement savings schemes such as 401-k's and IRAs in the US, Piketty also underreports their effect on wealth distribution.

Closing comments

Let me close by sharing a final concern, relevant both to Piketty's work itself – and to reading Piketty in Athens.

The topic: corruption's role in the distribution of wealth and income. Piketty knows full well its importance, but discusses it only briefly in the closing pages of *Capital*. I briefly want to raise the issue of corruption, but specifically in one particular (but by no means corruption's only) form: systematic tax evasion, and most especially evasion through "off-shoring". You will, I hope, understand why it is on my mind here in Athens.

Off-shoring, we all know, distorts (by under-reporting) the measurement of income and wealth (which is both a technical issue, in the narrowest sense, and – as Piketty has so brilliantly shown, a window onto much larger issues). It also short-changes public revenues (a broader macroeconomic question in its own right) *and* erodes public confidence in the integrity of government and markets alike (a very broad and very, very important issue).[28]

---

[27] For country and OECD social spending,, see http://stats.oecd.org/Index.aspx?DataSetCode=SOCX_AGG

[28] Transparency International's surveys of perceptions of corruption in countries around the world are a starting point for understanding how widespread the problem is, and its multi-dimensional consequences. See http://www.transparency.org/research/cpi/overview

I hardly need point to Russian oligarchs, the new billionaire relatives of Chinese Communist leaders, or Third World kleptocrats of myriad ilk to make the point; here in Athens, shipowners often are the first mentioned. Across human history (as earlier Greeks tell us – among them, Solon, Thucydides, Socrates, Herodotus come to mind effortlessly), corruption has always been a significant factor in income and wealth distribution, more so in some countries and some times than others. But public attention today – and public alarm that demands changes – is rising even faster than inequality, although it's not yet at a point that leads to large-scope national (let alone international) reforms.

Let me here just underscore one enormous aspect to provoke attention: the "offshoring" of income and wealth in tax havens with strict secrecy laws or opaque institutional protections. The Cayman Islands, Monaco, Switzerland, the Isle of Man are all among the 80 or so mostly small, even micro, states involved.

If these offshore havens are small in size, the amounts they're holding are not, as Gabriel Zucman, a young LSE-based protégé of Piketty, has recently shown. In a forthcoming paper (which Piketty generously shared with me this summer)[29], Zucman estimates that 8% of the world's total personal financial wealth is now held offshore, costing governments at minimum $200 billion annually in lost public revenue.[30] Additionally, he finds that offshoring lets 20% of US corporate profits escape American taxation each year – a tenfold increase in (legal) tax evasion in the past fifteen years that accounts for seven of the ten percentage points by which corporations have reduced their effective tax rates on average from 30% to 20%.

One might note here – although Zucman politely doesn't – that over those same fifteen years, the cumulative public debt of the US government, and hence the ultimate tax liabilities of its citizens, trebled from roughly $7 trillion

---

[29] For "Taxing Across Borders", forthcoming in *The Journal of Economic Perspectives*, as well as several other papers authored by Zucman (including some with Piketty), see http://gabriel-zucman.eu/.

[30] The NGO Tax Justice Network estimates that in toto some $21-32 trillion in financials assets may currently be held offshore.

to $21 trillion.[31] One should also note that Zucman's work joins that of a number of NGOs which have been researching and advocating reforms for more than two decades. (In contrast to the NGOs, academic economists have given almost no attention to off-shoring – or to corruption more generally. Searching the top five American economics journals over the past five years[32], and using any combination of the terms 'corruption,' 'tax haven' and 'offshore', I found just six papers; five – the exception, an earlier Zucman paper – touch only tangentially on the issues.)

Significantly, although economists aren't paying attention, a growing number of governments are listening, some inspired by criminal concerns, others more pragmatically focused on the governments' revenue losses from taxes evaded.

That governmental attention has in turn led to some barely-known legal and administrative advances in a number of countries, including Germany and France, and even Italy and Greece, where tax evasion approaches a way of life.[33] The United States has quietly entered this arena as well, most recently in 2009 with passage of the suggestively-initialed FATCA (for Foreign Account Tax Compliance Act), which though barely known by the public or the economics profession, now requires 77,000 non-US banks to regularly report transactions of US account holders to US tax authorities. The bill, while weak in several respects, has shown its bite. Credit Suisse, in the largest (but by no means only) FATCA settlement to date, earlier this year agreed to pay $2.6 billion to settle its role in helping American account holders evade US taxes.

---

[31] On gross federal debt, 1999-2014, see http://www.usgovernmentdebt.us/spending_chart_1999_2014USr_15s2li111mcn_H0t

[32] The search was done using Google Scholar's ranking of economic journals at http://scholar.google.com/citations?view_op=top_venues&hl=en&vq=bus_economics

[33] For a summary of EU and member countries' efforts, see the 2013 European Parliamentary study "European Initiatives on Elimination of Tax Havens and Offshore Financial Transactions and the Impact of These Constructions on the Union's Own Resources and Budget" at http://www.europarl.europa.eu/RegData/etudes/etudes/join/2013/490673/IPOL-JOIN_ET%282013%29490673_EN.pdf

Yet the scale of estimated offshoring vastly exceeds enforcement penalties, and Zucman and the NGOs are finding that serious tax haven depositors are responding with clever new means for concealing their wealth and income.

I've raised corruption here as a coda, to underscore just how broadly issues of income and wealth distribution extend beyond their central role as measures of how societies allocate material reward among its members.

In that, I mean to expand our imaginative horizons as we think about how, over the coming years, we might contribute to building on the questions Thomas Piketty has so usefully placed in front of us.

What we will do with that gift remains our challenge as much as his.

Pondering the hurdles for the Mexican economy while reading *Capital in the Twenty-First Century*

Alicia Puyana Mutis [FLACSO, Mexico]

Introduction

I do not intend to simply add one more to the many papers so far published on Piketty´s *Capital in the Twenty-First Century*. There is no need to add further comment regarding the importance of Piketty´s contribution to the actual economic debate. Krugman (2014) states "This is a book that will change both the way we think about society and the way we do economics". However, he also calls attention to the political factors that may render it a version of Palley's *Gattopardo* economics (Palley, 2014)[1]: "Sometimes it seems as if a substantial part of our political class is actively working to restore Piketty's patrimonial capitalism. And if you look at the sources of political donations, many of which come from wealthy families, this possibility is a lot less outlandish than it might seem." Krugman considers *Capital* "a call to arms – a call, in particular, for wealth taxes, global if possible, to restrain the growing power of inherited wealth" (Krugman, 2014 op cit). Very well. But may we ask what the arms might be? The arguments from Smith, Marx, Keynes or those from the Washington Consensus? I am afraid Piketty's work is closer to the principles of the Consensus than it may appear at a first reading.

Rather than cover the same ground as other contributors, in this paper I will explore issues relevant to Piketty's *Capital* based on the Mexican case. Mexico is mentioned only once in *Capital.* In Mexico income concentration remains high despite economic reforms that responded to the debt crisis in the early 1980s, including entry into GATT and the implementation of NAFTA. After presenting some ideas about inequality and poverty in

[1] I would like to add that Palley values Piketty's work, stressing: "The book has already had an enormous positive political impact" and suggesting that criticizing it would help to better understand his arguments (Pally, op cit 2014).

economics, and discussing some points of disagreement with Piketty, the paper will refer to topics he does not analyze or does not consider with sufficient detail. These include differential levels of development and the effects of trade liberalization in some Latin American economies on those differentials. This raises issues regarding path convergence both within and between countries, and also the impacts of education and technology. Mexico offers a relevant case to consider the significance of *Capital* because the country fully embraced neoliberal doctrine and did so at an intense pace. The policies implemented from 1985, induced many changes in the sectoral structure of GDP, in the allocation of labour by sectors, and its distribution between the formal and informal economy. These structural elements are not considered in Piketty's *Capital*, nor does he discuss the path of real wages, labour productivity and its intensity. Bringing these issues to the fore is not necessarily to critique Piketty but it is to add to the explanatory context in which his work might be assessed.

Looking back to the debate on inequality and poverty

At least since the end of the Second War World up to the end of the 1970s both inequality and poverty were considered a malady affecting developing countries, a temporary disorder to overcome if adequate policies were implemented. That optimism about the market economy was fuelled by the works of several authors from different and sometimes conflicting perspectives (Arrow Solow, Kuznets, Rostow ...). Experts from other social sciences also contributed to the aim of confronting socialism and preventing newly independent states from leaning too far to the left. So inequality was relegated to a back corner and attention was given to extreme poverty, as a woe of underdevelopment. After the 2008 crisis, it was evident that inequality and poverty and informality were no longer distinctive characteristics of underdevelopment. Almost all multilateral organizations started to study the effects of increasing wealth and income concentration upon the stability of national economies, globalization and neoliberal doctrines. Works focused on wealth concentration and economic policies and analyzing the effects of wealth and income concentration on growth and poverty reduction through the trickle-down effect. One of the most negative effects of inequality, according to the International Monetary Fund, is political since a minority are able to control a disproportionately large share of resources and "... high inequality also has the potential to alter the political process, giving the rich a relatively greater voice than the less homogenous majority. This imbalance of power can produce policies and economic institutions that benefit a few at the expense of broader society. These policies can in turn further skew the income distribution and ossify the political system, leading to even graver political and economic consequences in the long run" (Ramcharan, 2010). The inverse relation between income concentration and growth has been analyzed by scholars and by practically all multilateral institutions. A general conclusion has been that far from being detrimental some inequality of income distribution benefits growth.[2] So, the topic was not first reintroduced by Piketty, neither did Piketty put it on the agenda of economic debate or link for the first time economic power to political power. As many others have suggested the importance given to *Capital in the Twenty-First Century* can be explained because it analyzes inequality from a neoclassical perspective, and where the proposed solutions are restricted to taxes on hyper salaries and inheritances, in the context of education, technology, trade liberalization and an open door to foreign investments, caveats notwithstanding. Although Piketty critizices neoclassical economics, he also prescribes its principles as a way to breach the inequality trap (Piketty, 2014 p. 55). His prescriptions and those from the OCDE or FMI are pale compared with those proposed by F.D. Roosevelt (1910) in a speech commemorating the Civil War. Quoting Lincoln (1861) the president laid the foundations of the welfare state as the only way to reduce, or to manage, the conflicting interests between non-organized labour and ever-expanding concentrated capital:

> "Labor is prior to, and independent of, capital. Capital is only the fruit of labor, and could never have existed if labor had not first existed. Labor is the superior of capital, and deserves much the higher consideration" (Lincoln, 1861).

While recognizing the rights to own property he affirms, with Lincoln: "Capital has its rights, which are as worthy of protection as any other rights. ... Property is the fruit of labor; ...."

[2] Krugman has insisted on it in a large number of pieces in the NYT. Stiglitz and Galbraith FMI, (2012) OCDE (2011, 2013 and 2014A) ECLAC (2010). Private think-tanks also added to the debate for instance the New Economic Foundation (NEF).

From here Roosevelt explains the need to reduce inequality if the USA wants to preserve the freedom gained with the Civil War. "One of the chief factors in progress is the destruction of special privilege," (Roosevelt, 1910). For the president, the elimination of all privileges was also to achieve practical equality of opportunity for all citizens. Roosevelt's practical equality or *square deal*, did not mean fair play under existing rules but a radical change of them. He proposed raising, even at a confiscatory level, taxes on income and undeserved gains and inheritance, since these led to greater inequality. And since he connected the concentration of wealth with politics, he proclaimed:

> "Today this task (to guarantee *square equality*) means that our State and National governments should free themselves from the influence and from the sinister control of vested interests... today, large business interests frequently control and corrupt the men and methods of government for their own interests. We must expel these interest groups from politics" (Roosevelt, 1901).

How far behind the republican Lincoln and the democrat Roosevelt, we all are today.

In this context, Piketty adds argument to Arrow's claim that if income and property are the basis of freedom, its concentration implies an unequal distribution of liberty, and the possibility of exercising it. This obliges one to consider redistribution as an economic as much as a social and political problem. This aim detracts from the neo-classical proposition that redistribution eliminates the incentive to produce. Even accepting that redistribution might slow down the rhythm of economic growth, the moral and ethical arguments in favour of redistribution should not be underestimated. The values of a society are central to the application and success of development and growth policies. What prevents us finding a solution to the crisis are arguments against distribution provided, for example, by Lucas: "Of the tendencies that are harmful to sound economics, the most seductive, and in my opinion the most poisonous, is to focus on questions of distribution" (Lucas, 2004).

According to the OECD (2011), inequality has a negative effect on the trajectory of an economy. It unleashes social resentment and instability and encourages protectionism and populist anti-globalization sentiments. If the majority loses and a small group absorbs ever greater segments of the gains, the system loses legitimacy and the economic model loses support. So, equity stops being a social and political end and turns into an instrument to maintain the *status quo*, which seems to be Piketty´s position. Literature on the subject also recognizes the socio-political impact of inequality:

(a) The economically powerful groups have greater access to the State (they capture it) they collect the gains and induce policies to perpetuate inequality and low income growth (Arrow, 2013; Barro, 1999; Bénabou, 1996).
(b) Inequality fosters 'clientelism' thereby reducing the quality of democracy (World Bank quoted in Murillo, 2008).
(c) It weakens democratic values by corroding trust and by restricting compensating social mobility (Arrow, 2013; Friedman, 2012).
(d) It has led to the degradation of the environment (Sachs, 2003).
(e) It disrupts the social order by allowing poverty to intensify, which then becomes the basis for social movements and for currents of economic and political migration. (Murillo, 2008; Sachs, 2003).

The conclusions drawn from all these contributions suggest that concentration of wealth and poverty is not just a humanitarian problem, but a geo-strategic one. What political and economic problems would derive from the awareness of the end of the American dream and of an egalitarian Europe is not yet clear; but the social stability of the post-World War II welfare state is fading. The re-emergence of right wing populist parties is a focal point of concern.

Mass inequality, the welfare state and the developing countries

For many, concern with the stratification of poverty and inequality appears to be a relatively new subject in the history of economic thought and politics. It is a problem that fades out and returns according to economic cycles, political concerns and paradigms. Poverty and inequality emerged as a serious concern for the developed world at the time of Indian independence, and later, in the aftermath of the Second World War, with regard to manifest poverty in various countries in Africa and the Caribbean. As Galbraith (1974) notes issues of global stability and a context of confrontation with socialism made it necessary to combat poverty. In the sixties, the concern was expressed through the Rostow *Manifesto*, the proposals for *economic modernization*, the World Bank basic needs programs, Kennedy's Alliance for Progress etc. (Valcárcel, 2007). The purpose of ameliorating inequality between nations and reducing poverty within them was sometimes explicit, but mostly implicit. The concepts of economic and social equality gained worldwide currency, and did so following the consolidation of the welfare state in the developed countries. Industrialization, import substitution and urbanization were taken as essential factors for modernization with the Development State as the leading actor. To consolidate their independence and the nation building process newly independent countries sought to consolidate their national identity. This included tackling inequality in reality or rhetoric. However, countries of the periphery only implemented a devalued version of the welfare state, which not fully integrated into economic and social policies (Mkandawire, 2011). The exceptions in Latina America were Argentina and Uruguay, where a full set of entitlements were implemented.

At the end of the Seventies, strong forces pushed for partial abandonment of the welfare state, the advance of neoliberal ideas and the establishment of elements of supply-side economics, which then sets the main axis of the economy regarding the return on capital. So, the central task of economic management and economic theory was reduced to the containment at all costs of inflations. The non-accelerating inflation rate of unemployment (NAIRU) led to greater labour flexibility and focused on wages as costs, rather than labour as a factor in demand (Laliberté, 2011). The liberal export model aimed mainly at elevating productivity by liberalizing trade, as well as capital and labour markets, reducing taxes and public expenditures, while controlling inflation. It failed to prevent economic crises and did not raising the rate of economic growth. However, in general it did increase inequality and many developing countries sank in the Lost Decade. The relatively short growth spells Latin America has experienced during some years of the 21st

Century have done little to restore the gains lost in terms of equality and well-being for the majority of the population (ECLAC 2012).

Liberalization and convergence in the real world

Piketty's analysis is entirely neoclassical. It assumes full employment of factors and remuneration to all factors according to their marginal productivity; although Piketty does also acknowledge that marginal productivity is a problematic concept. According to the argument, economies will tend to converge at a steady state growth rate, which equals the exogenous growth rates of the labour force and labour productivity at full employment. That is, convergence will occur, supposedly at a magic rate of 2%. Piketty suggests that convergence both internal and external will occur thanks to the full working of the markets induced by liberalizing the economy. The steady state growth rate, diminishing returns to capital and convergence have all previously been disputed by Helpman (2004).

Even acknowledging that total and per capita GDP of some less developed countries (poor countries in Piketty´s terminology) has tended to converge with developed ones, it is clear that the process has taken place in groups and in some instances seems to have lost pace or finished all together. International convergence took place at the cost of internal divergence, as in China. It is of little help to draw attention to the fact that inequality in this country is still lower than in the USA, inferring perhaps that it is a limit not to be surpassed (Piketty, 2014 p. 232). According to Piketty, GDP convergence ends when countries reach the technological frontier: "Similarly, once these countries had attained the global technological frontier, it is hardly surprising that they ceased to grow more rapidly than Britain and the United States or that growth rates in all of these wealthy countries more or less equalized" (2014, pp. 98-99). This assertion is contested by several authors, referred to in Helpman, although based on contrasting evidence (2004, chs 4 and 5). For OECD countries, several authors conclude that convergence has occurred since World War II. Simialrly, within the European Union, convergence took place before the Treaty of Rome came into force in 1958 and decelerated thereafter (Ben-David, 1993; Olivera et al, 2003). Other authors suggest that convergence goes back to the end of the 19th century and came to a standstill in the 1950s. This finding extends also to countries not part of the EU nor of the European Free Trade Association EFTA (Quah, 1995; Slaughter, 1998; Rodríguez and Rodrik, 1998).

Table 1. Per capita GDP growth rates of selected Latin American Countries and the USA, 1900-2013.

	Panel A				**Panel B**			
	Annual growth rate GDP/C				Annual rate as % of USA growth			
	1900-2013	**1900-1945**	**1945-1982**	**1982-2013**	**1900-2013**	**1900-1945**	**1945-1982**	**1982-2013**
Argentina	1.4	1.2	1.32	1.41	0.7	0.4	1.1	0.8
Brasil	2.2	1.7	3.35	1.05	1.1	0.6	2.9	0.6
Chile	2.0	1.5	1.36	2.99	1.0	0.6	1.2	1.7
Colombia	1.9	1.5	2.18	1.79	0.9	0.6	1.9	1.0
Mexico	**1.7**	**1.1**	**2.98**	**0.58**	**0.8**	**0.4**	**2.5**	**0.3**
Peru	2.0	2.5	2.15	0.82	1.0	0.9	1.8	0.5
Uruguay	1.7	1.6	1.36	1.67	0.8	0.6	1.2	1.0
Venezuela	2.7	4.6	2.21	0.41	1.3	1.8	1.9	0.2
8 L. America	1.7	1.7	1.92	1.29	0.9	0.7	1.6	0.7
EUA	2.0	2.6	1.17	1.76	1.0	1.0	1.0	1.0

Source: Own calculations based on Madisson 2001 and The Conference Board 2014.

As indicated in table 1, Panels A and B, between 1945 and 1981, the eight largest Latin American economies grew at rates faster than the USA and never before experienced. In general terms, it could be said that convergence manifested only during the post-war period and came to a halt when liberal reforms were implemented. Piketty suggests:

> "... historical experience suggests that the principal mechanism for convergence at the international as well as the domestic level is the diffusion of knowledge. In other words, the poor catch up with the rich to the extent that they achieve the same level of technological know-how, skill, and education, not by becoming the property of the wealthy. The diffusion of knowledge is not like manna from heaven: it is often hastened by international openness and trade (autarky does not encourage technological transfer)" (Piketty, digital version, p. 55).

But it is clear that from the early Eighties the liberalization of trade and the dismantling of industrial policies, had other and perhaps more important costs than the reduction in government receipts, including the costs of deindustrialization both of productive capacity and employment (Bertola y Ocampo, 2014; Thorp, 1999).

Convergence linked to free trade or to liberalization policies has been disputed at length (Rodríguez and Rodrik, 1999; Quah, 1995; Slaughter, 1997 and 2001; Olivera Herrera, 2002; Rodríguez et al, 1999 and 2013; Puyana et al, 2004). The direct relation between free trade and convergence has not been fully established. It seems where economies first grow and then liberalize subsequent convergence is rather an exception than a norm – it is hard to achieve in the neoliberal economic model (Rodrik, 2013). This can be illustrated using Latin America. Consider figure 1, where convergence is measured as the standard deviation of the logarithm of per capita GDP.

Figure 1. Per capita GDP convergence of selected Latin American countries and the USA, 1946-2013.

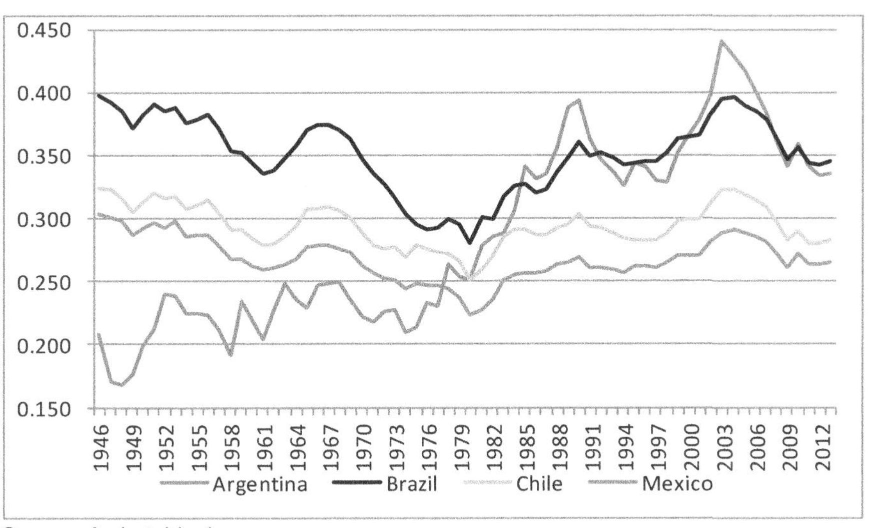

Source: As in table 1.

The situation is similar for income per head. From 1970 to 1981, Mexico's income per head was nearer as a % of USA income than subsequently. After 1981 divergence occurred – as it did in Brazil and, to a lesser extent, in Colombia. Chile is the exception.

The *divergence* of per capita GDP and per capita income after the liberal reforms of the early eighties invite the question: have Latin American countries, for instance Mexico, reached a technological frontier and is convergence no longer possible?

Figure 2. Convergence between per capita income of some Latin America Countries and the USA, 1970-2012 (in percentages).

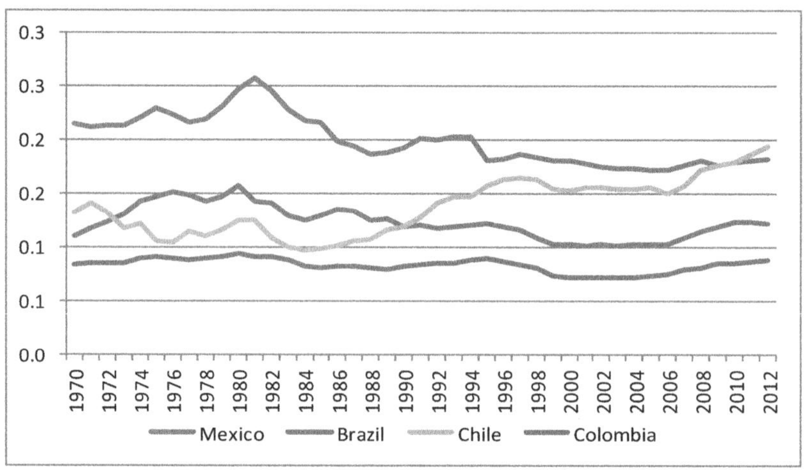

Source: Own elaboration bases on WB WDI 2014.

Is it liberalization?

For all countries included in figures 1 and 2, convergence ended after liberal economic reforms and liberalization of trade and capital accounts were in place. None recovered the level reached in the Seventies. The principal sources of convergence for Latin American countries has been gross capital formation, the share of manufactures in GDP; liberalization of trade is negative for Mexico and positive for Chile and in both cases not significant. Convergence factors declined after reforms. The elimination of state intervention in markets, leaving untouched the concentration of assets, production, distribution and human capital, was itself a real manifestation of the political power of big capital. Education has not demonstrated any explanatory value (Puyana and Romero, 2004; Romero 2014). In general terms, the countries with the largest increases in the trade/GDP ratio, Mexico amongst others, were the ones with lower economic growth (Puyana, 2014)[3]. Fiscal policy, taxation and public expenditure brings to light the political muscle of big economic interests. The income distribution after taxes and fiscal expenditure is practically identical, with a reduction of the Gini index of only a small fraction of a percentage (OCDE, 2014 B). The structure of taxes, in which indirect taxes, especially VAT, are highly prominent demonstrates that income taxes and corporate taxes are relatively low, resulting in regressive taxation.

Figure 3. Latin America. External coefficient and GDP growth, 1960-2013.

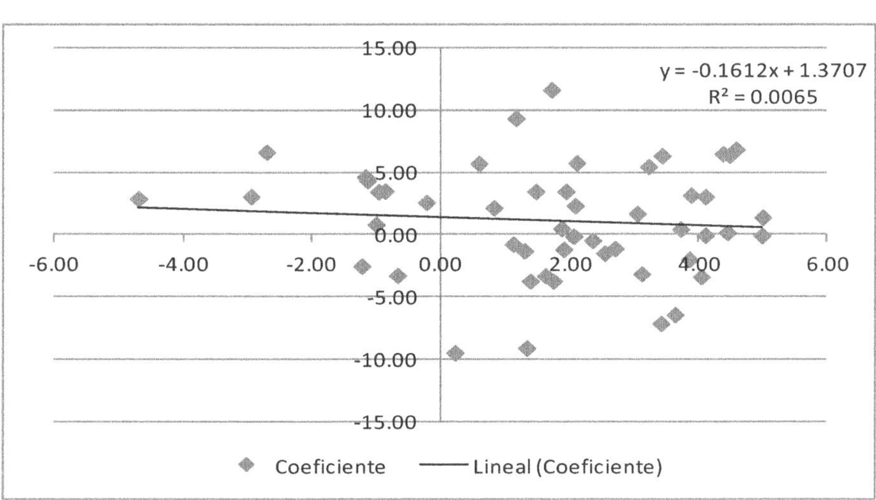

Source: Own elaboration based on WB WDI 2014

In Latin America, liberalization measured as the external coefficient of GDP (imports + exports/GDP), does not seem to be strongly related with faster GDP expansion (figure 3) and, therefore, neither with convergence. During

[3] The data and the results from a growth model calculated for Argentina, Brazil, Chile, Colombia and Mexico, covering 1960-2012 discussed in Puyana 2014 are available upon request.

1980-2013, the total external coefficient of Mexican GDP expanded from 23 to 64%. In 2013 the exports coefficient was 32.4 and imports 31.7 of total GDP, resulting a deficit which has been constant since 1983. We found that the labour productivity gap between Mexico (and other L.A. countries) and the USA has grown larger since the reforms. So at least in Mexico, but as well in other Latin American Countries, free trade and open borders have not meant that "...the less developed countries have leapt forward in productivity and increased their national incomes. The technological convergence process may be abetted by open borders for trade, but it is fundamentally a process of the diffusion and sharing of knowledge – the public good par excellence – rather than a market mechanism", (Piketty, 2014, p. 21 digital version).

The Latin American data is approximately replicated for Mexico, where the relation is inverse, although not significant. This is also confirmed by the trajectory of imports and exports as a percentage of GDP and contrasting per capita GDP growth. External coefficients have little explanatory significance, but the relation is negative as figures 4 and 5 bear out.

Figure 4. Mexico, GDP, exports*, imports* growth rates 1960-2013.

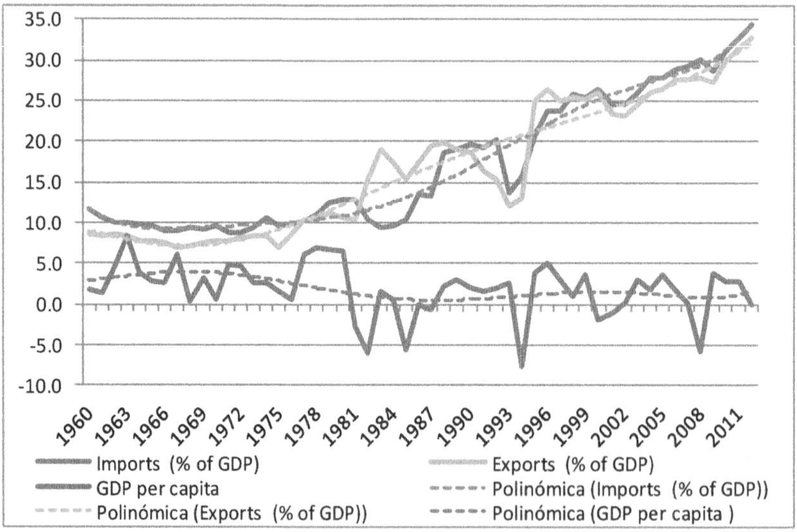

Source: Own elaboration based on WB WDI 2014

Figure 5. Mexico. Relation between GDP/C- external coefficient, 1962-2012.

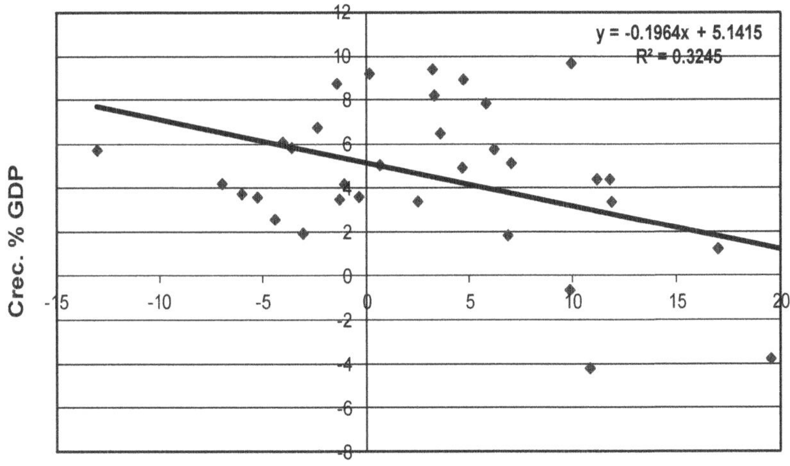

Source: Own elaboration based on WB WDI 2014.

Mexico did expand its exports, mainly manufactured ones, which contributed 85% of total external sales. Total exports grew from 26 to 338 billion constant 2005 dollars that is at an annual average rate of 8.4%.

How does one explain the inverse relation between external coefficient and exports and GDP growth, given that the aim of liberalizing foreign trade and capital and labour markets was to increased productivity (by eliminating the distortions induced by industrialization policies changing the allocation of productive factors in accordance with comparative advantage and resource abundance)? First, an impact noticeable all over Latin America, México included, has been the fall in tradable sectors, manufactures and agriculture as sources of total GDP and employment (Puyana, 2014). In the period 1983-2013 Mexican manufactures contribution to GDP and employment fell from 25% to 15% and from 24 to 10% respectively. For agriculture the contraction started during the import substitution process and the reforms failed to provide a reversal. In 2013 the contribution of agriculture to GDP was 3% and to employment around 14%, suggesting low productivity and low income.

Second, the tradable sectors contribution to GDP and employment has been low and falling and total labour productivity has not increased substantially, vis-à-vis the USA and its major competitors in this market, where Mexico directs almost 80% of its total exports (see figure 6). In general, since around 1983, rather than as a result of increases in productivity (the main driver 1950-1982), the Mexican economy has grown more as a result of increases in employment, the rate of participation of the labour force and because of numbers of hours per worker[4].

Figure 6. Mexican labour productivity as % of USA productivity, 1950-2013

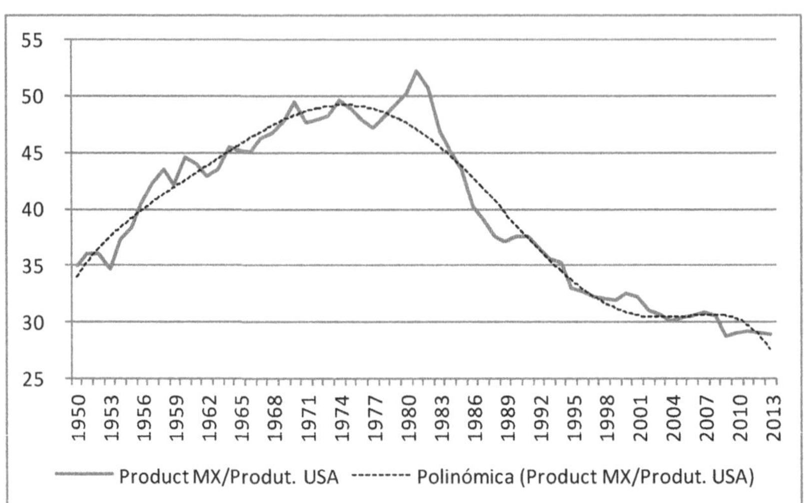

Source: As in table 1.

Several reasons help account for this trajectory:

- persistent low productivity in the agriculture sector (accounting for 14% of total employment);
- the movement of labour from agriculture to informal trade and personal services and construction in urban areas (sectors employing contemporary surplus labour);
- the fall of total investment per worker after 1982: in 2010, total investment per worker was 2.5% lower than in 1982 (a record year

[4] Mexicans worked in average 30% more hours a year than the USA. Intensification of labour is a way to confront declining real wages.

for private national and public investment based on data going back to 1940).

The fall both in public and private investment per worker in the second period suggests there has been no crowding-out effect. Considering that during 1940-1982 total GDP expanded faster (6%) than total investments, it could be assumed that resources were efficiently used. Labour productivity fell in the post reform period as investment failed to manifest and grew at a lower pace than employment (see table 2). Given these conditions, it is not possible to conclude with Piketty (2014, p. 398) that liberalization induces technological convergence: "The overall conclusion of this study is that a market economy based on private property, if left to itself, contains powerful forces of convergence, associated in particular with the diffusion of knowledge and skills".

Table 2. Total investments per worker. Total, public, private national and foreign, 1940-2010 (in thousand 2000 dollars)

	GDP	Emplyt	GDP/L	Total	Private	Private Nal.	FDI	Public Nal.	Total Nal.
1940	325.6	5,858	55.57	3.22	1.64	1.37	0.27	1.58	2.95
1982	4,047.1	22,813	117.40	33.78	16.05	15.01	1.04	15.42	30.42
2010	7,453.7	47,138	158.13	33.83	23.19	20.38	2.81	9.29	29.68
Annual average rates of growth in percentages									
	GDP	**Emplyt**	**GDP/L**	**Total**	**Private**	**Private Nal.**	**FDI**	**Public Nal.**	**Total Nal.**
1940-1982	5.99	3.26	2.66	5.68	7.00	8.59	18.95	5.76	5.75
1983-2012	2.48	2.73	-0.12	1.58	4.06	5.49	8.54	0.65	2.75

Source: Own estimations based in Presidencia de la República, Informes presidenciales, several years. figures in brackets are negative rates.

A third factor explaining the lack of convergence between Mexico and the USA is the structure of exports. These are heavily concentrated in manufactured products inserted within global value chains and with little domestic value added, relatively low labour intensity per unit of product, and limited technological significance. Total exports in 2012 represented almost 34% of GDP, whilst exports of manufactures comprised 85% of total external sales, they accounted for only 3% of total GDP. Mexican manufactures for exports are linked to global value chains. The country is a cost reducing center and not a centre of innovation and development. Decisions regarding when, where and how quickly to decentralize and where to export to are a controlled matrix. In 2012 foreign owned companies accounted for around 66% of total Mexican exports of manufactures. With small demand for domestic labour and other inputs, manufactures do no generate employment and do not have important linkages with the rest of the economy. As Arndt suggests, based on fragmentation of the productive process, the most technological segments of production moved to developing countries during an import substitution process but moved again to the central matrixes; the more intensive processes are transferred to lower wage countries, as fragmentation has resulted in a de facto *death of distance* (Arndt et al, 2001) enabling, for example, companies to move from the Mexican-USA border area to China, even if their total production is exported to the North American Market..

Mexican foreign trade is an intra-industry trade but also a Ricardian-type trade, since Mexico imports high-tech manufactures and exports low-tech ones for low income markets in the USA. Rather than technological up-grading, Mexico is a consumer of technology not a technology producer, analogous to countries specialized in commodities, which according to Piketty (p. 55) are "... areas without much prospect of future development". Mexican has embraced a second generation import substitution model. The income elasticity of demand for imports is 4.5% making it impossible to have the needed high rates of GDP growth (around 6%) to accommodate in the formal sector the over one million entrants to the labour force. The current account deficit stands at around 1.5% of GDP. With lower growth, let's say 4%, exports should grow steadily at an impossible annual rate of 18 percent over a long period. For Mexico to maintain the actual current account, the long-term growth of the product cannot exceed 1.6%, a rate that creates negative effects upon employment and labour income, as we will see. Other Latin American countries, such as Argentina, Brazil, Colombia, Uruguay, Bolivia, all two-hundred-year-old republics and not the new ones (to which Piketty refers, p. 55), are specializing in exports of commodities, in a 21st Century version of old forms of specialization. We contend that this reversion is a logical and intended effect of liberal reforms and the liberalization of trade. The potential effects of *extractivismo* on income concentration internal and external inequality are not always positive, as many authors have concluded along the years. Latin America followed the Washington consensus by the book, ignoring List's 1885 warning regarding policies to implement development.

To conclude: impacts on the labour market

After reform, Mexican informal employment exploded to more than 61% of total employment, while rural migration fed the services and construction sectors (the major part of the annual increases of the PEA and of employment displaced from manufactures). In 2012, the service sector constituted 69% of total employment. The country has entered an open economy deindustrialization path. This is an effect of depressed aggregate demand and interaction with the international economy (Patnaik, 2003) rather than full employment. In developing countries, even in the most dynamic emerging countries, full employment has not been and is not now the norm. Mexico and practically all Latin America fully liberalized their economies. The movement of goods and capital is totally free but labour is not and economic international migration is costly. This partial factor liberalization accelerated the mobility of capital and increased the capital/labour mobility ratio. In this context, capital is relatively more scarce, labour more abundant and the relative profitability of capital higher.

Table 3. Index of minimum and medium real wages, 1980-2013
(Year 2000 = 0)

	Minimum Real wage	Medium Real wages
1980	312	114
1990	145	89
2000	100	100
2010	97	113
2013	99	114

Source: own estimations based on Puyana and Romero (2009) and STSP ENOE several years.

From 1980 to 2012, the Mexican real minimum wage collapsed and medium wages stagnated. Table 3 presents the index of real minimum and medium wages during 1980-2013. The index of minimum wages in 2012 was 68.3% lower than in 1980. Argentina shows a similar trajectory for the indexes of real minimum and average wages, with the former falling from 100 in 1970, to 53 in 2012 and the latter to 99.

What is really preoccupying is that in Mexico the fall in real wages took place despite improvements in education. In effect, the structure of the labour force by years of education changed radically during 1991-2010; the rates for annual growth of workers with high tertiary education was 6.7% while that of workers with only one year decreased by 1.2%.

Table 4 shows how the salary gap between the L0 to L3 groups and the L5s decreased because the wages for the most educated grew at a lower pace - and not because of any increases in wages for the less educated resulting from increased demand. Better educated workers are being employed in activities which require lower levels of education and training.

Table 4. Structure of Mexican labour force by years of education, 1991-2010.

	1991	1995	2000	2005	2010	G*
L0	3.4	3.6	3.1	2.4	2.2	-2.52%
L1	12.7	13.3	13.9	12.5	12.0	-0.31%
L2	5.5	6.7	8.7	10.8	11.1	3.95%
L3	4.0	4.6	5.6	5.9	6.3	2.47%
L4	2.7	3.2	4.8	8.7	8.9	6.95%
L5	0.1	0.2	0.3	0.5	0.5	7.48%
Total	28.5	31.6	36.3	40.8	41.0	2.04%

L0: no education; L1: between 1 and 6 years education (Primary); L2: between 7 and 9 years (Secondary) + Technological education: L3: between 10 and 12 years; L4: one or more years university; L5: one or more years of post-graduate education.

As a result of liberalization, fragmentation and the high concentration of production and distribution, salaries in the manufacturing sector have fallen while productivity shows only small gains. This is due more to the reduction in employment than increases in productivity and in the volume of product. The effect of liberalization has been to reduce costs, mainly labour costs. The combination of liberalization of trade and the revaluation of the peso (and almost all Latin American currencies), has been to maintain stability, suppressing wages. One percent of revaluation of the Mexican peso reduces real wages and consumer prices by about 0.50%. Since 1980, the peso has been protractedly revalued by almost 20%. Between 1994-2003, labour productivity and real wages in manufactures grew at an annual rate of 1% and 0.5% respectively.

Figure 7. Share of labour and capital in national income, 1960-2012.

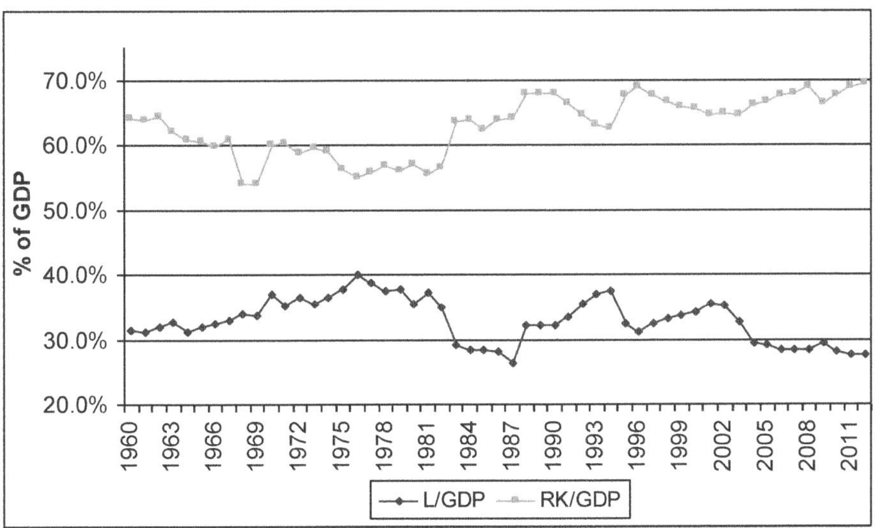

Based on the above exploration of the Mexican case we can now draw some conclusions regarding the evolution of Piketty´s inequality r>g; which explains why capitalism tends to increase inequality by reducing the share of labour in the functional distribution of income (see figure 7). In the case of Mexico this is linked with the liberalization of trade, capital and labour markets, and the entire set of liberal reforms. We suggest that for developing countries similar to Mexico, free trade and liberal policies may *not* lead to internal and external convergence.

The production of manufactures presents a similar path: larger rates of growth of income (g) and lower rates in wages (r). In effect, for the period 1990-2012 the value of r-g was -13.48, signalling a mayor expansion of g. If comparing: for the period 1995-2013, we found gains in annual productivity, which contrast with declining real annual wages per worker, see figure 8.

Figure 8. Mexico: annual productivity per worker and real annual average wages per worker, 1995-2013 (in thousand pesos 2010).

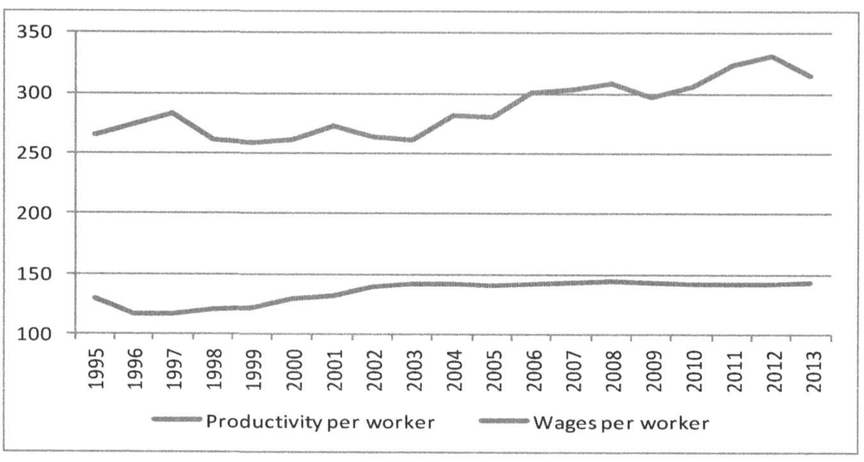

Source: Secretaría de Trabajo y Previsión Social, Encuesta de empleo y salarios, varios años

References

Arndt, S.W. Kierzkowski, H. (2001), *Fragmentation : New Production Patterns in the World Economy: New Production Patterns in the World Economy*, Oxford UP, Oxford, London

Bertola L. y Ocampo, J. A. (2014) El desarrollo económico de América Latina desde la Independencia. FCE, México

CEPAL (2010) *La hora de la igualdad*: brechas por cerrar, caminos por abrir. www.cepal.org/.../100604_2010-114-SES.33-3

Krugman, P. (2014) "Why we're in a New Gilded Age", *The New York Review of Books*, May 8/2014

Lincoln A. (Dic 3 de 1861) "First Annual Inform", recuperated September 1(2014) from: http://teachingamericanhistory.org/library/document/new-nationalism-speech/

List, F. (1885) *The National System of Political Economy Book IV, Chapter XXXIII* http://www.econlib.org/library/YPDBooks/List/lstNPE33.html #Book IV, Chapter 33

Lucas, E. R. (2004) "The Industrial Revolution: Past and Future", 2003 Annual Report Essay, The Federal Reserve Bank of Mineapolis, Mayo 2004 acceded at http://www.minneapolisfed.org/publications_papers/pub_display.cfm?id=3333&

Madisson, Agnus (2001) The World Economy: Historical Statistics, GGDC databases http://www.ggdc.net/

OECD (2011), Divided We Stand, Paris

OECD (2014 A), "OECD@100: Policies for a shifting world" (ECO/CPE(2014)11)

OCDE (2014 B) Statistics,publicbalance and public debt acceded at http://www.oecd.org/eco/public-finance/

OECD (2013), "Crisis squeezes income and puts pressure on inequality and poverty"

Olivera Herrera (2002), Cuarenta Años de Crecimiento Económico en la Unión Europea: Factores Determinantes. Mimeo, Instituto Ortega y Gasset, Madrid.

Palley Thomas I. (2014) The Accidental Controversialist: Deeper Reflections on Thomas Piketty's "Capital", *Monthly Review*, 24.04.14, acceded at http://mrzine.monthlyreview.org/2014/palley240414.html

Piketty, Thomas (2014). *Capital in the Twenty-First Century.* Cambridge: Harvard University Press.

Puyana y Romero (2003). *Acuerdos comerciales.*

Puyana, A. and Romero, J. 'Is There Convergence Between North American Free Trade Agreement Partners?' acceded at http://www.networkideas.org/feathm/may2004/ft05_American_FTA_Partners.htm

Quah, Danny, T. (1995). 'Empirics for Economic Growth and Convergence'. LSE DP No. 253

Ramcharan, Rodney 2010 "Inequality Is Untenable", Finance and Development, September 2010, Vol. 47, No. 3, acceded at: http://www.imf.org/external/pubs/ft/fandd/2010/09/ramcharan.htm#author

Rodriguez & Rodrik (1999). *Trade Policy and Economic Growth: A Skeptic's Guide To The Cross-National Evidence.* NBER, WP No 7081

Slaughter, M. (1997)._'Per capita Income Convergence and the Role of International Trade' in *American Economic Review.*

Slaughter, M. (2001). 'Trade Liberalization and Per Capita Income convergence: A Difference-in-Difference Analysis' in *Journal of International Economics*, vol 55, pp. 203-28.

The Conference Board Total Economy Database™,January 2014, http://www.conference-board.org/data/economydatabase/

Thorp, R (1999), Progreso, pobreza y exclusión: una historia económica de América Latina en el siglo XX, IAB, Washington

WB WDI 2014, acceded September 4 2014 at: http://databank.worldbank.org/data/views/variableSelection/selectvariables.aspx?source=world-development-indicators#

Piketty's inequality and local versus global Lewis turning points

Richard C. Koo [Nomura Research Institute, Japan]

Thomas Piketty's *Capital in the Twenty-First Century* opened up an entirely new debate on the optimal distribution of wealth, an issue that was largely overlooked by the economics profession until now. Although I cannot claim to have understood all the implications of his enormous contributions, I do have one reservation about one of the historical points he makes. Namely, he claims that the extreme inequality that existed prior to World War I was corrected by the destruction of two world wars and the Great Depression. He then goes on to argue that the retreat of progressive taxation in the developed world starting in the late 1970s ended up creating a level of inequality that approaches that which existed prior to World War I.

Although he has ample data to back his assertions, I would suggest that the pre-1970 results he obtained may also be due to the urbanization that drove the industrialization taking place in the developed world. Similarly, his post-1970 results may be attributable to urbanization in Japan and subsequently in other parts of Asia. In this paper I would like to propose that there are two relevant Lewis turning points (LTPs) – one for local economies (i.e., for the developed world) and one for the global economy – and that these two overlap Piketty's two observations on inequality.

The LTP refers to the stage in the industrialization of a nation's economy where urban factories finally absorb all the surplus labor in rural areas. From the standpoint of a capitalist or business owner, whether domestic or foreign, the pre-LTP world is an extremely lucrative one, since it is possible to secure a boundless supply of labor from rural districts simply by paying the going wage. In this world, capitalists need not worry about a shortage of labor and can expand their businesses essentially without limit as long as they have the necessary production facilities and a market for their products. Capitalists able to supply products in demand before the LTP is reached can therefore earn huge profits, further increasing their incentive to expand.

Figure 1 illustrates this from the perspective of labor supply and demand. The labor supply curve is almost horizontal (DHK) until the Lewis turning point (K) is reached because there is an essentially unlimited supply of rural laborers seeking to work in the cities. Any number of such laborers can be assembled simply by paying a given wage (DE).

In this graph, capital's share is represented by the area of the triangle formed by the left axis, the labor demand curve, and the labor supply curve, while labor's share is represented by the rectangle below the labor supply curve. At the time of labor demand curve D_1, capital's share is the triangle BDG, and labor's share is the rectangle DEFG. The inequality arises from the fact that the capital share BDG may be shared by a few persons or families, whereas the labor share DEFG may be shared by millions of workers.

Figure 1. The Lewis turning point

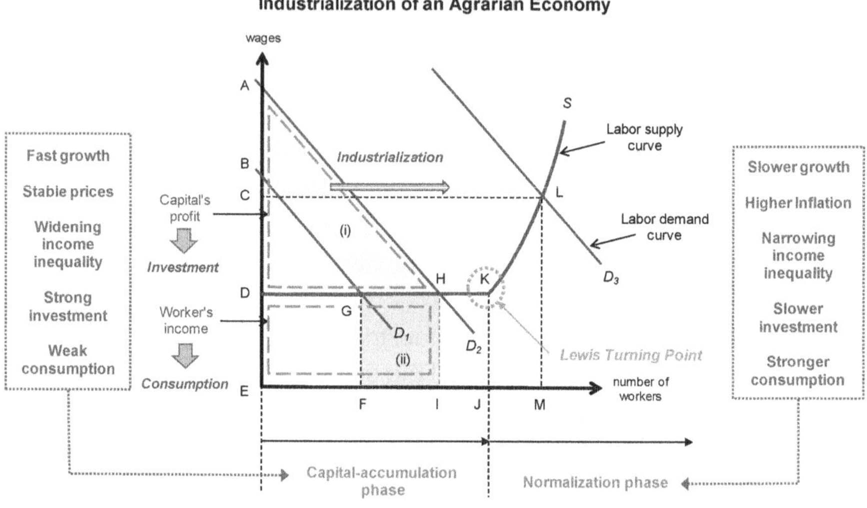

Source: Nomura Research Institute

Successful capitalists in this world will continue to invest in an attempt to make even more money. That raises the demand for labor, causing the labor demand curve to shift steadily to the right (from D_1 to D_2) even as the labor supply curve remains flat. As the labor demand curve shifts to the right, total wages received by labor increase from the area of the rectangle DEFG at time D_1 to the area of rectangle DEIH at time D_2 as the length of the rectangle below the labor supply curve grows. However, the growth is linear. The share of capital, meanwhile, is likely to increase at more than a linear rate as the labor demand curve shifts to the right, expanding from the area of the triangle BDG at D_1 to the area of the triangle ADH at D_2.

Until the LTP is reached, GDP growth increases the portion of GDP that accrues to the capitalists, exacerbating inequalities. A key reason why a handful of families and business groups in Europe a century ago and in Japan prior to World War II were able to accumulate such massive wealth is that they faced an essentially flat labor supply curve (wealth accumulation in North America and Oceania was not quite as extreme because these economies were characterized by a shortage of labor). Inequality in China has worsened in recent decades for the same reason.

Inequality worsens with growth until LTP is reached

During this phase, income inequality, symbolized by the gap between rich and poor, widens sharply as capitalists' share of income (the triangle) increases much faster than labor's share (the rectangle). Because capitalists are profiting so handsomely, they will continue to re-invest profits in a bid to make even more money. Sustained high investment rates mean domestic capital accumulation also proceeds rapidly. This is the takeoff period for a nation's economic growth.

Until the economy reaches the Lewis turning point, however, low wages mean most people will still have hard lives, even though the move from the countryside to the cities may improve their situations modestly. Business owners, in contrast, are able to accumulate tremendous wealth during this period.

Marx and Engels, who lived in pre-LTP Europe, were incensed by the horrendous inequality and miserable working and living conditions for ordinary people they saw and responded by inventing the theory of communism, which called for capital to be shared by the laborers. In that sense, the birth of communism may itself have been a historical imperative of sorts.

Today's so-called developed economies all started out as agrarian societies before the industrial revolution. As Piketty points out, economic growth was slow in the agrarian centuries, and upward mobility was very limited. With few technological breakthroughs, investment opportunities were limited if not non-existent – the only opportunities involved the acquisition of new territories, mainly through colonization. The absence of investment opportunities at a time when people were trying to save for the future meant these economies were constantly confronting what Keynes called the paradox of thrift.

The advent of the industrial revolution, which was in essence a technological revolution, opened up tremendous investment and employment opportunities in the cities where factories were being established. The massive growth in investment opportunities pulled these economies out of a multi-century paradox of thrift, and economic growth picked up sharply. That also kick-started the process of urbanization that continued until the LTP was reached. However, it was no easy transition for the average workers with 14-hour work day not at all uncommon until the end of 19th century. According to the OECD, the yearly working hours in the West in 1870 were 2950 hours or double the present level of 1450 hours. Access to capital and financing, together with the expertise needed to produce and sell products, was also limited to the educated elite, which in those days was a very small group. Those having this access and the right skills did very well indeed.

Inequality improves and economy matures after passing LTP

As business owners continue to generate profits and expand investment, the economy eventually reaches the Lewis turning point. Once that happens, the total wages of labor – which had grown only linearly until then – start to increase rapidly since the labor supply curve now has a significant positive slope. For example, even if labor demand increases just a little, from J to M in Figure 1, total wages accruing to labor will rise dramatically, from the area of rectangle DEJK to the area of rectangle CEML.

Once the LTP is reached, labor finally has the bargaining power to demand higher wages, which reduces the profit share of business owners. But businesses will continue to invest in the economy as long as they are making good returns, leading to further tightness in the labor market. It is at this point that the inequality problem begins to correct itself.

As labor's share increases, consumption's share of GDP will increase at the expense of investment, and with reduced capital accumulation, growth will slow as well. From that point onward the economy begins to "mature" and "normalize" in the sense in which we use those terms today.

A significant portion of the European and American populations still lived in rural areas until World War I, as shown in Figure 2. Even in the US, where – unlike Europe – workers were always in short supply, nearly half the population was living on farms as late as the 1930s. The mobilization of two world wars then pushed these economies beyond the LTP, and standards of living began to improve dramatically. With workers' share of profits increasing relative to that of capital, inequality diminished as well, ushering in the so-called Golden Sixties in the US.

Marx and Engels' greatest mistake was to assume that the extreme inequality they witnessed (points G and H in Figure 1) would continue forever. In reality, it was just one inevitable step on the path towards industrialization. Ironically, those countries that adopted communism before reaching their LTPs ended up stagnating because the profit motive needed to promote investment and push the economy beyond its LTP was lost.

US-led free trade changed the game and enabled Asia's emergence

In the pre-1945 world, there was an important constraint that slowed down the progression described above – a shortage of aggregate demand and markets. If the workers constituted the main source of consumption demand, they could not have provided enough demand for all the goods produced because their share of income was so low, while capitalists typically had a higher marginal propensity to save. Consequently, aggregate supply often exceeded aggregate demand.

Figure 2. Urbanization* continued in the West until the1960s...

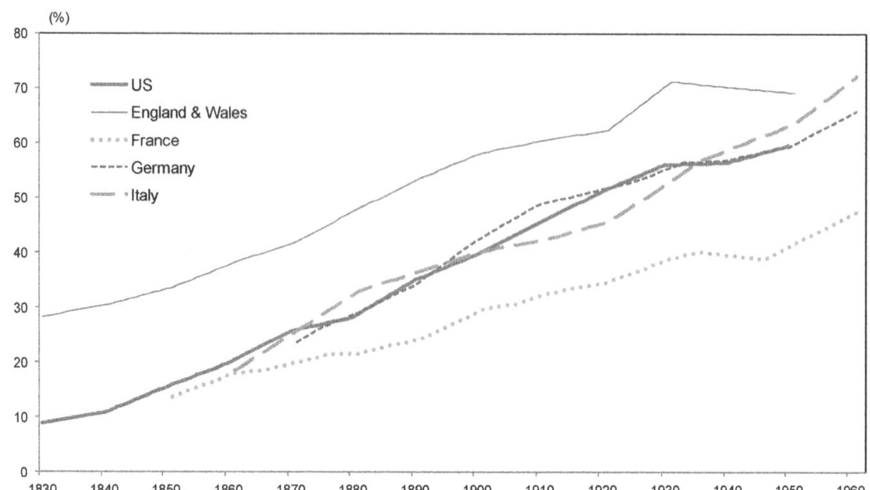

* Percentage of population living in urban areas with 20,000 people or more in England & Wales, 10,000 or more in Italy and France, 5,000 or more in Germany and 2,500 or more in the US.
Sources: U.S. Census Bureau (2012), *2010 Census*, Peter Flora, Franz Kraus and Winfried Pfenning ed, (1987), *State, Economy and Society in Western Europe 1815-1975*

To overcome this constraint, European powers turned to colonization in a bid to acquire both sources of raw materials and captive markets where they could sell the goods they produced. Indeed, it was believed for centuries that national economies could not grow without territorial expansion.

That led to constant wars and killing until 1945 when the victorious and enlightened Americans introduced a free-trade regime that allowed anyone with competitive products to sell to anyone else. The US took the lead by opening its own market to the world. Although the US initiative was motivated to a great extent by the need to fend off the Soviet threat by rebuilding western Europe and Japan, the free-trade regime allowed not only Japan and Germany, which had lost all their colonies, but also many other countries to prosper without the need to expand their territories.

The advent of free trade made obsolete the notion of territorial expansion as a necessary condition for economic growth. While the victorious allies after World War II were busy fighting indigenous independence movements in their colonies at enormous expense, Japan and Germany – which had lost all of their overseas and some of their domestic territories – quickly grew to become the second and third largest economies in the world. In other words, post-war Japan and Germany have proved that what is really needed for economic growth is markets, not territories. Economic growth will accelerate if markets can be accessed without the expense of acquiring territories.

The relative infrequency of wars between countries that had been fighting since history began may be due to the fact that free trade meant territorial expansion was no longer a necessary or sufficient condition for economic growth. Indeed, colonies became more of a liability than an asset after the free-trade regime took hold.

In Asia, it was the Japanese who discovered in the 1950s that an economy could grow and prosper simply by producing quality products for the US market. Japan reached its LTP in the mid-1960s, when the mass migration of rural graduates to urban factories and offices, known in Japanese as *shudan shushoku,* finally came to an end. Then the share of labor began to rise sharply, and the nation came to be known as the country of the middle class, with more than 90 percent of the population considering themselves to be part of the middle class. The whole country was proud of the fact that it had virtually no inequality. Some even quipped in those days that Japan was how communism was *supposed* to work!

The Japanese success then prompted Taiwan, South Korea and eventually the rest of Asia to follow the same export-oriented growth formula in a process dubbed the "flying geese" pattern of industrialization. The biggest beneficiary of all, of course, was China, which was able to transform a desperately poor agrarian society of 1.3 billion people into the world's second-largest economy in just 30 years.

The 30 years following Deng Xiaoping's opening of the Chinese economy probably qualify as the fastest and greatest economic growth story in history, but it was possible only because the US-led free-trade system allowed Chinese firms and foreign companies producing in China to sell their products anywhere in the world. It was that access to the global market that prompted so many companies from around the world to build factories there. Were it not for the markets provided by the free-trade regime, it could have taken many times as long for China to achieve the same economic growth.

Local and global Lewis turning points and Piketty's inequality

This increase and decrease in inequality before and after the LTP may explain the first part of Piketty's historical observation that inequality in the West increased until World War I but subsequently decreased until the 1970s. Although Piketty attributes this to the destruction of wealth brought about by two world wars and the introduction of progressive income taxes, this was also a period in which urbanization came to an end in most of these countries.

Figure 3. Urbanization in the West slowed down in the 70s

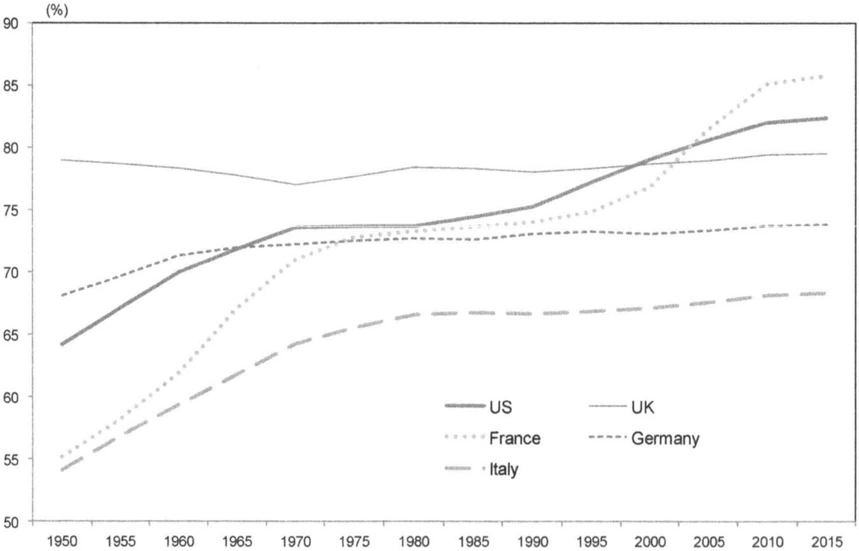

Source: Population Division of the Department of Economic and Social Affairs of the United Nations Secretariat, World Population Prospects: The 2010 Revision and World Urbanization Prospects

The post-1970 increase in inequality in these countries noted by Piketty may also be due to the fact that Japan and later other Asian countries began exporting to the West as they reached their own LTPs. For western capitalists able to utilize Asian resources, it was a golden opportunity to make money. But for manufacturing workers in the West whose employers had to compete with cheaper imports from Asia, this was not a welcome development at all.

The Japanese ascent disturbed the US and European industrial structures in no small way. As many workers lost their jobs, ugly trade frictions ensued between the US and Europe on one side and Japan on the other. This was the first case of western countries that had passed their LTPs being chased from behind by a country where wages were much lower.

Some of the pain western workers felt were of course offset by the fact that, as consumers, they benefitted from cheaper imports. And soon enough, Japanese wages reached western levels. The Asian "tigers" reached their own LTPs by the late 1980s.

The end of the Cold War then brought China and India into the global trading framework. Both countries were still far from their LTPs, and each had more than a billion people. Although India is taking time to get its economy moving, China wasted no time in integrating itself with the global economy. That enabled it to attract an astronomical amount of foreign direct investment, not just from the West and Japan but also from Taiwan and Hong Kong.

Those in the West and elsewhere who have the skills needed to take advantage of the opportunities in China are operating like the capitalists in their own countries' pre-LTP eras and are making tremendous amounts of money. It also means those who have to compete with Chinese (and eventually Indian) workers are experiencing zero or even negative income growth. Foreign businesses that are expanding rapidly in China are also likely to be investing less at home, which will have a depressing effect on domestic economic growth and wages.

Moreover, the skills not easily replaced by cheap labor elsewhere are likely to be highly technical and require long years of investment in human capital. Not everybody in the developed world is willing to put up with the hardship required to acquire such skills, especially when they already enjoy a reasonably comfortable life.

The result has been the renewed increase in inequality that Piketty observed during the last three decades in the industrialized world. In other words, this is a story of a global LTP which still has some ways to go because there are many countries in the world that have not reached their LTPs.

The above suggests that there are at least two relevant LTPs for a country's development: the country's own turning point and the *global* turning point. For a capitalist in the developed world, the existence of developing countries that have yet to reach their LTPs represents an opportunity to make money by lowering production costs. For workers in the developed world, the same globalized environment means more competition from low-wage developing countries.

That, in turn, will increase inequality in the developed world until everyone in the world is gainfully employed, i.e., when all countries in the world have moved beyond their LTPs. The fact that China passed that point around 2012 should come as a relief for workers in the developed economies, but there are still other countries, such as India, that can continue to exert downward pressure on developed-world wages.

Global competition and the happiness of nations

The real issue for growth and inequality in the developed world, therefore, is how to fend off the countries chasing these economies from behind. The West faced this problem for the first time when Japan emerged as a formidable competitor in the mid-1960s.

It is well known that many US industries and companies disappeared under assault from Japanese competition, but the same phenomenon was also observed in Europe. The German camera industry, the world's undisputed leader until around 1965, had all but disappeared by 1975 due to Japanese competition. West German camera production that year was virtually zero.

The disappearance of good manufacturing jobs was not helpful in reducing inequality in these countries.

Today the same challenge confronts Japan. Whereas it was once a country where 90 percent of the population considered itself middle class, more and more people are now worried about inequality. Millions of manufacturing jobs have migrated to Southeast Asia and China. The jobs that remain are often not particularly highly paid, and many have actually been taken by workers from abroad, such as Japanese Brazilians and young Chinese who came to Japan as students.

Many displaced workers who had to find jobs in the service sector are now considered "working poor." Regional cities that once prospered as centers of industry have become ghost towns with shuttered shopping streets, reminiscent of the US Rust Belt.

The same phenomenon can now be observed in Taiwan where a huge number of factories had moved to China. As a result, those who can utilize resources in China are doing well while those who cannot are doing poorly.

This is a natural result of the progression of industrialization at the global level. And this process has been accelerated by the global free-trade regime and continuous technological innovation.

This global perspective also implies that nations are at their happiest – i.e., inequality is shrinking and people are enjoying the fruits of their labor – when they are either well ahead of other nations or are chasing other countries but are not being pursued themselves. The West was at its happiest until the 1970s because it was ahead of everybody else – until Japan started chasing it. It was a French person who said before the Berlin Wall came down that the world would be a much nicer place if there were no Japan and no Soviet Union.

The Japanese were at their happiest when they were chasing the West but nobody was chasing them. When the Asian Tigers and China began pursuing Japan in the 1990s, the nation's happy days were over.

This also suggests that the favorable income distributions observed by Piketty in the West before 1970 and in Japan until 1990 were also transitory phenomena. These countries enjoyed a golden era not because they had the right kind of tax regime but because the global economic environment was such that nobody was chasing them.

Just because such a desirable world was observed once does not mean it can be preserved or replicated. Any attempt to preserve that equality in the face of international competition would have required massive and continuous investments in human and physical capital, something that most countries are not ready to implement. It is not even sure whether such investments constituted the best use of resources. And businesses would be too ready to move to lower-cost countries to remain competitive.

The US experience in fending off Japan

Assuming that free trade is here to stay, the real issue for the developed world is how to maintain growth momentum when it is being pursued from behind. Here the US experience in trying to fend off Japan is instructive. The US pursued a two-pronged approach that involved keeping Japanese imports from coming in too fast while at the same time trying to make its industry more competitive.

The US utilized every means available to prevent Japanese imports from flooding the domestic market. Those measures included dumping accusations, Super 301 clauses, gentlemen's agreements of all sorts, and exchange rate depreciation via the Plaza Accord of 1985. Trade frictions between the two countries got so bad during this period that it began to resemble a racial confrontation.

At the same time, so-called "Japanese management" was all the rage at US business schools. Many of those schools eagerly recruited Japanese students so that they could discuss Japanese management techniques in their classes. Ezra Vogel's *Japan as Number One: Lessons for America* published in 1979 was widely read by people on both sides of the Pacific Ocean. Combined with the debacle of the Vietnam War, the self-confidence of Americans had fallen to an all-time low, while their consumption of sushi went up sharply.

As a resident of Japan who had worked for the Federal Reserve as an economist and also held American citizenship, I was frequently asked and briefed by the US Embassy in Tokyo to explain the US trade position to Japanese audiences. I was a frequently invited onto television programs in Japan to discuss economic issues. Although I tried my best to explain to the Japanese why it was in their own interest to find compromises with the US, I will never forget the intense mutual hostility that characterized the US – Japan relationship from the mid-1980s to mid-1990s.

After trying everything, however, the US seems to have concluded that when the country is being pursued from behind the only solution is to run faster – i.e., to stay ahead of the competition by continuously generating new ideas, products and designs. The supply-side reforms of President Ronald Reagan were indeed a way to maximize the incentives for such innovators so that their number and output would be maximized. Although the reforms, which included significantly lower taxes, took a long time to produce results, they began to pay handsome dividends in the 1990s when the US started to regain its leadership role in many high-tech sectors.

The real challenge for the developed world

The problem is that not everyone in society is capable of coming up with new ideas or products. And it is not always the same group that is coming up with new ideas. It also takes an enormous amount of effort and perseverance to bring new products to market. But without innovators who can come up with new ideas and industries, the rest of society will be relegated to stagnation or worse.

Reagan's reforms allowed the US economy to grow at a respectable pace during the two decades leading up to the global financial crisis (GFC) in 2008, but for 80 percent of the population there was no increase in real income at all during this period. In other words, the growth was accruing mostly to the 20 percent who were able to come up with new ideas and products.

Admittedly, some of the 20 percent actually made their money by riding increasingly deregulated Wall Street with clever financial manoeuvers that had little to do with adding value to society, as the collapse of the market for toxic CDOs in 2008 amply demonstrated. But the problem of "financial capitalism" – excessive financial assets relative to GDP chasing too few real investment opportunities – is not only a separate issue that goes beyond the scope of this paper, it also runs counter to Piketty's assertion that the return on capital is almost always higher than economic growth. Indeed it was precisely the drive to achieve such returns that led to excessive risk taking and eventually the GFC.

The post-GFC re-regulation of the financial sector, including the Volcker Rule, is the right way to contain such excesses in the financial market. To the extent that some of the gains from financial transactions are zero-sum in nature, a country may also want to limit remuneration in the financial sector so that its best and brightest are not entirely absorbed by zero-sum or near zero-sum activities.

In any case, the real question is whether the 80 percent would be better off with higher taxes on the wealthy 20 percent, as proposed by Piketty. If a higher tax rate discouraged the 20 percent from taking huge risks to develop new ideas and products, their expenditures would fall. That would reduce the income of the 80 percent who provide products and services to the 20 percent. With no new products or industry, the whole economy might be overtaken by competition from the emerging world.

Viewed in this way, Piketty may be underestimating the tremendous costs and hard work involved in developing new products and ideas. A vast majority of new ventures fail. But – at least in the US – people keep on trying because they have a dream of making it big. Piketty will have to prove that the innovating 20 percent will work just as hard even if a much smaller reward awaits them at the end. The track record of generating new products and industries in Japan and Europe, both of which have taxes that are more progressive than the US, does not seem to support Piketty's position.

Conclusion

At least some parts of Piketty's historical observations on inequality can be explained with reference to two Lewis turning points: the western economies' own turning points and the not-yet-reached global turning point. Passing the country's own LTP reverses the worsening trend on inequality brought about by industrialization that was present prior to the LTP. But that improvement may be short-lived or even reversed by the subsequent competition from countries that are yet to reach their LTPs.

Viewed in this way, Piketty's favorite period of income distribution from the end of World War I to the 1970s may have been a transitory phenomenon when the West was ahead of everybody else and nobody was chasing the West. That happy period ended when Japan started chasing the West in the 70s, and the same happy period for Japan ended in the mid-1990s when China started chasing Japan.

For developed countries that are now being pursued from behind, the challenge is to maximize the output of the 20 percent of the population capable of developing new ideas and products so that they can both stay ahead of the competition and allow the remaining 80 percent to live off the new industries created by the 20 percent. Given the huge risk and hard work involved in bringing new products to market, Piketty's push for higher taxes on the wealthy could turn out to be detrimental for developed nations trying to fend off competition from the emerging world.

The growth of capital: Piketty, Harrod-Domar, Solow and the long run development of the rate of investment

Merijn Knibbe [Wageningen University, Netherlands]

> After considerable hesitation by many of our traditionally inclined and appropriately cautious colleagues, the desirability and feasibility of an integrated comprehensive system of national accounts, which includes a balance sheet as a necessary component, seems now to be generally accepted (R.W. Goldsmith, 1966).

Introduction

Piketty and Zucman use a concept of capital based upon the System of National Accounts (SNA) definitions which, like the concept used by Harrod-Domar and Solow, includes fixed depreciable capital, but which also encompasses 'land', 'natural resources' and financial capital. This makes it fit to estimate the flow of capital income including rents. Which is what Piketty and Zucman do: it's an income flow consistent concept. Unlike the Harrod-Domar model the ideas of Piketty and Zucman are not expenditure flow consistent as they do not contain an explicit link to measured investment expenditure and, therewith, the level of aggregate demand. A first step towards making the Piketty-Zucman concept of capital expenditure flow consistent is made comparing the long term historical flow of investment with the development of the stock of capital which shows that the 'U' shaped development of total capital, measured as a percentage of GDP, identified by Piketty and Zucman is inversely related to the rate of investment while the stock of depreciable capital – part of total capital - seems to show a slight positive relation with the rate of investment. A comparison with 'Piketty consistent' long term capital estimates for the Netherlands shows that the 'U' shaped pattern as well as the inverse relation with investment is robust. The declining part of the 'U' can be explained by technological and market developments in agriculture which caused a large decline of the value of agricultural land. The increase can be explained by increases of the price of land underlying buildings induced by money-creating lending and borrowing and is, i.e., inflationary. Neither the decrease nor the increase shows a large and direct connection with either 'r', or capital income and 'i', the rate of investment. Depreciable capital however does show a small positive relation with the rate of investment. The decrease and the increase are, however, connected with changes in the concept of capital and the distribution of wealth and power.

1. Growth theory and the concept of capital

The 'workhorse' concept of capital used in mainstream economics is largely based on growth theory and, therewith, limited to fixed depreciable capital. In 1946 Evsey Domar stated that a high rate of net fixed investment does not only lead to an increase of the stock of capital and therewith potential supply but also contributes to aggregate demand which, as investments increase potential supply, has to increase, too, to ensure full employment. As such, this was a clear and conscious attempt to write down an intertemporal stock/expenditure flow consistent model which related the (change of) the stock of capital to expenditure and potential as wel as actual production as defined and estimated in the new national accounts (Domar, 1946).[1] Somewhat earlier, Harrod was less explicit about this but he, too, tied investment expenditure to the stock of capital, therewith connecting the demand side of the economy to the intertemporal development of the supply side (Harrod, 1939). In more modern parlance: Harrod and Domar used a 'perpetual inventory method' to estimate the macro stock of capital using the flow of fixed investment to estimate the stock of capital *as well as* to analyse aggregate demand in relation to potential output - an important theoretical step for economics. Domar as well as Harrod however used a restricted definition of capital as they only took depreciable fixed assets into account, though their method holds as well when non-depreciable and/or unproduced assets like 'land' or 'oil' are added to their stock of capital. They also discarded the liability side of the balance sheet as well as financial flows and

---

[1] He already used the phrase 'embodied technological progress'.

stocks, which disabled a genuine analysis of the distribution of capital income.

The same restricted concept of capital was used by Solow who, in his famous 1956 article, however purged flow consistency from growth theory by *assuming* neoclassical general equilibrium: whatever the flow of monetary investment expenditure, full employment would be maintained as wages and interest rates and employment and profits would change, miraculously, just enough to assure 'knife edge' full employment (see also Fazarri e.a., 2012). This decoupling of investments from aggregate demand was a clear scientific retrogression as it made a lot of questions difficult to pose. And while Harrod and Domar *chose* to use a limited concept of capital and to discard unproduced assets, the general equilibrium view of Solow *forced* him to do this as wages and profits would only change with the right magnitude when no rent incomes would exist. He therefore had to state: "*The community's stock of capital takes the form of an accumulation of the composite commodity*" and "*there is no scarce nonaugmentable resource like land*" (Solow, 1956, pp. 66-67).[2] Aside: the very idea behind distinguishing 'capital' from consumer and intermediate goods is of course the fact that the composition, use , span of life and 'span of production' of fixed depreciable assets is *not* equal to the composition, use or span of life of either final consumption goods or intermediate inputs. A bridge is not a strawberry. But even understanding Solow's definition of capital as a convenient modelling strategy instead of a serious definition it still seems to exclude houses, roads and other buildings, including the land below these structures. More than thirty years after the publication of his article Solow cited the empirical long run estimates by Wolff (at that time still preliminary) very approvingly in his Nobel lecture (Solow, 1987). Checking the work of Wolff it turns out that he uses long term estimates of capital obtained from Maddison (Wolff, 1991, footnote 5). Checking the Maddison estimates it turns out that these exclude houses, land, natural resources, international assets, gold, and farm animals (Maddison, 1982, Annex D).[3] Restricting our attention to the seemingly trivial item 'farm animals' it turns out that, around

[2] It's interesting to know if this last remark was inspired by Solow's friend Paul Samuelson – it has a very Samuelsonian ring to it.

[3] Maddison continuously revised and extended his data, however (Maddison, 1992; Maddison, 1994).

1885 and according to Goldsmith, these still made up about 13% of the total stock of reproducible assets (Goldsmith, 1985, table 45) – and the importance of the other items not included in the operationalization of capital used by Wolff was often even larger. Considering this importance it's clear that any long term estimates of capital and labour productivity, like those of Wolff, should include not just the wagons but the horses, too. The Wolff estimates don't. And a quick check of a number of macro textbooks reveals that the Harrod/Domar/Solow/Wolff approach to tangible capital, i.e. implicitly restricting it to (a subset of) produced depreciable capital and discarding the liability side of the balance sheet, is still dominant in economic thinking. Modern growth theory of course often does include 'human capital' or even 'health' in the definition of capital, I'll pay more attention to this below. The point here is that many kinds of capital are left out of the equations, just like balance sheets. Which leaves us with the conclusion that, despite early attempts at stock/flow consistent estimates of capital which combined the demand and the supply side of the economy serious, the modern concept of 'capital' applies to a subset of the total amount of tangible capital only while it's, despite excellent data on the flow of investments and capital income as well as, much more recently, the total stock of capital, focused on the supply side only. Clearly, this concept does not have solid macro-foundations.

2. Combining different concepts of 'capital' with flows of income and expenditure: Piketty-Zucman and Harrod-Domar

2.1 The contrarian results of PIketty and Zucman

Modern national accounts, unlike those of the days of Harrod and Domar, do not only contain data on monetary flows of expenditure and income but, since about 10 years, also on (net) financial flows as well as stocks of financial and non-financial assets. This information is the basis of the estimates of Piketty and Zucman (Piketty and Zucman, 2013; Piketty 2014). They base their approach hook, line and sinker on the concept and definition of capital as stated in the 'System of National Accounts' (SNA) (SNA, 2008). Following the pioneering work of Goldsmith, who in 1985 still had to base his approach on his own estimates of balance sheets of different countries (Goldsmith 1985), they extend SNA estimates of capital backwards to 1800 and even further. They frame these data in a theory of distribution, which is possible as their concept of capital is much broader and more conceptually consistent (i.e. balance sheets based, note the plural here) than the 'growth theory' concept described above. This leads to some 'textbook ready' results. They show that the long term development of 'total capital', or wealth, expressed as a percentage of GDP, shows a 'U' shaped historical pattern: high in the nineteenth century, low between about 1910 and 1985 and high afterwards with the development in the USA as the exception (Piketty and Zucman, 2013; Piketty, 2014).[4] They combine data on the flow of capital income ('r') with these estimates and state that 'r', especially when growth is low, might(!) lead to an increase of the wealth/GDP ratio and a self-perpetuating pattern of high and /or increasing wealth/GDP ratio's and maybe even to the rise of a powerful class of rentiers: back to the 'régime ancienne'. And, not entirely coincidental, to a science of economics which, once again, pays serious attention to the relation between 'wealth' and the distribution of income.

These findings are however critically dependent upon the concept of capital used by Piketty and Zucman (and the national accounts statisticians). The U-shaped pattern might indeed be surprising to people accustomed to the concept of capital used in growth theory. The period between 1910 and 1985 is (in the west) characterized by uniquely high rates of economic growth *as well as investment* and mainstream growth theory suggests that this process should or at least could have led to *higher* instead of *lower* capital/output ratios. A rise in the investment ratio will, according to the neoclassical model of capital accumulation engineered by Solow, lead to a transitory period of higher growth and, eventually, also to a higher capital output ratio, even more so (though Solow does not stress this) when a larger share of investments ends up in capital goods with a low rate of depreciation like

[4] Compare Maddison, 1992, on savings (i.e. investment plus the surplus/deficit on the current account): "US long run experience has not conformed to the norm for the other countries. In most of the other cases it is possible to discern an upward trend in the long term savings rate, whereas in the USA this is not the case. The atypicality of US experience is important because a good deal of the theorizing about savings (or consumption) behavior emanated from the USA and was clearly influenced by the historical evidence (see Friedman ... and Modigliani... explaining how they came to reject Keynes' notion of that savings rise with income - because there was no upward trend in the savings estimates developed by Kuznets)".

houses (Solow, 1956). The combination of a 'U' shaped pattern of the capital/output ratio as estimated by PIketty and Zucman and an 'Λ' shaped pattern of the rate of fixed investment however suggests an *inverse* relation between 'capital' and the rate of fixed investment, a suggestion which gains credibility when we realize that the Λ-pattern of gross fixed investment was quite but not entirely universal: the USA, with a flat long run rate of investment was, *again*, the exception while the Netherlands, not included in the Piketty and Zucman estimates, *also* showed the same investment and capital growth pattern as the other countries, as will be shown below. Arithmetically, the problem of investments leading to a lower capital:output can, using the Solow growth model, easily be solved. Just assume that high rates of investments also lead to high rates of technological progress and/or positive returns to scale and add a positive relation between the rate of investment and the technology parameter of the Solow model to your spreadsheet – anything which makes the denominator increase faster than the numerator (see also the statements of Piketty and Zucman about this (Piketty and Zucman, 2014, p. 38)). But Wolff's 'vintage' models of (part of) the stock of fixed depreciable capital show that though productivity of capital often does increase, while high rates of investment do seem to foster these productivity increases the capital/output ratio as measured by him did not decrease. To the contrary: he had to state: *"On average, capital:output ratios trended upward between 1880 and 1979"* (Wolff, 1991, p. 577) while countries with relative low investments (the UK, see below) showed less increase than other countries – the very opposite of the results of Piketty and Zucman, whose main results include a *downward* trending capital/output ratio! How come?!

2.2 The modern , flow consistent concept of capital

This remarkable difference in findings might well be due to the differences in the concept of capital used. As we've seen, 'growth economists' tend to restrict 'capital' to (part of) fixed depreciable capital, though they sometimes also extend it with 'human capital', i.e. education and/or training on the job. Piketty and Zucman however use the SNA definition. To be able to show the differences, it's necessary to discuss this definition at some length. The SNA defines assets as:

> "a store of value representing a benefit or series of benefits accruing to the economic owner by holding or using the entity over a period of time. It is a means of carrying forward value from one accounting period to another. All assets in the SNA are economic assets" (SNA 2008, 10.8).

'Value' relates to future benefits (more precisely: to the ownership rights of these benefits) but also to the future monetary value of the asset itself, 'carrying forward' means that an asset can (1) either be kept by the owner until the next period and/or can be sold and used in the next period (land, ships, planes, vehicles, buildings, military equipment) and/or can be transferred to the 'next generation' (city roads, dykes and levees are default examples). This definition encompasses the 'fixed depreciable assets' of growth theory but is much broader. Items like 'human capital' and 'health' *(*Arrow e.a., 2010*)* are however excluded, as these are neither transferable nor tradable. A distinction is made between a legal owner (the landlord) and the economic owner (the tenant farmer) who decides how an asset is used and runs upside and downside economic risks connected with the way the asset is used. In this case, the landlord is economic owner of the rent contract, a financial 'unproduced asset'. The SNA definition also includes net financial assets which, on the national scale and as domestic debts and liabilities cancel out (at least in an accounting sense…) means that the national stock of fixed capital is augmented with the (positive or negative) 'net international investment position' of its inhabitants, its companies and the government of a country. Non-financial assets are distinguished into produced assets (houses, roads, machinery, equipment, stocks, livestock) and non-produced assets, like stocks of hydrocarbons, agricultural land, land underlying buildings, 'goodwill' and some contracts and leases. Which is necessary to ensure accounting consistency and which, de facto, is a return to the classical dichotomy between capital and 'land'. Ponder that sentence. As the estimates of Piketty and Zucman are totally consistent with the concepts of the national accounts they are stock consistent and enable, unlike analyses just based upon fixed depreciable capital, an analysis of capital income. As a very important part of their analysis indeed hinges on 'r', the return to capital, they are also flow consistent – quite a step ahead compared with mainstream growth models, which, as they do not distinguish unproduced capital from other kinds of capital, disable a proper analysis of rent incomes. When it comes to expenditure flows, Piketty and Zucman however scarcely pay attention to the level of investment, which means that their ideas are not flow consistent with the expenditure side of the accounts. Just the opposite situation as with the Harrod and Domar models which did not pay attention to capital income but which do encompass the flow of investment while the Solow model is neither income or expenditure flow consistent . There is however nothing that prevents us using Harrod-Domar kinds of ideas about the relation between capital and investment while also using the SNA concept of capital. The SNA concept of capital can, i.e. be flow consistent on the income as well as on the expenditure side. And it's also totally possible that the difference between the findings of Piketty and Zucman on one side and Wolff on the other side are caused by the difference in the concept of capital used. An increase in the rate of fixed investment can, theoretically, be *positively* related to the stock of depreciable capital but *negatively* to the total stock of capital (or, looking at the other side of the balance sheet, wealth) which of course means that there should be a quite strong though negative relationship between 'non-depreciable capital' and high rates of investment. It is, however, also possible that the 'U' shaped- pattern is just a historical coincidence. The rest of this article will be devoted to an investigation of this problem which, on a meta level, can also be understood as a somewhat rude attempt to impose investment flow consistency upon the estimates of Piketty and Zucman.

To do this we will first establish the long run pattern of fixed investments, i.e. those kinds of expenditure which lead to an increase of the stock of fixed capital, to investigate if there indeed a Λ-shaped pattern of addition to the stock of depreciable capital. As we're interested in capital as a percentage of GDP we will express investment as a percentage of GDP, which means that, as fixed investment is part of final demand, we'll also get some information about the changing importance of fixed investment to GDP. We will compare this data with data on the long run development of the stock of capital as established by Wolff and Piketty and Zucman. As we need in-depth knowledge about the metrology behind this information to establish if any relations are spurious or not and as, in my experience, such knowledge can best be gained by constructing such series yourself and as Piketty nor Goldsmith present long term series for the Netherlands I also constructed long term capital series for the Netherlands, using the same methodology as

Piketty and Zucman. With the help of this information, the problem posed above (is there an inverse relation between the total stock of capital and fixed investment but a positive relation between the stock of depreciable capital and the rate of investment) will be discussed.

3. The rate of investment: a long run view

3.1 Introduction

Piketty and Zucman present data on capital for about two centuries. This means that we have to assemble investment data for about the same period. Knowledge about the rate of investment is not just important in relation to the change in the amount of depreciable fixed capital (the Solow approach) but, as (business) investment is the most volatile component of total aggregate demand, also for the level of aggregate demand (the Harrod-Domar approach). *Knowledge about long run changes in this ratio is i.e. crucial to our understanding of capitalism as we know it* – and it was something of a surprise that constructing comparative long run series required a bit of an effort. The countries shown were chosen because of their size (Italy, Spain), because they were included in the long run Piketty sample (USA, Britain, France, Germany, Sweden) or because of data availability and their proximity to other countries in the sample (the Netherlands, Denmark, Finland). Together, these countries clearly show the 'Atlantic' investment experience during the 1807-2013 period. The data are from before the 2014 GDP revisions, i.e. do not include R&D investment.

3.2 Intermezzo: capital, innovation, revolutions and all that

Before presenting these data a little more has however to be said about capital, especially because the very nature of capital and investment might change over a two century period. Like Piketty, we will stick to the SNA definition which, as stated, enables a much better understanding of the distribution of capital income but also of production than the mainstream definition. Several aspects of 'capital' are however not encompassed by the SNA definition. One is 'liquidity'. Over the centuries, the liquidity of 'capital' on the asset as well as the liability side of the balance sheet has increased, think of the rise of the stock market, securitization of mortgages and even the merger between precious metals and the unit of account, which led to: coins. *All of these innovations led to major economic and social changes* – which underscores the crucial position of capital and wealth in our society. An example of such a change is the connection between the introduction of tradable shares and the rise of the first privately owned listed multinational, the Vereenigde Oostindische Compagnie, after 1602. Without tradable shares, this company, which lasted two centuries, would never have lived that long as the owners would have had to 'liquidate' the company instead of selling the shares to get their money back. But as they could sell their shares liquidation was not necessary and, with its own private army, the VOC could take its time to establish a true commercial empire.[5] Another important aspect is 'revolution'. The protestant revolutions of the sixteenth and seventeenth centuries, the French revolution, the USA civil war or the Russian revolution al led to fundamental redistribution of ownership or de-owning of land, slaves or other kinds of capital – in the United Kingdom it was Cromwell who seized the monasteries for the crown, in the Netherlands the government (not 'the crown'!) also seized the lands of the catholic clergy. It's a bit too much to state that our present concept of capital was forged with blood and iron – the historical reality often was much more mundane. North and Weingast use the phrase 'evolution' in the title of their 1989 article about the capital consequences of the Glorious Revolution for a reason – an evolution which was however directly based upon the revolutionary expropriations of the monasteries executed by by Cromwell, more than a century earlier (North and Weingast, 1989). Biologists use the phrase 'punctuated evolution' to describe such processes, Marx and Engels simply called these punctuations: 'revolutions'. Somehow and sometimes, these revolutions did redistribute property and create the room for these mundane developments which contributed to the growth of interest bearing loans between 'burghers', stock exchanges, orphanages endowed with the land of the former catholic monasteries, a class of small farmers in France or larger farmers in the UK and the Netherlands ('The crown' in the UK as well as the Dutch government had to sell a lot of the seized lands). Early sixteenth century national sector accounts would not have had a separate sector 'Monetary financial Institutions' but they would have had distinct sectors 'The

[5] I owe this insight into liquidity to the posts by J.W. Mason on his slack wire blog, even though Mason does not relate liquidity to innovation but to capitalist behavior.

Crown' and 'The Church'! Note that these redistributions often did not lead to long or even medium term declines of production – even cotton production in The South of the USA recovered fairly fast, after the civil war! To use a Piketty device: one is reminded of the last scene of 'Gone with the wind', when Scarlett discovers that 'land' is an unproduced asset. A further, related aspect of the evolution of capital is the increasing dichotomy between private/communal and public capital. Revolutions, glorious or not, led to an ever sharper distinction between the property of the ruler and the property and the state while states, in a very uneven and punctuated process and in exchange for ever higher and surer taxes increasingly acted as guardians of private property (Wilterdink, 1984). In the Netherlands, the loss of wealth caused by Indonesian independence (1948, according to the Dutch, 1945 according to Indonesian historiography) and the nationalization of remaining Dutch property in 1958 comes to mind (Baudet, 1975). At the moment, the fight about the value of the financial assets of banks is clearly an example where the state levies ever higher taxes to protect the property of a limited number of companies and exemplifies the shift from a state which protects the property of its citizens to a state which protects the property of creditors. Below, I'll return to this.

3.3 Data

Standardized information about the rate of investment in current prices is one of the standard items in public macro-economic databases. These databases however cover relatively short periods (about the last 40 years for Eurostat) or do have somewhat longer series (the Penn data go back to 1950) but use international 'PPP' price-estimates which, partly because roads and houses are not really tradable on the international markets, are often quite distinct from data in national prices. A comparison of the Penn data with current price estimates yields that, except for the USA and Germany, differences between PPP-fixed investment ratio's and current national price ratios are often quite large (up to 7% of GDP). As the stock of capital as measured in the national accounts is, as far as possible, expressed in current prices the Penn data are discarded and Eurostat data were spliced to 'historical' estimates of the investment ratio in current prices. Eurostat data on investments are almost invariably a little higher than the historical data, possibly because they include changes in 'stocks' while historical series often don't. To account for this, the historical series have been increased with the difference between the series (see the Annex for the sources of the historical series). As the difference is bound to be variable, this does give a bias to the series: a 17,5% level in 1880 will only be roughly equal to a 17,5% level in 2012.

3.4 Results

The five graphs below cover 10 countries: the USA, France, Germany, the UK, the Netherlands, Sweden, Finland, Denmark, Italy and Spain. Some highlights:

A. The USA: exceptionalism

I. The USA graph shows series including and excluding military equipment – which clearly makes a difference and sometimes even a stupendously large difference. This serves to highlight a conceptual problem: how to define investments? As there is a clear primary and second hand market in military gear while countries replace equipment lost in wars, tanks and planes do have 'economic' value, which means that, *according to the SNA logic*, they have to be included in our concept of capital. The transfer of redundant material from the USA army to the USA police, which in an accounting sense is an economic transaction, underscores this idea. Not all historical series below however seem to include military equipment (Germany!). It also serves to highlight the importance of stock/flow consistent estimates of capital – these military investments did not increase the stock of productive capital (to the contrary) but they did end the Great Depression.

Graph 1

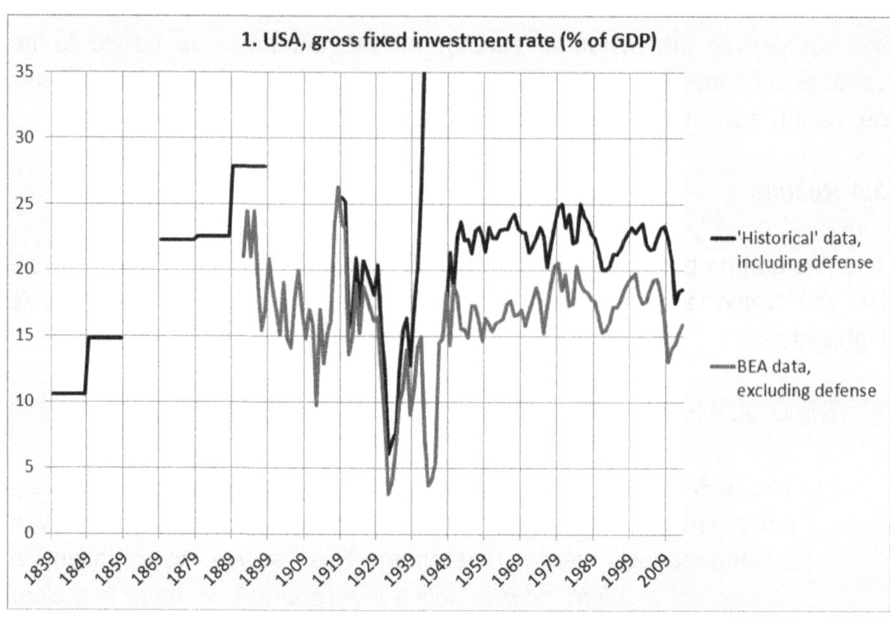

II. The most remarkable aspect of the USA series is the comparatively high rate of investment in the nineteenth century, mainly caused by a rapid increase of the urban as well as the agricultural population in combination with the extension of the system of railways.˙ This finding is consistent with the finding of Wolff (1991) of a comparatively high as well as stable {fixed depreciable capital /labour} ratio in the USA during this period. A clear sign of things to come! A more surprising aspect is the long run stability of the rate of (gross) investment. In the short run, gross investments were quite volatile and net investments even became negative during the Great Depression. In the long run it's the stability of the investment rate that catches the eye. However – as we will also see for Finland, Spain and, to a lesser extent, France – the post 2000 level of investment was driven by a housing bubble and as such unsustainable. The low post 2008 levels might be a clearer sign of things to come than the 2000-2006 levels. Investment levels which were sustainable in the sixties and seventies might not be sustainable today.[6]

B. France and the UK: catching up versus falling behind

France shows rather low but gently rising levels in the nineteenth century, followed by further increases post 1920 and, again, post 1945 which led to very high investment ratios in the sixties and seventies. Up to about 1930, this pattern might have been caused by a process of catching up. The UK experience is slightly anomalous: it shows, in a comparative perspective, low rates up to as late as 1920. Initially, these low rates might be explained by the already quite high {fixed depreciable capital/labour} ratio in the nineteenth century, but the increase of this ratio during the nineteenth century and up to about 1920 was clearly lower than in other countries. As a result, 1979 UK {fixed depreciable capital/labour} ratios were, contrary to the situation around 1870 and even 1890, way lower than for instance German ratios (Wolff, 1991). This serves to underscore the long run consequences of (changes in) the fixed investment rate as well as the relation between the investment rate and the stock of depreciable capital. The high French rate after especially 2005 is remarkable, too. Considering the, very recent, dramatic decline in housing starts in France it is to be expected that the French rate will go down soon.

---

[6] An argument can be made that 'bionics' (artificial hips, teeth and the like) have to be included in the concept of investment. An investment rate including bionics might show a somewhat different development. The remarks made in the text are clearly conditional on the definition of fixed investment – which does not make them less true.

Graph 2

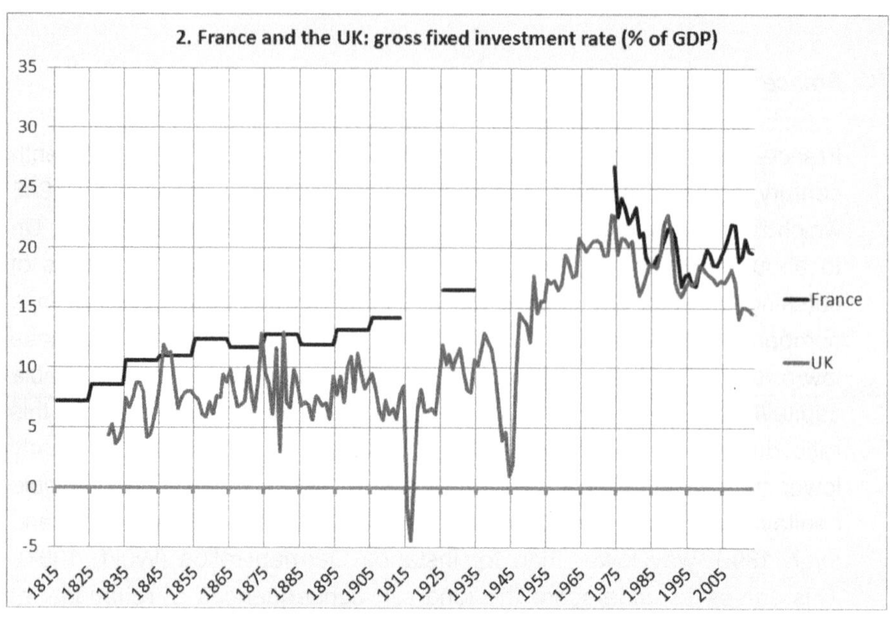

C. *Germany and the Netherlands: archetypes*

Note that the borders of Germany changed quite a lot during this period. Despite this the patterns are consistent: the rather late take-off of the Netherlands but a rather high level of investment before this period, the high German level during the German 'Gründerjahren' and a relatively high German level after World War II. The most remarkable aspect of the graph is the large and sustained post 1973 decline of the German and to a lesser extent Dutch investment rate – even despite German re-unification. The low level of German investments post 1991 corresponds with the glacial and for a decade even non-existent decline in the East-German unemployment ratio, this contrary to the fast decrease of West-German unemployment post 1950. As such, the 150 year wave-like pattern of German and the Netherlands seems to be rather typical for 'latecomers' to modern economic growth while the high level of German unemployment indicates a consistent pattern of underspending. After decades, this spending gap was filled by a large external surplus – a strategy which for obvious reasons can't be used by all countries at the same time. Note that the length of this wave corresponds with the length of the patterns identified by Piketty and Zucman. As net government investment in Germany is, at the moment of writing, negative a slight uptick might be expected.

Graph 3

D. The Nordics. More archetypes

The same long wave is visible in Denmark, Sweden and Finland. Take note of the 'Finnish bubble' after 1990, which, again, indicates that investment ratios which were sustainable in the sixties were unsustainable post 1980, maybe due to slower population growth.

Graph 4

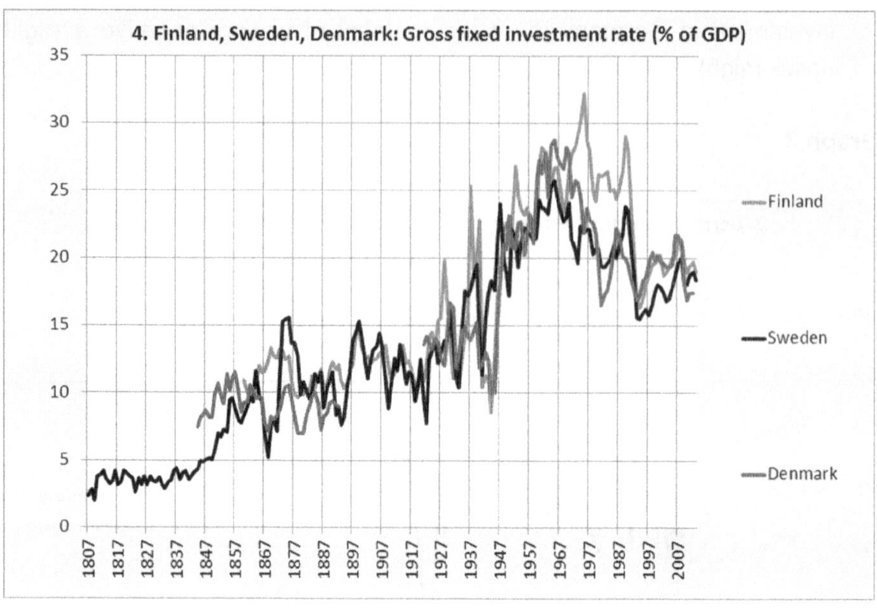

E. *Italy, Spain*

Both Italy and Spain show the same wave, albeit with Spain as a latecomer and, like Finland, at the end of the series clearly showing an investment bubble. The gap for Spain between 1958 and 1980 can be filled with the Penn series, which (as mentioned above) often show quite some differences with current price rates. These data suggest that, after a severe decline during the 1959-1960 depression, investments were relatively high throughout the sixties and especially in the seventies, declining a little thereafter. The Italian series show, especially after the Second World War, basically the same pattern as the Dutch, Swedish, Danish and German series.

Graph 5

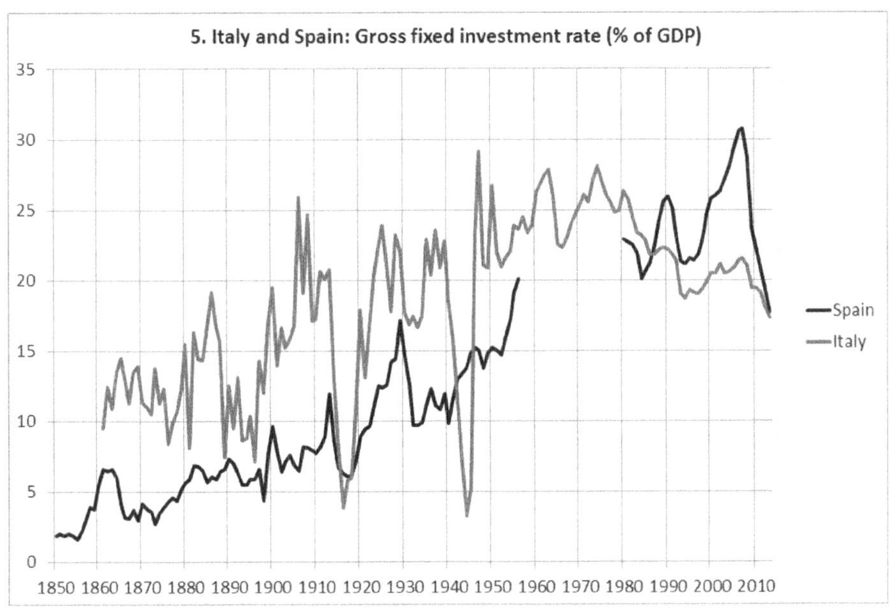

Summarizing: except for the USA all countries show, with relatively little difference in timing, a 150 year wave like pattern of the investment ratio, with exceptional high investment ratios during the period when, according to Piketty and Zucman, the {*total capital*/output} ratio is lowest but when, according to Wolff, the {*depreciable fixed capital*/output} ratio increased. Most countries show a decline of the investment rate after somewhere in the seventies or eighties, countries which managed to keep a stable or even increasing rate of investment after this period turned out to have had severe financial bubbles. There indeed seems to be an inverse relation between the investment rate and the total capital/output rate, spurious or not, while, according to the Wolff data, the relation with the stock of depreciable capital is, more predictable, slightly positive and even more so when we look at comparative data. To investigate these relations in more detail we will, in the next paragraph, present data on total as well as depreciable fixed capital/output ratios for the Netherlands, investigate if these show the same properties as the 'Piketty' and 'Wolff' data and, if so, investigate why the 'total capital' ratio behaves in ways contrary to the 'fixed depreciable capital' ratio.

4. Capital series for the Netherlands

Graph 6 shows the long term total capital/output ratio for the Netherlands. The series is, considering the goal of this article, only an intermediate result but for obvious reasons it is worthwhile to investigate it.

Graph 6

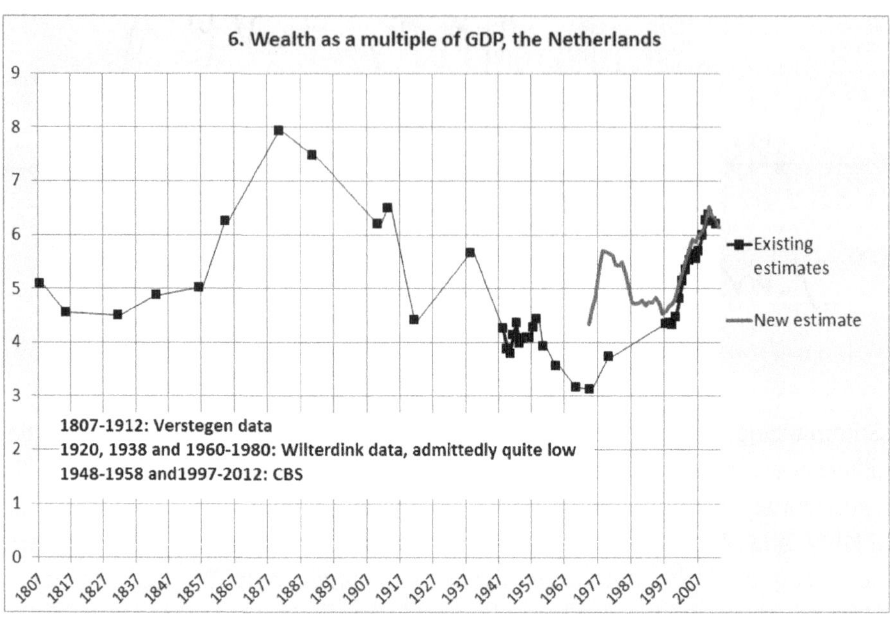

Sources: see annex.

The elephant in the room: however one mistreats and tortures the data the series clearly shows the same 'U' shaped pattern identified by Piketty and Zucman, albeit with a somewhat higher value during the fifties-seventies period.[7] Some minor anomalies show. The somewhat low level of and the decline after 1807 can be explained by the consequences of the French occupation of the Netherlands in combination with the demise of the Vereenigde Oostindische Compagnie and the loss (to the UK) of a number of territories like Sri Lanka (which became a crown colony) and the (rather

[7] Contemporaneous estimates show lower capital/output levels, mainly as houses are not valued at market but at a much lower 'collateral' value. See Wilterdink, 1984.

small) Cape Colony owned by this company. Even then, the rise between 1852 and 1880 is remarkable and asks for an explanation. This period was characterized by increasing and high agricultural prices and high gross land rents, 1882 marking the apex of nineteenth century agricultural prices in the Netherlands (Knibbe, 1993 and 1999). These increase led to an increase of the value of land. Decreasing land prices after 1882 clearly caused a rapid and marked decline of landed wealth and, therewith, of the total wealth to GDP ratio with about 300% of GDP, which is enough to explain the total decline of this ratio after 1880 (graph 7) and which, therewith, requires some special attention.[8]

Graph 7

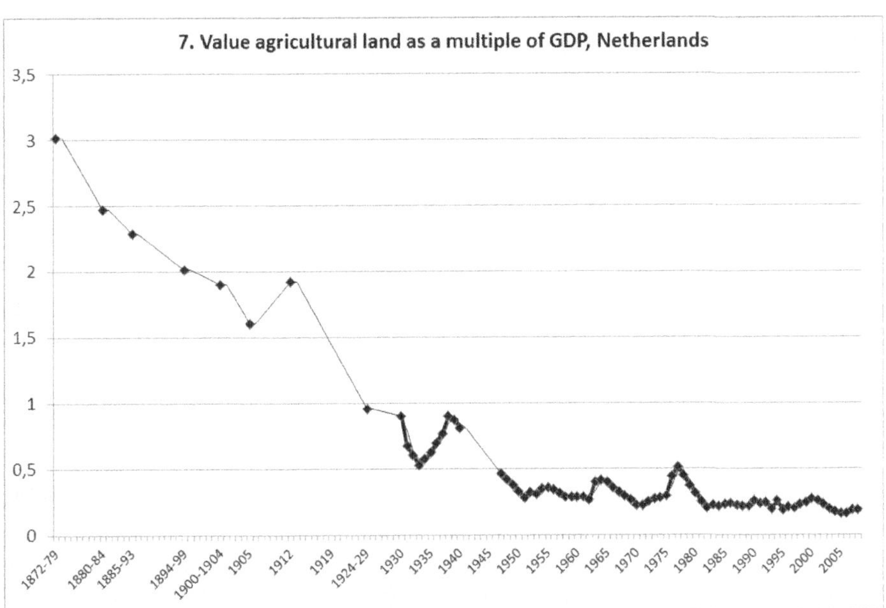

Sources: see graph 6

The decline of landed wealth is totally consistent with the findings of Piketty and Zucman. Was this decline in any way connected to the increasing rate

[8] My specific estimate of the value of agricultural wealth is not part of the estimates of the period before World War II, which are based upon Verstegen (1996) and Wilterdink.(1984).

of investment? This question is too simple and we have to reframe it, giving center stage to more complicated historical developments which were annex to what we measure as increasing investments in fixed depreciable capital (Knibbe, 1993 and 1999). It's clear that on one hand investments in ships and railroads enabled the development of hitherto virgin lands in countries like the USA, Argentina and India and, earlier, the Crimean area, which enabled an improvement in the food situation of the European population and (*almost* the other side of this coin) a decline of food prices vis-à-vis wages and, i.e., a lower share of the value of land as a share total production (or income). This is however only part of the story. Increased use of intermediate inputs (feed, artificial fertilizer) not only enabled an increase of the productivity of European agricultural land but *also led to increases in labour productivity* as, for instance, the gathering, storing, mixing and spreading of a multitude of organic fertilizer often required loads and loads of labour. In for instance the Netherlands this process led, despite a relatively fast increase of the population, to a near stability of the amount of per capita calories produced domestically. Dutch imports of food *improved* the availability of food but were not needed to compensate dwindling per capita production – as per capita production did not dwindle (Knibbe, 2006). In combination with rapid mechanization after 1950 and ever lower prices for purchased inputs (except for energy) this process enabled a decline of the cost price of the production of food and (much) lower prices for food products. This is a story about technical and organizational change which was only to an extent 'embodied' in new capital. Anyway – relative agricultural prices declined dramatically – and the price of land vis-à-vis the general price level declined, too. The total stock of fixed depreciable capital (ships transporting grain, railroads, roads) increased – to an extent as a consequence of a process which ultimately led to lower land prices and therewith to (considering the very large share of land in total wealth around 1880) much lower wealth/GDP ratios. As this (international) decline of the wealth/GDP ratio was concentrated in landed wealth it also led to large changes in the distribution of wealth which, especially in countries with some quite large land owners, of course led to large social and political changes.

The decline of the capital/GDP ratio up to about 1940 can be accounted for by looking at an *unproduced* asset: land. After World War II, capital/output ratios however stayed low for several decades, despite (at least in Europe) unprecedented fixed investment ratios – while they increased, depending on the country, after about 1970 or 1980, exactly when the investment rate started to decline. Graph 8 sheds a little more light on this process for the Netherlands.

Graph 8

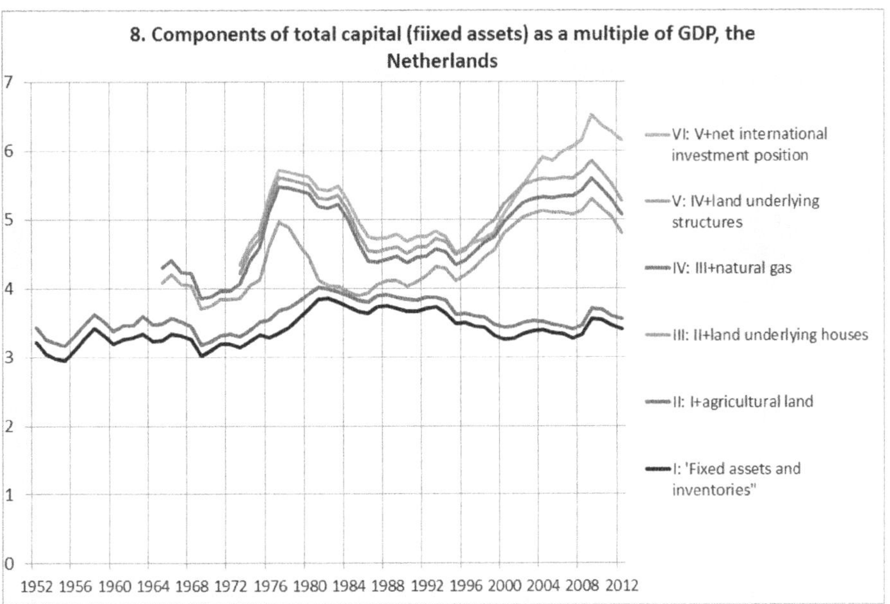

It shows total capital/output ratio using a consistent methodology for the 1965-2012 period as well as series on fixed depreciable capital including houses but excluding the value of land under houses back to 1952. To be honest to Solow, Harrod and Domar: when they wrote their classic articles, depreciable capital was by far the most important part of total capital. Since, then the situation has changed. Up to 1976 this depreciable capital series is more or less stable but after 1976, exactly when fixed investment ratio started to decline, this series started to *increase* a bit. This increase was mainly caused by a relative increase in the number and quality of houses (the average number of inhabitants per houses declined from 4 in the beginning of the twentieth century to three around 1965 to 2 around 2010).[9] But it was also caused by an increase in house prices triggered by deregulation of the banking sector, higher leverage and other events eerily similar to the recent housing bubbles (Frederik, 2012). Just like in the 1995-2008 period (the second Dutch housing bubble) this increase in house prices was enabled and to an extent even caused by a large increase in credit and (the other side of the balance sheet) the supply of money, not by an increase in the savings ratio. Which means that changes in the capital/output ratio can't be explained with a non-financial model which 'only' takes flows of income (i.e. the rate of capital income, Piketty's 'r') and expenditure (i.e. the rate of investment) into account. A 'flow of funds' kind of analysis which also looks at changes in (mortgage)credit is in place. As the housing bubble coincided with the oil crisis and higher oil and natural gas prices, and as the Netherlands had just discovered huge reserves of natural gas, this led to a kind of double Dutch total capital/output bubble – a clear sign of things to come. The 1982 Volcker crisis, characterized by the combination of high interest and high unemployment, in combination with lower prices for energy led to the deflation of this bubble. At the moment, the second Dutch bubble is deflating – at least when it comes to house prices. Just like in Ireland and Spain, mortgage debts however do not decline in tandem with house prices which means that the collateral of mortgage debts (which are about equal to GDP) is dwindling. This puts pressure upon the government to act to save banks or refinance banks or to prevent (in an environment with record low policy rates!) refinancing of mortgage loans – another example of the state functioning as the guardian of the property rights of creditors – to the detriment of the income of households.

Special mention has to be made of the development of the net international investment position (NIP) of the Netherlands. After 1971 the Netherlands had, except for 1978-1980, a persistent and often large surplus on the current account. This should, at first sight, have led to ever increasing net international wealth. As can be seen the NIP however deteriorated after 1990 and even became negative, due to revaluations of assets (Nieuwkerk and Sparling, 1985; Nieuwkerk and Sparling, 1987; Boonstra, 2008). It's worthwhile to summarize the data of Boonstra:

---

[9] A quality index of houses is missing, but each year around 0,5% of the total stock of houses was scrapped. These scrapped houses were often small and simple.

Table 1. The relation between the current account and the net international investment position of the Netherlands, 1987-2006 (Euro, billions)

Cumulative surplus on the current account, 1987-2006	321
Capital account balance	-19
Errors and omissions	- 63
Capital losses	-285
Resulting net change in international investment position	-46

Source: Boonstra, 2008, table 2.

Clearly, 'saving' explains only a part of what happened and even for this twenty year period price developments trumped volume developments. These data are however influenced by accounting methods (i.e. valuing shares of foreign subsidiaries owned by Dutch companies at book value instead of market prices and not counting retained profits by foreign subsidiaries) as well as by somewhat neglecting Special Purpose Entities. Data might understate the true value of the Dutch NIP (Vandervyvere, 2012; Claassen and Van den Dool, 2013). The NIP data are, therewith, opaque as well as unreliable.

Conclusion

The broad and national accounts oriented concept of capital used by Piketty and Zucman enables an income and investment flow consistent analysis of 'capital', this is contrary to the concept used in 'text book' growth theory. The 'U'-shaped pattern of the long term evolution of the capital-output ratio established by Piketty and Zucman is robust to new data: it's also clearly visible in the Dutch data (not included in the Piketty-Zucman sample). Looking at the details and SNA definitions it however turns out that the U-pattern is totally driven by changes in the value of unproduced assets. In the decades around 1900, land prices declined because of a process of intensive and extensive growth of agriculture which, in the end, was strongly land and labor saving and led to lower agricultural prices and, i.e., a lower value of land. Flows of capital income (Piketty's 'r') had little to do with this and flows of investments (ships, railways), though crucial, explain only a limited part of this process. After around 1880 an increase in the investment rate probably led, *despite the decline of the {total capital/output} ratio,* to slightly *increasing* {fixed depreciable capital/output} ratio's. After around 1985, the fixed depreciable capital/output ratio seems to have declined a little (at least in the Netherlands). Because of credit fuelled increases in the price of houses and land below houses and buildings the {total capital/output} ratio however increased which, however, has to be understood as a sign of the credit bubble of the nineties and noughties and not as a consequence of re-invested capital income, as Piketty and Zucman suggest. Which means that a expenditure flow consistent analysis of capital output ratio's should, in a state backed bank-money monetary environment, not just look at capital income but also at credit creation and all kinds of innovations which influence the credit-process and, therewith, the value of capital.

Annex: data and methods

I. General principles

The literature mentions four basic ways to estimate nominal 'wealth' or 'capital' which are used next to each other and which relate to different concepts of investment (as outlined by Gallman, 1986) and different kinds of capital goods:

- **Using book value** including the perpetual inventory method (and extensive description of this method in Groote, 1995). This method is, also known as valuing capital at acquisition costs, is based upon past investments. It uses the notion of capital as piled up savings, like retained profits, in the sense of consumption foregone (Gallmann, 1986). A problem with this method is that the capital stock consists of different 'vintages' with different implicit price levels and explicit use of price indexes has to be made to make prices of different capital goods comparable. It also requires the use of a depreciation rule. An advantage: it forces researchers to assemble scores of data on prices and volumes of investments and to be explicit about this.

- **Using reproduction costs**. This is of course not possible for non-produced capital goods. These estimates '*express the capital stock in terms of current productive resources rather than historical forgone consumption*' (Gallman, 1986, p. 174) and is related to the present. In that sense, it is closest to the concept of value added of the national accounts. A problem with this method is that worn out equipment with a low book value often might have high reproduction cost (consider the $14 billion costs to repair the New Orleans levees).
- **Using market prices** of capital goods (which are not always available). This is a future oriented method as the price is somehow related to benefits yet to come, either of a monetary or (in the case of houses) non-monetary. Sometimes, these future monetary benefits (or the estimated monetary value of non-monetary benefits) are discounted which, however, often (like in the case of natural gas) leads to unacceptable swings in the value of capital when the interest rate changes (Veldhuizen, Graveland, Van der Bergen and Schenau, 2009; Rossum and Swerts, 2011). In the case of houses, the monetary price of houses does not seem to be connected to future *benefits* but to the, considering incomes, regulations and the interest rate, maximum amount which can be borrowed, i.e. to future outlays.
- A fourth method is calculating depreciation (in fact a variant of the book value method) by using the discounted value of the stream of income of depreciable capital goods which, as it has to be equal to the present market, book or or reproduction value of a capital good, is *not* the same method as the discounting method mentioned above and in fact only one of many ways to calculate non-linear depreciation.

II. Sources for graph 1 to 5

Except for the USA, Eurostat data on 'gross capital formation' which include changes in inventories and which go back to somewhere between 1974 and 1980 are spliced to historical series. For Sweden, the Netherlands and the UK long run series on gross fixed investment were available via the websites of the Centraal Bureau voor de Statistiek (2, the Netherlands), The Bank of England (3, Great-Britain) and Sveriges Riksbank (1, Sweden).

1) http://www.riksbank.se/en/The-Riksbank/Research/Historical-Monetary-Statistics-/Historical-Monetary-and-Financial-Statistics-for-Sweden-Volume-II-House-Prices-Stock-Returns-National-Accounts-and-the-Riksbank-Balance-Sheet-16202012-/
2) http://www.cbs.nl/nl-NL/menu/themas/dossiers/historische-reeksen/cijfers/extra/historische-reeksen.htm
3) http://www.bankofengland.co.uk/publications/Documents/quarterlybulletin/threecenturiesofdata.xls

For the USA, NBER data were used back to 1919 (4, 5). For the 1897-1919 period, data from Levy, 2000 (which are ultimately based upon partial series from a 1955 study by R.W. Goldsmith not used in this article) were used. For the 1839-1900 period, data from Davis and Gallman, 1978 and Gallman, 1986 are used.

4) http://www.nber.org/databases/macrohistory/rectdata/08/a08165.dat
5) http://www.nber.org/databases/macrohistory/rectdata/10/a10037.dat

Additional data for Spain, Italy, Germany, Finland and Denmark were obtained from Mitchell (2005). Data for France are from Lévy-Leboyer (1978).

III. *Sources for graph 6 to 8*

The estimates presented in this study are somewhat preliminary and quite some improvements are possible. Care has been taken to stick as much as possible to the methods used by the Centraal Bureau voor de Statistiek (CBS), see below, but the specialists of the CBS can, no doubt, improve these series quite a bit. Aside – many of the background reports about estimating capital are nowadays available on the internet, which facilitates studies like this one more than a little bit. At this moment my estimates are, despite all possibilities to improve them, however, the best (in fact: the only) long run estimate of Dutch wealth available and the fact that quite different estimates from different authors (i.e. CBS, 1960, this study, Verstegen 1996) show comparable developments or developments consistent with my findings indicates that there is some merit to the data.

Systematic endeavors to estimate balance sheets for the Netherlands start with Tinbergen (1942). These comparative estimates for six countries are characterized by Maddison (1994, p.1), using a German translation, as: "His 'Kapitalmenge' could better be characterized as a heap than as a stock'. For the Netherlands, these estimates were however quickly replaced by a regular statistic of national balance sheets, see Derksen, 1946; CBS, 1947 and ultimately Korn and van der Weide, 1960 which contains consistent balance sheets for the 1948-1958 period. These estimates were, alas, discontinued (is there a relation with the Indonesian nationalizations of remaining Dutch property in Indonesia in 1957 and 1958 (Baudet, 1975)?) and it would not be until the end of the nineties when, spurred by the growing international consensus about the importance of balance sheets, new attempts ultimately culminated into national and sectoral balance sheets consistent with the SNA methodology. Two methodological studies: Pommeé and Maris, 1996 and Verbiest, 1997. See also Lith, 1999, about the interrelation between the capital value of houses and the estimation of imputed rents. In the meanwhile, however, Wilterdink had published his still monumental study '*Vermogensverhoudingen in Nederland*' (Wealth and its distribution in the Netherlands) which clearly sets out the relation between both side of the balance sheets (i.e. the value of assets and the value of property claims) and relates these to distributional issues (Wilterdink, 1984). One crucial aspect of this study is the analysis how, in the very long run, capital evolves – economists do have to pay attention to this. Eventually, the Dutch Centraal Bureau voor de Statistiek has published, in the national accounts, financial sectoral balance sheets which stretch back to 1990 as well as physical balance sheets stretching back to 1997. Though they have not published these, their series of depreciable fixed capital however stretch back to 1952 (to an extent using the information of the 1948-1958 series), which were kindly provided to me.

In this study, data on agricultural land, the value of houses, the value of land below houses, the Net international investment position, the value of natural gas have been added to the 1948-1952 data using sources and methods which are as comparable as possible with sources and methods used by the Centraal Bureau voor de Statistiek for the post 1997 series.

More specifically, the next methods have been used:

1) **Natural gas**. The amount of known reserves were based on interpolating existing data of the CBS, interpolation was based upon data on production which stretch back to 1946 (before the end of the sixties, production was very low). On the internet, a spreadsheet of the Centraal Plan Bureau (CPB), a kind of (semi) public financial watchdog, can be found which contains data about government natural gas income, including sales taxes and the like. As prices differ quite a lot between different kind of customers, households often paying a price which is multiples higher than prices paid by industrial companies, a unit value price has been calculated using these CPB data. Following the methodology of Veldhuizen e.a. (2009) and Rossum and Swerts (2011), a three year average has been used to calculate the value of reserves of natural gas; Veldhuizen e.a. explicitly do not use a discounting method as changes in interest rates (as well as, of course, future 'benefits') make such estimates extremely volatile.
2) **Agricultural land**. CBS methods for estimating the value of land are described in Bergen, Van den and De Haan, 2009. CBS series were extrapolated backwards by using volume data from Knibbe, 1993 and the CBS. Price data on the value of arms per hectare (including buildings) were obtained from Luijt and Voskuilen (2009). A comparison with post 1997 CBS data on the value of agricultural land yielded a very consistent difference of about 20% (my estimates being higher) which means that I calibrated my series by applying a 20% haircut to distract the value of farm buildings.
3) **Land below houses**. The CBS data contain data on the value of houses back to 1952. Comparing these with the 1948-1958 series mentioned above yields that for the 1952-1958 period the recent data are neatly in between the two series provided in the older estimate. Multiplying house prices with the number of houses shows, back to 1990, a very good correspondence with the CBS series for the value of houses plus the value of land despite the fact that the CBS uses tax value (WOZ-waarde) of houses instead of market

prices (Bergen, Van den and M. den Haan, 2009). This tax value is however, with a lag and somewhat smoothed, based upon market prices. This means that the value of land below houses was calculated by multiplying house prices with the number of houses for the period 1965-1989 and subtracting the value of houses. Data on house prices back to 1965 were kindly provided by Jesse Frederik, dependable older macro-series do not seem to be available (though the 'Kadaster' should have archives with data on literally all house transaction back to somewhere in the nineteenth century).

4) **Land below other structures**. This was extrapolated backwards from 1990 onwards, using official data on land below structures, price data are however missing.

5) Net international investment position. This is a tricky statistic as it is influenced by the net surplus or deficit on the current account (which is well known) but also by large changes in the value of shares and bonds as well as by earnings retained by foreign subsidiaries which do not show in the book value of these subsidiaries. According to Boonstra (2008) and Vandervyvere (2012) this means on one hand that surpluses on the current account can easily be offset by swings in the value of foreign capital (hence the negative value of the Dutch IIP during the 1997-2001 period) while, on the other hand, the value of foreign capital may be severely understated by book value. The 1973-1983 data are however based upon direct observation (though only of the value of foreign capital owned by companies, not of capital owned by individuals) while the more recent data also seem to be of ever higher quality as, for instance, more care is taken to take Special Purpose Entities into account. See Claassen and Van den Dool (2013).

6) Data from earlier studies. Nineteenth century data (up to 1910) are based upon Verstegen (1996). The Verstegen data are mainly based upon extrapolation on wealth data obtained from inheritances. Data for the 1910-1980 period other than my series are based upon Wilterdink, who however states that private capital is severely understated, mainly due to tax evasion pratices. The 1948-1958 data are based upon Korn and Van der Weiden, 1960.

References

Arrow, K.J., P. Dasgupta, L.H. Goulder, K.J. Mumford and K. Oleson (2010), 'Sustainability and the measurement of wealth', NBER working paper 16599.

Baudet, H. (1975), 'Nederland en de rang van Denemarken' in: *Bijdragen en mededelingen over de Geschiedenis van Nederland 90-3* pp. 430-443.

Bergen, D. van den and M. den Haan (2009), 'A balance sheet for land. Experiences for the Netherlands', LG15/11/2, 15th Meeting of the London Group on Environmental Accounting Wiesbaden, 30 November – 4 December 2009

Boonstra, W. (2008), 'National savings and the international investment position: what does the current account tell us?', *Proceedings of Rijeka Faculty of Economics, Journal of Economics and Business, Vol. 26, No. 1, pp. 9-40*

CBS (2013), *Nationale rekeningen 2012*. CBS, Den Haag/Heerlen.

CBS (1947), 'Uitkomsten van enige berekeningen betreffende het nationale vermogen van Nederland in 1938' in Statistische en econometrische onderzoekingen no. 3

Claassen, P. and G. Van den Dool (2013), 'The effects of including SPEs of BOP and FDI statistics', paper presented at the twenty-sixth meeting of the IMF committee on Balance of Payment statistics, Oman, October 28-30, 2013.

Davis, L.E. and R.E. Gallman (1978), 'Capital formation in the United States during the nineteenth century' in: *The Cambridge economic history of Europe VII-2* pp. 1-69. Cambridge.

Derksen, J.B. D. (1946), 'A system of national book-keeping illustrated by the experience of the Netherlands economy' , National Institute of economic and social research occasional papers X.

DNB, 'Monetair-financiële tijdreeksen 1982-2002', *Statistisch bulletin themanummer october 2012.*

Domar, R.E. (1946), 'Capital expansion, rate of growth and employment', *Econometrica 14-2* pp. 137-147.

Fazarri, S. M., P.E. Ferri, E.C. Greenberg and A.M. Varlato (2013), 'Aggregate demand, instability, and growth' in: *Review of Keynesian economics 1-1.*

Frederik, J. (2012), 'Twee keer dezelfde steen', http://www.ftm.nl/exclusive/twee-keer-dezelfde-steen/

Gallman, R. E. (1986), 'The United States Capital stock in the nineteenth century' in: Engerman, S.L. and R. E. Gallman, *Long-term factors in American Economic growth* pp. 165-214. Chicago.

Goldsmith, R.W.(1966), 'The uses of national balance sheets', *Review of Income and wealth 15-2* pp. 95-133.

Goldsmith, R.W. (1985), *Comparative national balance sheets. A study of twenty countries, 1688-1978.* Chicago.

Groote, P. (1995), *Kapitaalvorming in infrastructuur in Nederland 1800-1913.* Groningen.

Harrod, R. F. (1939), 'An essay in dynamic theory', *The economic journal 49* pp. 119-133.

Knibbe, M. (1993), *Agriculture in the Netherlands 1851-1950: production and institutional change.* Amsterdam.

Knibbe, M. (1999), 'Landbouwproductie en productiviteit 1807-2000' in: Van der Bie, R. and P. Dehing, *Nationaal goed. Feiten en cijfers over onze samenleving*pp. 37-55. Voorburg/Heerlen.

Korn, B. and Th. D. van der Weide (1960), 'Het nationale vermogen van Nederland, 1948-1968' in: Statistische en econometrische onderzoekingen' 1960-no. 3.

Levy, D. (2000), 'Investment-saving comovement and capital mobility: evidence from century long U.S. time series', *Review of economic dynamics 3* pp. 100-136.

Lévy-Leboyer, 'Capital investment and economic growth in France, 1820-1930' in: *The Cambridge economic history of Europe VII-1* pp. 231-295.

Lith, E. van (1999) 'De raming van diensten uit eigen-woningbezit', CBS M&O.011. - Voorburg/Heerlen.

Luijt, J. and M. Voskuilen (2009), 'Langetermijnontwikkeling van de agrarische grondprijs', LEI nota 09-014, LEI Wageningen UR, Den Haag.

Maddison, A. (1982), *Ontwikkelingsfasen van het kapitalisme.* Utrecht/Antwerpen.

Maddison, A. (1992), 'A long run perspective on saving', Scandinavian journal of economics 1992-2, pp. 181-196.

Maddison, A. (1994), 'standardised estimates of fixed capital stock: a ix country comparison', Research memorandum 570 (GD 9). Groningen.

Mitchell, B. (2005), *International historical statistics 1750-2000: Europe.* London.

Nieuwkerk, M. van and R.P. Sparling, 'De internationale investeringspositie van Nederland', DNB, *Monetaire monografieën Nr. 4*

Nieuwkerk, M. van and R.P. Sparling, 'De betalingsbalans van Nederland: methoden, begrippen en gegevens (1946-1985), DNB, *Monetaire monografieën Nr. 7*

Piketty, T. (2014A), *Capital in the Twenty First century,* Harvard.

Piketty, T. (2014B), 'Technical appendix of the book 'Capital in the twentieth century', Harvard University Press, available at http://piketty.pse.ens.fr/capital21c` (assessed July 10, 2014).

Piketty, T. and G. Zucman (2013), 'Capital is back: wealth-income ratios in rich countries 1700-2010. Full paper and appendices'.

Piketty, T. and G. Zucman (2014), 'Wealth and inheritance in the long run', forthcoming in *Handbook of Income distribution 2*, downloaded 28/8/2014 from: http://www.google.nl/url?sa=t&rct=j&q=&esrc=s&source=web&cd=1&cad=rja&uact=8&ved=0CCMQFjAA&url=http%3A%2F%2Fgabriel-zucman.eu%2Ffiles%2FPikettyZucman2014HID.pdf&ei=oTQAVJe1EaSP7AboyYDICw&usg=AFQjCNFiigZrwbZI98Z_9jPsML__ERI7Xw&bvm=bv.74115972,d.ZGU

Pommée, M. and W. Baris (1996), 'Balance sheet valuation: Produced intangible assets and non-produced assets', CBS, NA-081 P-30/1996-4.

Rasmussen, M.W. and Marvin Towne (1960), 'Farm gross product and gross investment in the nineteenth century' in: Conference on Research in Income and Wealth, *Trends in the American economy in the nineteenth century'* pp. 255-316. Princeton University Press.

Rossum, M. van and O. Swerts (2011), 'De Nederlandse aardgaswinning' in: CBS, *De Nederlandse economie in 2010* pp. 232-254. http://silverberg-on-meltdown-economics.blogspot.nl/2014/06/nitpicking-piketty-productively-part-i.html

Solow, R. M. (1956), 'A contribution to the theory of economic growth', *The quarterly journal of economics 70-1* pp. 65-94.

Tinbergen, J. (1942)'De groei van den voorraad van eenige kapitaalgoederen in zes landen vanaf omstreeks 1870', *Maandschrift van het CBS*, 1942, pp. 113-121, 296-299, 497-509

United Nations/Organisation for Economic cooperatioin and development/European commission/Internationa Monetary Fund/World bank (2009), *A system of national accounts 2008*. New York.

Veldhuizen, E., C. Graveland, D. van der Bergen and S.J. Schenau (2009), *Valuation of oil andgas reserves in the Netherlands 1990–2005*. Voorburg/Heerlen.

Vandervyvere, W. (2012) 'The Dutch current account and net international investment position', European Commission, Directorate for Economic and financial affairs, Economic papers 465.

Verbiest, P. (1997), 'De kapitaalgoederenvoorraad in Nederland'. CBS Nota M@O 007.

Verstegen, S. (1996), 'National wealth and income from capital in the Netherlands 1805-1910' in: *Economic and social history in the Netherlands 7* pp. 73-108

Wilterdink, N. (1984), *Vermogensverhoudingen in Nederland. Ontwikkelingen sinds de negentiende eeuw*. Amsterdam.

Wolff, E. N. (1991), 'Capital formation and productivity convergence over the long term', *The American Economic Review 81-3* pp. 565-579.

Piketty vs. the classical economic reformers

Michael Hudson [Institute for Study of Long-Term Economic Trends and University of Missouri, Kansas City, USA]

Thomas Piketty has done a great service in collating the data of many countries to quantify the ebb and flow of their distribution of wealth and income. For hundreds of pages and tables, his measurements confirm what most people sense without needing statistical proof. Across the globe, the top 1% have increased their share of wealth and income to the steepest extreme since the Gilded Age of the late 19th and early 20th century.

The Federal Reserve's 2013 *Survey of Consumer Finances* shows that economic polarization has accelerated since the 2008 crash. The 0.1% of Americans have pulled even further ahead of the rest of the 1%, who in turn have widened their gains over the remainder of the 10%. At the bottom of the pyramid, the poorest 10% have faired even worse than the next lowest. The economy is operating like a centrifuge separating rich from poor. But neither Piketty nor the Fed makes an attempt to explain the dynamics causing this polarization. They merely measure its broad parameters.

Some reviewers have labeled Piketty's statistics and policy proposals as Marxist, partly because the title of his book – *Capital in the Twenty-First Century* – suggests that it might aim at updating of Marx's *Capital.*[1] Even Martin Wolf writes of Piketty's book that, "in its scale and sweep it brings us back to the founders of political economy."[2] But apart from seeing inequality as a social threat, there is little similarity either in Piketty's analysis or in his proposed policy remedies.

Marx followed in the classical tradition of Francois Quesnay, Adam Smith, David Ricardo and John Stuart Mill in defining economic rent (including natural resource rent and monopoly rent from legal privileges or control of access point to key infrastructure monopolies) as the excess of price over intrinsic labor-cost value. Volumes II and III of Marx's *Capital* extend value

---

[1] See for instance Steven Erlanger, "Taking on Adam Smith (and Karl Marx)," *The New York Times*, April 20, 2014.
[2] Martin Wolf, "Inequality time," *Financial Times*, April 19, 2014.

theory to the exploitation of industrial wage labor by capitalists. Using the labor theory of value to define extractive rentier or capitalist exploitation is what distinguishes classical political economy from the post-classical reaction against Marx and other reformers and critics gaining political influence by the turn of the 20th century.

The statistical sources used by Piketty reflect this reaction against treating *rentier* income as unearned. Post-classical theory insists that all income is earned productively, with no source of gain less productive than any other. Making money by privatizing public monopolies and cutting services, or simply price gouging to cover higher costs of interest and dividends, management fees, higher executive salaries and stock options is treated as economically productive as building new factories and hiring employees.

Limiting Picketty's reform proposals to what anti-reform statistics reveal

Piketty sought to explain the ebb and flow of polarization by suggesting a basic mathematical law: when wealth is unequally distributed and returns to capital (interest, dividends and capital gains) exceed the rise in overall income (as measured by GDP), economies polarize in favor of capital owners. Unlike the classical economists, he does not focus on *rentier* gains by real estate owners, their bankers, corporate raiders and financiers, privatizers and other rent seekers.

Piketty is limited by the available statistical sources, because any accounting format reflects the economic theory that defines its categories. Neither the National Income and Product Accounts (NIPA) nor the Internal Revenue Service's *Statistics on Income* in the United States define the specific form that the wealth buildup takes. Most textbook models focus on tangible investment in means of production (plant and equipment, research and development). But industrial profits on such investment have fallen relative to more passive gains from asset-price inflation (rising debt-fueled prices for real estate, stocks and bonds), financial speculation (arbitrage, derivatives trading and credit default insurance), and land rent, natural resource rent (oil and gas, minerals), monopoly rent (including patent rights), and legal privileges topped by the ability of banks to create interest-bearing credit.

A byproduct of this value-free view of wealth is that Piketty suggests an equally value-free remedy for inequality: a global estate tax with a progressive wealth and income tax. Not only is this almost impossible to enforce politically, but a general tax on wealth or income does not discriminate between what is earned "productively" and what is squeezed out by rent extraction or obtained by capital gains.

The advantage of classical economic theory's focus on rent extraction, financialization and debt-leveraged asset-price ("capital") gains is that each form of "unearned" wealth and income has a different set of remedies. But to Picketty's sources – and hence to his analysis – wealth is wealth, income is income, and that is that. He is obliged to make his solution as general as his statistics that define the problem.

Taxing all forms of income or wealth at the same rate does not favor industrial investment over financial engineering. It does not reverse today's fiscal subsidy treating interest as tax-deductible. This tax preference for buying companies on credit – using their earnings to pay interest to bondholders and bankers – enables the 1% to obtain a much higher payout in the form of interest than by dividends on equity financing. The tax collector loses in favor of creditors – and taxes consumers and wage earners to make up the shortfall. Meanwhile, low taxes on capital gains encourage corporate managers to use earnings for stock buybacks to bid up their prices. Piketty's book does not address these tax preferences and distortions favoring the 1%.

Why is inequality increasing? False leads that Piketty avoids, but does not controvert

Piketty shows that inequality is rising, but his broad formula relating overall financial returns (*r*) to the overall rate of economic growth (*g*) does not explain how policies have driven the turnaround since 1980. But at least his broad treatment of *rentiers* does not succumb to apologetics based on age and educational levels.

The "life cycle" theory of savings depicts individuals borrowing to consume more when young, and repay out of incomes expected to rise during their working life. They pay interest to "patient" savers who defer their own consumption in order to earn interest. This "abstinence" theory blames debtors for their plight of needing credit to get by in today's world. Inherited wealth seems to play no role, as if everyone starts from the same economic point. Also absent from this "pay later" view is the fact that real wages have stopped rising since 1980. Upward mobility is much more difficult to achieve, and most debtors have to pay by working even harder for lower wages.

It is not by deferring consumption that inheritors obtain their wealth. As Marx put it, it is absurd to view the Rothschilds as growing so rich simply by being Europe's most "abstinent" consumers. And on the macroeconomic level, this individualistic "life-cycle theory" of interest ignores the fact that the economy is an overall system whose volume of debt grows exponentially from one generation to the next as savings accrue and are augmented by new electronic bank credit – extracting interest from debtors.

Another diversionary explanation of wealth disparity is educational status, duly dubbed "human capital" on the logic that each academic step adds to the stream of future earnings. The idea is that better-educated individuals at the best schools earn more – justifying student debt. One CEO of a Fortune 500 company has assured me that the reason he is so rich is because he is so smart and well educated. Other corporate executives tell me that the reason they hire economics PhDs is that it shows that the prospective employee is willing to work hard for a goal to get a better job. The tacit message is that such PhDs have learned to accept writing economic fictions to get ahead. But all you really need is greed, and that can't be taught in school.

On the negative side of the relationship between education and net worth, schooling has become so expensive and debt leveraged that the burden of student loans is keeping recent graduates living at home with their parents instead of being able to start families in homes of their own. For-profit technical schools such as the University of Phoenix have notoriously low graduation rates, but use government-guaranteed loans to create an artificial market selling dreams that end in jobless student-loan peonage taking its place alongside debt serfdom for homebuyers paying mortgages.

Matters are even worse than Piketty's measure of inequality shows. He refers to gross income, not the net earnings *after* meeting basic expenses. To make wages conceptually symmetrical with profits or rents – corporate profits or cash flow *after* meeting the costs of production – the appropriate measure would be wages after meeting basic living expenses. That is why net worth measures are more important than income.

What U.S. official statistics call "disposable income" – paychecks *after* taxes and FICA withholding – is not all that disposable. Recipients must pay their monthly "nut": debt service on bank loans and credit cards, home mortgages or rent, pension fund and health insurance contributions, and other basic expenses needed simply to break even, such as food and transportation to and from work. Faced with these monthly obligations, a rising proportion of the labor force finds itself with scant savings. Hence the "traumatized worker" effect, "one paycheck away from homelessness," too fearful to strike or even to complain about working conditions or the lack of wage increases.

The upshot is that most wealth takes the form of what classical economists characterized as unearned income, mainly from the FIRE (finance, insurance and real estate) sector: interest and various forms of economic rent, inherited wealth and "capital" gains, not to speak of tax avoidance, stock options and other favoritism for *rentiers*.

Piketty's statistics show a number of turning points in the share of wages compared to returns to capital (interest, dividends and capital gains). The Gilded Age was followed by a move toward greater equality during 1914–50. A progressive U.S. income tax was legislated in 1913, taxing capital gains as normal income – at a high rate. (Only about 1 percent of Americans initially had to file tax returns.) The Great War was followed by the financial crash of 1929, the Great Depression and World War II that destroyed capital or taxed it more heavily. A period of relative stability followed in the 1960s and 70s as progressive taxes and public regulation were maintained.

The 1980 turning point in wealth and income distribution

The great turning point occurred in 1980 after the victory of Margaret Thatcher's Conservatives in Britain and Ronald Reagan in the United States. Progressive taxes were rolled back, public enterprises were privatized and debts soared – owed mainly to the wealthy. Interest rates have been driven down to historic lows – and after the crash of 2008 the aim of Quantitative Easing has been to re-inflate asset prices by reviving a Bubble Economy aiming mainly at "capital" gains for wealth-holders. These trends have led wealth to soar and become concentrated in the hands of the top 1% and other wealthy families, first during the post-1980 bubble and even more during its post-2008 collapse.

1. Interest rates and easier credit terms promoting debt leveraging (pyramiding)

Interest rates determine the rate at which a given flow of income, interest or dividends is capitalized into mortgage loans, bond or stock prices. Rising steadily from 1951, loans by U.S. banks to prime corporate customers reached a peak of 20 percent by yearend 1979. At that rate it was nearly impossible to make a profit or capital gain by borrowing to buy housing, commercial real estate, stocks or bonds.

Then, for more than thirty years, interest rates plunged to all-time lows. This decline led bankers and bondholders to lend more and more against income-yielding properties. As mortgage interest rates fell, larger bank loans could be afforded out of existing income and rent, because a property is worth whatever a bank will lend against it. This "creates wealth" by purely financial means – an explosion of bank credit financing capital gains over and above current income. Prices for bonds enjoyed the greatest bull market in history.

In addition to lowering interest rates, banks stretched out the maturities and also required lower down payments to attract more customers hoping to get rich by going deeper into debt. And until 2008, real estate – the economy's largest asset – rose almost steadily. But a byproduct of debt leveraging is that mortgage holders receive a rising proportion of the rental income of property. Home ownership was becoming a road to debt peonage, as owners' equity declined as a share of the property's price.

Much the same phenomenon was occurring in industry after 1980. Innovations in leveraged buyouts enabled corporate raiders, management teams and ambitious financial empire-builders to buy companies on credit, paying earnings to bondholders instead of reinvesting in the business (or paying income taxes). Capital gains were achieved by bidding up stock prices by share buybacks and higher dividend payouts, while cutting costs by downsizing and scaling back pension plans.

Most money is not being made by tangible capital investment but financially. Stock buybacks are being financed even with borrowed funds – going into debt to create short-term capital gains for managers whose pay is tied to stock options. "In 2012, the 500 highest paid US executives made on average $30.3 [million] each ... More than 80 per cent of it came in the form of stock options or stock awards. Their incentives are skewed towards extracting value from the companies they run, rather than creating future value."[3]

Gains by the 1% of this sort are not an inherently natural law. "Greed will always be with us. Dumb laws are optional," the *Financial Times* writer just quoted observes. This perception is missing in Piketty's analysis. Thinking about inequality simply in terms of comparing the return to capital to overall economic growth leaves little room for public policy. And in the absence of government taking the lead, planning shifts to Wall Street and other financial centers. The result is as centrally planned an economy as Hayek warned against in *The Road to Serfdom*. But it is planned financially, for purely pecuniary gain, not for economic growth or industrial capital formation as such.

This means that in order to preserve its momentum, financialization evolves into Bubble Economies, requiring ever larger injections of credit to bid up asset prices by enough to cover the interest charges falling due. Wealth-holders can gain only as long as asset prices grow as exponentially as the

---

[3] Edward Luce, "The short-sighted US buyback boom," *Financial Times*, September 22, 2014.

compounding of interest. This requires that banks continue to lend, or that governments bail out financial markets, *e.g.* by the Federal Reserve's Quantitative Easing or Mario Draghi's "Whatever it takes" at the European Central Bank.

Bankers promote fiscal policies to encourage debt leveraging by focusing the public's attention on personal gains to be made by borrowing to buy assets expected to rise in price. What is suppressed is recognition that the wealthiest layer of the economy gets most of the gains while homebuyers, industry and governments go deeper into debt.

2. *Privatization and rent seeking*

The second major trend concentrating wealth in the hands of the ultra-rich since 1980 has been privatization. Led ideologically by Margaret Thatcher in Britain after 1979 (applauding Chile's "free market" privatization at gunpoint under General Pinochet after 1973), the pretense is that private management is inherently more efficient than public enterprise. Yet in contrast to the public interest in lowering prices – by subsidizing basic services to make economies more competitive – the aim of private owners is to install tollbooths to extract economic rent.

Under the neoliberal Pinochet-Thatcher style privatizations, capital investments in transportation, power, communications and other basic commanding heights were sold off, mainly on credit. This was the opposite of reform policy a century ago socializing pensions and health care, water, roads and other essential services. Key infrastructure was to be kept in the public domain or (in the case of heavy industry such as British steel) nationalized. But since 1980 infrastructure has been privatized into "tollbooth" opportunities to extract financial returns (interest and capital gains) and monopoly rent.

The richest individuals in the former Soviet Union and many Third World countries have gained their wealth by insider dealings to obtain such *rentier* privileges. In Mexico, Carlos Slim's fortune comes from charging high telephone rates increasing the cost of living and of doing business. This is how America's railroad barons became the Gilded Age elite, the last time that wealth inequality was as high as it is today. The U.S. stock market was largely a market in shares for railroads, much as stock markets in other countries dealt mainly in canals and commercial monopolies or trusts.

This concentration of wealth was achieved by rent extraction, bribery and fraud, facilitated by ideological patter that claims any way of transferring property into private ownership would help society grow richer faster. Piketty's point is simply that having been appropriated, such wealth takes a financial form, which should be taxed to rectify matters. He sees no need to reverse privatization, to change today's tax favoritism for *rentiers*, regulate monopoly prices, enact an excess-profit tax or minimum wage laws, full employment policies, debt writedowns and other specific remedies.

3. The tax shift off wealth and capital gains onto wages and consumer spending

An array of tax shifts has favored the wealthy. In addition to rolling back progressive income tax rates, the "small print" gives special exemptions for the FIRE sector (finance, insurance and real estate). Corporate industry and the wealthy are emulating the oil industry's pioneering tactics to declare their profits in offshore tax-avoidance centers. Real estate investors can pretend that their buildings are depreciating so fast that this fictitious book-loss offsets their otherwise declarable rental income. (Homeowners are not allowed to make such a deduction; only absentee owners can do so.)

Permitting interest payments to be tax-deductible subsidizes debt leveraging at the tax collector's expense. Capital gains are not taxed if they are invested to buy yet more property, or bequeathed when the owner dies. The effect is that in addition to receiving the lion's share of tax cuts, the 1% to 10% receive most of the interest and asset-price gains bid up on bank credit.

Governments are obliged to make up the fiscal shortfall resulting from favoring the wealthy by raising sales taxes on consumers and wage earners, *e.g.*, by Europe's value-added tax (VAT). U.S. state and local governments have replaced the property tax (which provided three-quarters of their fiscal revenue a century ago, but now accounts for only one-sixth) with local sales and income taxes that fall mainly on consumers.

Un-taxing *rentier* wealth favors the 1% who hold the 99% increasingly in debt. To make matters worse, taxing labor and industry instead of *rentiers* increases the cost of living and doing business, shrinking the economy and hence employment and wage rates.

4. Financing budget deficits via bondholders instead of government money creation

World War I (like America's Civil War) showed that governments could finance their own spending by "greenbacks" instead of borrowing from bondholders. But the latter wanted to keep government debt financing for themselves – and to keep governments on a short monetary leash as a means of controlling their policies.

At issue is whether economies will depend on credit creation by and for the 1%, or whether governments will self-finance deficits to promote full employment. Opponents of central bank money creation accuse central bank financing of being inherently inflationary, leading almost inexorably to Weimar-era style hyperinflation. The claim is that private bankers provide more responsible funding. But in practice the 1% promote policies that augment their own wealth by inflating asset prices on credit owed mainly to themselves.

Meanwhile, blocking government self-financing is *de*flationary. By running a budget surplus in the late 1990s, the Clinton administration obliged the U.S. economy to rely on commercial banks for its increased money supply. The result was a sharp rise in the debt overhead (at rising interest rates). Likewise in today's Eurozone, the European Central Bank's refusal to finance government deficits – and limiting budget deficits to only 3% of GDP – is turning the continent into a dead zone.

In contrast to public spending to promote growth and employment for the economy at large, bank credit "creates wealth" mainly by lending against property and financial securities and thus inflating asset prices, not by funding new tangible capital investment. This underlying contrast is a major factor explaining why the 1% advocates policies that increase the market valuation of its wealth vis-à-vis labor's wages. Any reform policy to reverse today's economic polarization needs to address this monetary and fiscal contrast.

5. Debt deflation

The main long-term dynamic holding back recovery in Europe and North America is the debt overhead – a flow of interest upward to bank bondholders and other creditors and "savers." The economy has become a debt pyramid diverting rent and profits as well as wages to pay debt service. Like corporate profits, a rising bite out of wages is being paid out as debt service, especially as wages have merely moved sideways since the late 1970s. Wages hitherto spent on consumer goods are paid to creditors, shrinking markets in the "real" non-*rentier* economy.

Despite his criticism of the financial sector, Piketty does not address the debt, credit or monetary dimensions of economic polarization. He proposes simply to tax the financialized economy that this debt pyramid has created, leaving in place the debt corner into which the 1% have painted the economy. It is difficult to see how a progressive income and estate tax alone can reverse the trend toward polarization without writing down today's debt overhead.

A major reason why the 1% have increased their gains since 2008 is that the Treasury and Federal Reserve bailed out banks, their bondholders and uninsured large depositors instead of obliging them to absorb the loss from having lent much more than borrowers were able to pay. These bailouts, and the Federal Reserve's subsequent Quantitative Easing to re-inflate real estate and other asset prices, were the only occasions on which banks have applauded government money creation – when it is to pay *them*, not to spur tangible investment and employment in the non-*rentier* economy.

These government policies are not the result of an inherent mathematical law about the return to capital vis-à-vis that of the non-*rentier* economy – GDP and wages. Reversing the widening inequality between finance capital and wage labor entails going far beyond Piketty's advocacy of more progressive income and wealth taxation. While certainly desirable, these taxes by themselves would leave in place the political, financial and privatized rent-extracting structures that serve the 1% to support their debt claims and tollbooth charges on the economy at large.

Piketty's narrow solution reflects the limited scope of his analysis. The 2008 crisis offered an opportunity much like wartime and the Great Depression to wipe out the financial buildup. But the response was to prevent financial losses by bankers and bondholders. Instead of governments acting to restore prosperity, they imposed austerity to squeeze out enough revenue to save banks from insolvency.

Piketty does not call for reversing the debt leveraging that has inflated asset prices, much less writing down the debts that hold the 99% in financial bondage. He accepts the status quo but would tax inherited wealth and restore an 80 percent tax rate such as typified the 1940s and '50s on incomes above $500,000 or $1 million, as if the wealthy will not circumvent such policies by the stratagems put in place in recent decades.

Ideological support for the 1%'s conquest of the 99%

Despite Piketty's focus on today's financial *rentiers* instead of landlords as the major idle rich class, he does not see that sustaining its dominance over the rest of the economy involves the political sphere. He accepts the political and legal environment for granted. His limited vision is what attracts a New York fund manager writing in the *Wall Street Journal*: "Thomas Piketty likes capitalism because it efficiently allocates resources. But he does not like how it allocates income."[4] As if the two can be separated!

The economy is polarizing because of how the 1% use their wealth. If they invested their fortunes productively as "job creators" – as mainstream textbooks describe them as doing – there would be some logic in today's tax favoritism and financial bailouts. *Rentier* elites would be doing what governments are supposed to do. Instead, today's financial oligarchy lends out its savings to indebt the economy at large, and uses its gains to buy control of government to extract more special privileges, tax favoritism and

[4] Daniel Shuchman, "Thomas Piketty Revives Marx for the 21st Century," *Wall Street Journal*, April 22, 2014.

rent-extraction opportunities by political campaign financing in the United States (unlimited since the Supreme Court's Citizens United ruling) and by lobbying.

Politics and the legal system have become part of the market in the sense of being up for sale. As in consumer advertising, ideological engineering is used to "manufacture consent," using the mass media to broadcast an anti-tax and anti-regulatory ethic. Thorstein Veblen described the tactic a century ago in *Higher Learning in America* (1904). Business schools have been endowed, economic prizes awarded and public relations "think tanks" staffed with credentialed spokesmen to shape popular perceptions to accept widening financial inequality as natural and even desirable.

Piketty's statistics show that inequality of wealth and income distribution is higher in the United States than in Europe, but he does not explain that this is largely because public spending and subsidies to promote employment and living conditions are much stronger outside of the United States. His proposed tax remedy does not include structural reforms, much less a public option for banking and de-privatization of the infrastructure still being sold to rent-extractors on credit.

Focusing mainly on the exponential accrual of inherited wealth, Piketty rightly warns of a lapse of economic democracy back into "patrimonial capitalism," a *rentier* economy controlled by hereditary dynasties. The world is seeing a retrogression of economic democracy back into *rentier* oligarchy. This prospect makes it all the more important to understand the dynamics that are endowing such dynasties. But Piketty's formula about the rate of return on capital (*r*) exceeding the rate of economic growth (*g*) does not explain how this political maneuvering over public policy affects this ratio. His statistics on inequality in themselves say nothing about the tactics of class warfare to prevent the minimum wage from being raised in the United States, or to impose austerity rather than full employment policies.

As Adam Smith pointed out, the rate of profit is often highest in countries going fastest to ruin. If there are internal contradictions, what may bring the rate of return (Piketty's *r*, increasingly based on debt service and asset-price inflation) back in line with the ability to pay out of growth (Piketty's *g*)? Would his proposed global tax on wealth and high incomes be sufficient to reverse today's widening inequality without changing the fiscal and social-economic structures that the financial oligarchy has created to prevent such a reversal?

It was by dealing with these structures to free industrial capitalism from the vestiges of feudalism that the classical economists were revolutionary, above all by taxing absentee-owned land. So radical was this drive to subordinate the growth of *rentier* wealth to serve society at large that despite almost winning by the early 20th century, it faltered. Marx extended this post-feudal revolution to the industrial economy in a way that reflected the interest of the working majority. But progress along these lines is now in danger of being rolled back under pressure of financial austerity.

When it comes to proposing an alternative, Piketty is no such radical. His version of a singular tax solution – a heavy estate tax and a global tax on the higher wealth and income brackets – does not follow the classical reformers' key distinction between *rentier* "free lunch" income and wealth earned productively. It does not counter the financialization of industry, reverse privatization carve-outs from the public domain, or see a need for a public option to finance budget deficits and retail banking. In that respect his remedy is in line with the post-classical "value-free" reaction denying that any forms of income are unearned and outright predatory.

Piketty's book provides a comprehensive description of the symptoms of pro-*rentier* policy as measured by the inequality of overall wealth and income distribution. But without analyzing or diagnosing the array of strategies by which *rentier* wealth has rolled back earlier policies toward greater economic equality of after-tax income and wealth, it cannot prescribe a remedy to stop today's economic polarization at its taproot.

Is *Capital in the Twenty-First Century, Das Kapital* for the twenty-first century?

Claude Hillinger [Germany]

1. Introduction

With *Capital in the Twenty-First Century*, (hereafter *Capital*) Thomas Piketty clearly intended to produce a book that will stand as a landmark in the history of economic thought. In his title he alludes to Karl Marx's *Das Kapital* and there is indeed a strong similarity between the two books. Both support the agenda of the political Left and both predict the demise of the capitalist system. A difference is that with Marx this prediction is an unconditional historical necessity, while Piketty believes that the outcome could be avoided through political action. Also, Piketty clearly believes that his work is based on a much more solid scientific foundation both regarding the voluminous data on which his inferences are based, as well as the theory that he uses to interpret it. The overwhelming positive response that the book has elicited from both the public and the economics profession would seem to validate this claim.

From a purely empirical point of view, *Capital* does not contain anything that is essentially new. The data on which the book is based has already been analyzed in a book and several journal articles by Piketty himself as well as in journal articles by associated researchers. This literature has been highly influential and popularized the expressions "the one percent" and "the 99 percent". The sensation caused by *Capital* is undoubtedly due to what is novel in it: the claim to have presented a theory of the evolution of a capitalist economy. Remarkably to my mind, none of the rave reviews of the book that I have seen seriously examines this claim. Many dutifully reproduce $r > g$, the rate of return on capital greater than the growth rate of the economy, but that by itself is no more than an assertion, not a theory. Understanding the reception is in my view at least as important as understanding the book and in this review I treat both aspects.

2. Piketty's theory of the evolution of capitalism

In my review of *Capital* I concentrate on a single issue: did Piketty present a valid, or at least interesting, theory of the dynamics of a capitalist economy. The question of whether the book deserves the overwhelming praise that it has received depends entirely on how this question is answered. Regarding that theory, Paul Krugman wrote in a much cited review in the *New York Times*:

> ...a unified field theory of inequality, one that integrates economic growth, the distribution of income between capital and labor, and the distribution of wealth and income among individuals into a single frame.

"Unified field theory" is the name that Albert Einstein had given to the theory he was seeking during the latter part of his life, in order to unify general relativity theory with quantum mechanics. He never found this theory, nor did he claim to have done so.

Let us look at Piketty's theory. He defines an economy's capital/ income ratio $\beta = K/Y$ and the ratio of the return on capital/total income $\alpha = rK/Y$. With these definitions he formulates his "first fundamental law of capitalism".[1] This and other assumptions are listed in the following table. At the head of each assumption is an indication of what type of statement is being made.

Piketty's theory of the dynamics of capitalism

(1) Identity: "The first fundamental law of capitalism" $\alpha = r\beta$
(2) Empirical statement: In a capitalist economy the rate of return of capital tends to be permanently above the rate of grows of the economy. This is the already famous $r > g$.
(3) Definitional statement: The inequality $r > g$ implies that β will increase.

[1] Piketty's "Second Fundamental Law of Capitalism" refers to a possible steady state equilibrium of the economy. It does not have an important function in his book.

(4) Empirical statement: The rate of return on capital is relatively stable. This implies that as β increases, so will α. More precisely, it follows from (1) that α will increase if r does not proportionately decline more than β increases.

As Piketty recognizes, (1) is simply a definitional identity. It is rather unusual to refer to an identity as a fundamental law.

The statement (3) is definitional because it is true only if r is defined as the growth rate of capital, i.e. $r = K'/K$. Piketty defines r as "...the average annual rate of return on capital, including profits, dividends, interest, rents, and other income from capital..." He does not mention capital gains or losses as part of his definition. Nor does he mention the fact that much investment in capital markets does not come out of capital returns. Think, for example, of public and private pension funds. Even if these omitted factors were judged to be irrelevant, the statement would still not be true unless *all* of the returns from capital are reinvested, i.e. if there is no consumption out of capital income. But, Piketty himself describes at some length, and with literary allusions, the luxurious style of living of the rentier class. To illustrate the problem with a simple example, assume $= 5\%$, $g = 3\%$ so that $r > g$. Assume further that the recipients of capital income consume 60% of it, leaving 40% to be reinvested. This makes an investment rate of 2%, less than the 3% growth of the economy. This implies a shrinking, not a growing, β.

Strangely, I have found no review that noticed this fundamental flaw in Piketty's theory. The closest that I have found is the following confused remark in (Milanovic 2014):

> ...as α increases, not only do capital owners become richer, but, unless they consume the entire return from their capital, more will remain for them to reinvest. (p. 522)

As the numerical example above shows, a quite reasonable rate of consumption can invalidate Piketty's analysis.

My conclusion is that Piketty does not have a theory in any formal sense of that term. In the framework of econometrics, he does not have a model that could be evaluated by fitting it to data. That said, the stylized facts which he postulates and projects into the future may very well be valid. They do not depend for their validity on his theory. A secular rise in both α and β remains a possibility. The discussion in reviews by professional economists has in fact concentrated on assessing the plausibility of these stylized facts rather than on Piketty's theory.

The basic data on which Piketty bases his conclusions had already been published and analysed in previous publications by him and associated researchers. They consist of time series for France, The United Kingdom, Germany and the United States, reaching from 1870 to 2010. In all four countries the data exhibit a similar pattern which can be described by distinguishing three periods which I will designate I, II, III. Period I ran from 1870 to the First World War. It was characterized by high levels of β and α, and the inequality $r > g$ was satisfied. Inequality of incomes and wealth was high. It was the time described as *Belle Epoque* in France and as Gilded Age in the United States. Period II goes from the First World War to 1950. During this period β and α decline, r declines and eventually fell below g. The distribution of income and wealth became more equal. Finally, in Period III, which goes from 1950 to 2012, the trends of Period II are reversed, but the levels of Period I have not yet been reached. Piketty extrapolates this trend to the year 2100 and predicts even more extreme values than characterized the Gilded Age (Figure 5.8.).

There is one significant deviation from these stylized facts that has been noted by a numberof reviewers, but also by Piketty himself. This is the fact that much wealth in recent decades is the result of the exorbitant rise in the salaries and bonuses of top executives, particularly in the financial sector. In my view, neither Piketty, nor the reviews that I have read, describe this situation correctly. The wealth gained in the financial sector, is best described as the distribution of the loot resulting from the defrauding of the public. The Libor scandal has been described as the biggest fraud in the history of mankind, in terms of the magnitudes involved. As I am writing, a consortium led by the asset managers Blackrock and PIMCO is suing some of the world's largest banks for *250 billion* dollars. None of the top executives involved in this incredible amount of fraud has gone to jail. That is the heart of the problem!

There is a further substantial problem with Piketty's stylized facts. Throughout the history of capitalism huge fortunes have been made by entrepreneurs who created successful enterprises. These fortunes did not result from the return on capital. They are in large measure the result of entrepreneurial talent, risk taking and hard work. This applies also to the fortunes made in information technology in recent decades.

A further very fundamental problem is Piketty's definition of "capital" is that it is an amalgam of real and financial capital. Such a construct has no role in economic theory. The magnitude of this construct fluctuates with the prices of financial assets and is not a measure of the productive capacity of the economy.[2]

Even more difficult than the determination of stylized facts is the identification of the causal factors involved and their projection into the future.. (Milanovic 2014) cites several economic historians who interpret the period under consideration differently from Piketty. Economists who reviewed *Capital* also expressed skepticism regarding Piketty's projection. It is based on the assumption that r remains stable as β increases, which implies near perfect substitutability of capital for labor, an assumption that goes against economic theory and as (Summers, 2014) points out is also contradicted by empirical studies. One can argue however, that as we advance further into the age of information technology and robotics, there may be few barriers to the substitution of machines for humans.

I prefer to adhere to the wisdom of Groucho (not Karl) Marx who remarked that "Predictions are difficult, especially about the future". Nor is this in my opinion the central question. That inequality has risen to levels that are much too high for the health of democratic societies has been widely agreed upon. There is no form of social pathology that is not aggravated by high levels of inequality (Wilkinson und Pickett 2009). Regardless of what we predict for the future, the time to act against inequality is now.

---

[2] Galbraith (2014) deals in some detail with this problem.

To combat inequality, Piketty would rely entirely on redistribution via taxation. His two proposed measures:

(a) A steep increase of the income tax, rising to 80% at the top.
(b) A comprehensive, progressive, global tax on total wealth.

Regarding (a), it was the policy pursued by governments of the Left (and nearly all governments were of the Left) in the post-WWII era. The policy was largely abandoned because the disadvantages were found to exceed the advantages. The disadvantages are: (1) The policy goes against entrepreneurship and innovation. This is because incentives are reduced and also because it becomes more difficult to amass substantial fortunes that could be invested in business enterprises. (2) Political conflict increases as earners of high incomes use political influence to lower their tax rates, or they look for schemes to avoid paying them altogether. (3) The revenue that can be obtained from "soaking the rich" is way below the expectations of a naïve public.

Regarding (b), Piketty himself calls his proposal "utopian". I believe that a more feasible and desirable alternative is a flat tax on financial assets. It would not require assessing the total wealth of individuals.

I am all in favor of taxing capital. Piketty and most reviewers fear that unless such a tax is levelled globally, capital would flee the locations where it is taxed. I believe that this fear is much exaggerated. The most important element in the choice of location by both firms and individuals is the quality of the location, which has many dimensions. That quality has a price which all residents of the location have to pay. A much bigger problem in my opinion has been the unwillingness of the political classes to close blatant loopholes for tax evasion. The most obvious sign of this is the continuous existence of tax havens, which have no function other than to cheat governments out of the taxes due them.

The political economies, both of nation states, of supra-national organizations such as the European Union, and last but not least our interconnected world economy are badly in need of deep structural reforms. Piketty has no blue print for such fundamental reforms.

3. The reception of *Capital*

I believe that the reception of *Capital* tells us as much, or more, about the current state of our society as does the book itself. A convenient place to study this reception is on Amazon.com. On the page for *Capital* excerpts are given from around 100 editorial reviews of the book. They read like a competition of who can think up the most extravagant superlatives. Following are some examples taken from the beginning of the list:

- "A seminal book on the economic and social evolution of the planet... A masterpiece. 'This book is not only the definitive account of the historical evolution of inequality in advanced economies, it is also a magisterial treatise on capitalism's inherent dynamics.'"
- "Anyone remotely interested in economics needs to read Thomas Piketty's *Capital in the 21st Century*."
- "Defies left and right orthodoxy by arguing that worsening inequality is an inevitable outcome of free market capitalism."
- "Rarely does a book come along... that completely alters the paradigm through which we frame our worldview. Thomas Piketty's magisterial study of the structure of capitalism since the 18th century, *Capital in the 21st Century*, is such a book..."

Of course, this is a biased list. Amazon apparently felt that they could maximize sales by selecting only positive reviews. However, when a list of some 100 reviews can be assembled, many in prominent publications, that praise the appearance of a masterpiece; then there is a collective message, though not necessarily the one the reviewers intended.

Amazon also provides customer reviews, of which at this writing there are 968. These reviews rate the book on a scale of 5 stars (maximum positive), to 1 star (maximum negative). Here is how the book was rated:

5-stars 566, 4-stars 124, 3-stars 51, 2-stars 39, 1-star 188

The overall tendency is clearly very positive. Interestingly, the first two 1 star reviews are warnings that most 1-star reviews are part of a right wing propaganda campaign and written by people who did not buy the book and probably did not read it. My own sampling of 1-star reviews confirmed these warnings.

That Piketty is loved by the Left and detested by the Right is not surprising. However, the exaltation on the Left, which in my view is not even remotely justified by the content of the book, requires an explanation. The Piketty phenomenon reminds me of another one, the euphoria that exploded internationally when Barak Obama campaigned for the presidency against McCain in 2008. Obama had no executive experience whatever and no record of any political achievements. Millions wanted to believe his promises of reforms and bought into his repetitive slogans of "Change", "Hope" and "Yes we can!" Via an innovative internet campaign Obama collected about 100 million dollars for his election. Hopes were high that he would initiate the fundamental economic and financial reforms that, following the financial crisis of 2007-8 were obviously needed.

In a paper that I wrote on the needed financial and economic reforms (Hillinger, 2010) I argued that Obama was unlikely to make any basic reforms. I pointed out that he had received more campaign contributions from industry than McCain. Particularly the finance and health industries, where major regulation was needed, supported him heavily. Surely, the lobbyists for these industries were better informed about his plans than the millions of small donors.

How can the Obama, Piketty phenomena be explained? I believe it is the yearning on the part of the Left, as well as of a wider public tending in that direction, for a Messiah to lead them out of their valley of tears. The Left has not had a dominant intellectual figure since Marx; that dominance vanished along with communism in Russia and China. In the post WWII era intellectual dominance passed first to the conservative philosophers Friedrich Hayek and Karl Popper, augmented later by the neoliberalism of Milton Friedman and the Second Chicago School. There followed the politicians who implemented the neoliberal policies: Ronald Reagan in the United States, Margaret Thatcher in the United Kingdom. A bit later they were followed by converts from the Left: Tony Blair in the UK and Gerhard Schröder in Germany.

Mainstream economics evolved into the neoclassical mold. With its demonstration of the efficiency of (mathematical) competitive markets it provided and additional support for neoliberal politics. Economics went through a number of research paradigms in the post WWII period that shone brightly for a while, produced their Nobel laureates, and then faded. More and more economists are turning to very specific problems, without any new and seemingly important research program in sight. Piketty now offers a vast new research paradigm, and for the first time, at least since Keynes, it is a research program that resonates with the concerns of the Left. No wonder, those prominent economists who sympathize with the Left, like Paul Krugman lauded *Capital* in the highest terms.

4. Conclusions

Piketty is a respected economic historian. The research project on the distribution of income and wealth which he organized has gained him wide recognition even beyond the confines of academia. With *Capital* he is clearly inviting a comparison of himself with Marx. This comparison he fails. Marx Invented concepts such as "class", "ideology", "alienation" that have remained central to sociology. I have found no novel concepts or ideas in *Capital* that can be imagined to play such a role.

By treating inequality as an economic problem, Piketty diverts attention away from what it really is – a political problem. His own discussions illustrate the following: Of the three sub-periods of his data set, the two with high or increasing returns to capital and rising inequality were periods with governments friendly to capital. The period with a rising income share going to labor and declining inequality had governments friendly to labor.

My own view is that the trend towards rule by wealthy elites is probably irreversible. Since the rise of the first empires about five thousand years ago rule by narrow elites has been the rule. Wars and revolts changed the elites, but these struggles were between different elites, or factions. Any revolts by the lower classes were brutally put down. Today, most of the world's populations feel that they have no influence on how their societies evolve and that feeling reflect reality.

The movement to empower the individual began with Greek philosophy, continued with the Enlightenment and led to political and social reforms that empowered ever wider segments of the population. That movement has ground to a halt and is reversing. Largely unnoticed, the elites have done away with the idea of a liberal education that would empower the population by giving them an understanding of social and political realities. Instead, we have what is essentially vocational training.

The Twentieth Century witnessed a unique window of opportunity for the establishment of genuine and lasting democracy. It came about when a large and homogeneous work force, produced by the industrial revolution, was organized into powerful unions. They supplied parties of the Left with money and manpower, equal in power to the money and institutions such as army and police at the command of parties of the Right. As the labor force fragmented and unions declined, the parties of the Left turned to the corporate sector for financial support and became indistinguishable from the parties of the right. The fruitless ideological debates between Left and Right and the failed policies that they are pursuing when in power are destroying democracy itself. I agree with (Wolin, 2008) who predicted that the United States would develop similarly to the late Roman Empire – the symbols of democracy would be maintained, but they would become empty of content. On this path, the United States are only taking the lead. As the elites consolidate their power, the distributions of income and wealth are naturally skewed in their favor; why else would they seek power?

References

Galbraith, James K. 2014. “Kapital for the Twenty-First Century?” *Dissent*. http://www.dissentmagazine.org/article/kapital-for-the-twenty-first-century.

Hillinger, Claude. 2010. “The Crisis and Beyond: Thinking Outside the Box”. *Economics: The Open-Access, Open-Assessment E-Journal* 4: 1–61. doi: http://dx.doi.org/10.5018/economicsejournal.ja.2010-23

Milanovic, Branco. 2014. "The Return of 'Patrimonial Capitalism': A Review of Thomas Piketty's Capital in the Twenty-First Century". *Journal of Economic Literature* 52 (2): 519–34. doi:10.1257/jel.52.2.519.

Piketty, Thomas (2014) *Capital in the Twenty-First Century*. Cambridge: Harvard University Press.

Summers, Lawrence H. 2014. "The Inequality Puzzle". *Democracy Journal*. http://www.democracyjournal.org/33/the-inequality-puzzle.php?

Wilkinson, Richard G., und Kate E. Pickett. 2009. "Income Inequality and Social Dysfunction". *Annual Review of Socioloy* 35 (1): 493–511.

Wolin, Sheldon S. 2008. *Democracy incorporated: managed democracy and the threat of inverted totalitarianism*. Princeton University Press.

Piketty and the resurgence of patrimonial capitalism

Jayati Ghosh [Jawaharlal Nehru University, New Delhi, India]

The wave of media enthusiasm and academic interest that has surrounded the publication of Thomas Piketty's massive tome reflects a wider resurgence of public interest in and concern with inequality. Over the last few years in particular, a significant and growing number of reports of international organizations[1], academic treatises[2] and more popularly oriented books[3] have dealt with this subject, at global, regional and national levels. The greater attention that Piketty's work has received may have come as a surprise to some, but it is certainly nonetheless greatly to be welcomed, as everything that draws highlights and gives prominence to this critical recent trend of growing inequality across most economies is important.

The empirical work of Piketty (together with others such as Emmanuel Saez and others using the Global Top Income Database that they have developed) has already been a resource of much value for both academics and policy makers for some time now. The book brings together much of this work, but also adds to it by seeking to provide an explanation of the broad trends uncovered by the empirical study.

The recognition that broad measures of inequality such as the Gini coefficient relying on periodic surveys of income or consumption provide at best a limited and sometimes even misleading idea of true inequality is an important insight. The creative use of tax returns to derive income shares of total national income across the population, particularly at the top, is another major contribution of this work. The focus on the shares received by top incomes – of the top percentile and on occasion the top 0.1 per cent –

---

[1] For example, UN (2013); UNCTAD (2011); UNICEF and UN Women (2013); OECD (2008); World Bank (2006); ILO (2008); even IMF (2007).
[2] To name just a few, Milanovic (2005, 2011); Cornia (2011, 2013); Galbraith (2012); Khan (2012); Lim (2013).
[3] Such as Wilkinson and Pickett (2010), Cohen (2008).

generates significant and even startling conclusions that support in often dramatic fashion the popular perceptions of the "Occupy" and similar movements. The spotlight on asset inequality, and particularly on the role of inheritance, is revealing. The insights on the competing claims of "patrimonial" versus "meritocratic" sources of inequality are rewarding.

The ambition and effort required to unearth such data over a longer historical sweep, in some cases several centuries using whatever different sources can be put together, is also of major interest and provides a longer term perspective on these issues that is often lost in an examination of just the past few decades, even if in some cases the consequent generalizations are somewhat too sweeping and therefore problematic. And of course the book (even in English translation) is very well-written and absorbing, with many literary references (dominantly Jane Austen and Balzac, but also bits of popular culture like the television series "Mad Men") thrown in for added interest and to drive certain points home in a telling way.

The historical/empirical points made by Piketty are both striking and persuasively presented. They are most conveniently summarized in the now-famous U-shaped curves that he describes for the income and asset shares of the top decile and the top percentile of the population (and even the top 0.1 per cent in some instances) in developed capitalist economies. These indicate relatively high inequality (expressed as high shares of these top income groups in total national income) in the early part of the 20th century, followed by a period of decline particularly during and after the second World War, and then a surge in inequality from around 1980 to the present, in some instances far surpassing even the high inequality observed in the late 19th/early 20th centuries.

The main contribution of the book – beyond the body of impressive historical and empirical research that has been published by Piketty and his colleagues in several articles – is the attempt to explain these observed patterns through a broad theory of long run capitalist development that is then also used to explain tendencies in contemporary capitalism. This is an ambitious task indeed, especially when it is evident that Piketty's conceptual framework is implicitly confined by a limited and ultimately ahistorical neoclassical approach towards the distribution of income shares.

Piketty is clearly conscious of the complexity of the various forces that determine economic inequality. He notes (p. 20)[4] that "one should be wary of any economic determinism in regard to inequalities of wealth and income" since this has always been deeply political. He also notes that "the dynamics of wealth distribution reveal powerful mechanisms pushing alternately toward convergence and divergence", and "there is no natural, spontaneous process to prevent destabilizing, inegalitarian forces from prevailing permanently". Notwithstanding these warnings, he then proceeds to make a very economically deterministic generalization about a basic tendency of capitalism, which he posits as "the fundamental force for divergence".

This is the argument that $\boldsymbol{r > g}$, where r is the annual rate of return on capital expressed as a percentage of its total value, and g is the (presumably real) rate of growth of national income. He notes (much in the spirit of Evsey Domar) that "when the rate of return on capital significantly exceeds the growth rate of the economy... then it logically follows that inherited wealth grows faster than output and income" (p. 26). Furthermore, this tendency is then reinforced by other mechanisms, such as the savings ratio of the economy increasing as wealth increases. Since "the share of capital in national income is equal to the product of the return on capital and the capital/income ratio" and "the capital/income ratio is equal in the long run to the savings rate divided by the growth rate" (p. 33), we effectively get a steady growth path in which both the capital/income ratio and the income share of those who own capital and receive a return from it keep increasing. Implicit in this argument is a theoretical model in which capital and labour are factors of production that are paid their marginal products.

The question obviously arises: what explains this supposed "law" of capitalist development? Piketty argues that growth rates of the economy tend to decrease particularly as population growth slows (thereby implicitly assuming some sort of full employment growth path in which exogenously determined population growth forms the "natural" rate of growth) but there is no equivalent decline in the rate of return on capital. This is a problematic argument for many reasons. For example it assumes that full employment prevails on this growth path (at least in a long run sense) and that labour

[4] All page numbers for Piketty relate to the Kindle edition of the book.

supply is exogenous, unlike the historical experience that has shown us that capitalism has always generated a supply of labour to adjust to demand, whether through migration or the changing work participation of women and children, or other means. Indeed, this formulation, relying on the ultimate determination of growth through exogenously given population growth and exogenous technological progress, is rejected by almost all modern growth theory, as Patnaik (2014) has pointed out in a very insightful critique.

This treatment of capital also ignores all the problems associated with the measurement of capital, which were highlighted by Piero Sraffa (1966) and others. Piketty himself seems blissfully unaware of the fundamental analytical challenge posed by this position, which pointed out that when capital is seen as a sum of values, the determination of these values or prices requires that distribution (including the profit rate) is already known. Therefore any attempt to determine profit as a marginal product of capital is circular and invalid (Bharadwaj, 1968). Simply put, you cannot explain something in terms of itself. Instead of recognising this basic critique, Piketty blithely describes the Cambridge controversies on capital as the result of the mistaken belief of economists in Cambridge England (such as Joan Robinson, Nicholas Kaldor and Luigi Pasinetti) that the Solow model argued that growth is always perfectly balanced. This is a completely wrong interpretation of their position that leaves out their basic argument. Piketty further states that by the 1970s, "Solow's so-called neoclassical growth model definitively carried the day" (p. 231). But indeed, Solow himself conceded the theoretical battle in the late 1960s, and most serious growth theorists today, especially those using endogenous growth theories, do not use the Solow model. And in any case, just because the mainstream profession has chosen to ignore this logical problem does not mean that it no longer exists.

On a steady growth path, Piketty's claim for the continuous increase in the capital/income ratio requires that the income elasticity of substitution of capital for labour is greater than unity – and indeed Piketty argues that it has historically been between 1.3 and 1.6. However, it has been pointed out that this assumption is questionable and furthermore is not actually supported empirically (Rowthorn, 2014; Semeniuk, 2014). Even more crucially, Patnaik (2014) has shown that a stable steady state trajectory, where the growth rate equals the sum of the exogenous rate of growth of the workforce and the exogenous rate of growth of labour productivity *does not exist* when the elasticity of substitution between capital and labour exceeds unity.

Neither is there strong evidence for the statement that the capital/income ratio continuously rises, since this also depends crucially on how capital is valued. Rowthorn (2014) has correctly argued that this is probably the result of a valuation effect reflecting a disproportionate increase in the market value of certain real assets, especially housing and real estate. Indeed it could be noted that the very fact that Piketty provides a U-shaped curve also for the capital/income ratio undermines his own argument, for at least on the downward slope of the U curve there was clearly a period (a fairly prolonged period of more than half a century, as it happens) when the capital/income ratio declined!

Piketty's own explanation for the downward-sloping portion of the curves (the period when the incomes shares of the top decile or percentile came down, or when the estimated ration of capital to income declined) is less than satisfactory. He sees the downward movement as something of a historical aberration from the opposite long-term trend, the result of the collapse of capital values (related to both the destruction of physical equipment and the decline in prices of financial assets) because of wars, depression and socio-political changes after the Second World War. But this explanation is both partial and unconvincing: as Galbraith (2014) has pointed out, physical and price changes are indeed very different and cannot be treated as aspects of the same thing. Further, the post-war improvements in labour shares of income in many developed capitalist economies were due to significant social and political changes, reflecting Piketty's own more nuanced formulation in an earlier chapter, that income and asset distributions reflect more than material forces but also political and cultural forces in society. And the prolonged period of the downward part of the curve does undermine the notion that – at least as expressed empirically in historically observed patterns – this is a necessary aspect of capitalist growth.

But what exactly is capital for Piketty, and what is the rate of return that he is talking about? Piketty uses the terms "capital" and "wealth" interchangeably, and defines them very broadly: "the sum total of nonhuman assets that can be owned and exchanged on some market. Capital includes all forms of real property (including residential real estate) as well as financial and professional capital (plants, infrastructure, machinery, patents and so on) used by firms and government agencies" (p. 45). So it includes "all forms of wealth that individuals (or groups of individuals) can own and that can be transferred or traded through the market on a permanent basis. ... Capital is not an immutable concept: it reflects the state of development and prevailing social relations of each society" (p. 46).

This brings to mind Marx's conception of capital as a social relation, though such a comparison would no doubt horrify the author. Capital here is also defined as including patents and other forms of intellectual property and similar "immaterial" forms such as stock market valuation, which therefore incorporates the changing valuations of both physical and financial assets by markets. But treating capital in this manner as a sum of prevailing values that reflect prevailing social relations sits very uneasily with the idea of the return on capital being in some sense its "marginal product", which is the underlying conceptual basis for his theoretical formulation. In particular, the very notion of the marginal product of changes in, say, stock market valuation or housing prices, is analytically absurd.

And there is a further twist, when Piketty clarifies that the returns are simply the rents on capital, defined as "the income on capital, whether in the form of rent, interest, dividends, profits, royalties or any other legal category of revenue, provided that such income is simply remuneration for ownership of the asset, independent of any labour" (p. 422). How can this motley combination reflect a marginal product of an equally motley combination of tangible and intangible "assets", especially when problems of valuation are so extreme?

It takes a while for the reader to figure out that, despite the implicit requirement for a marginal productivity theory of distribution to provide some logical consistency to this supposed "law" of capitalist development, Piketty himself does not rely on this. It is not until page 361 that we finally get a clear statement of his admittedly slippery position on this most fundamental issue: "The inequality r > g should be analysed as a historical reality dependent on a variety of mechanisms and *not as an absolute logical necessity*. It is the result of a confluence of forces, each largely independent of the others … g tends to be structurally low (generally not more than 1 per cent a year once the demographic transition is complete and the country reaches the world technological frontier, where the pace of innovation is fairly slow). … *r depends on many technological, psychological, social and cultural factors*, which together seem to result in a return of roughly 4-5 per cent (at any rate distinctly greater than 1 per cent)" (p. 361, emphases added).

At this point, the reader who has ploughed through the material in the vain hope of getting at a theoretical basis for this "law of capitalism" can be forgiven for thinking: WHAT???!!! All this fancy footwork, only to result in a vague and sweeping historical generalisation that makes no claims to logic, identifies no mechanisms of causation, but is only based on supposed "fact" – and is anyway disproved for prolonged periods not just by the disparate experience of some capitalist countries but by the author's own data for different countries? With this bizarre (and surprisingly delayed) admission, Piketty may have sidestepped some of the criticism of the logical fallacies exposed by Patnaik, Rowthorn and others, but he does so at the cost of accepting that there is in fact no logic to his argument!

Supposing then, we forget about Piketty's theoretical claims (which now indeed appear to be rather brazen) and focus instead on the empirical and historical insights that he does provide. Of course there is scope for some disagreement about long run historical trends, especially when data on such issues for the very long run exist only for a handful of countries. But the aspect relating to the latter part of the past century up to the present is of particular interest: the rapid rise of the top income shares across several developed economies, albeit to different degrees (with the US and the UK providing the most extreme examples). This is corroborated by other careful empirical work (e.g. Stockhammer 2012, 2013) on the declining shares of wages in national income, as well as work (Cornia 2012, 2013) pointing to increases in wage inequality driven by incomes at the top of the spectrum that are really managerial in nature.

The decline in wage shares of national income, and the associated rise of "surplus" in various forms (which Piketty broadly refers to as returns to capital) has been explained along a variety of lines: the expansion of the "global" labour supply through greater trade integration and cross-border mobility of capital that have together dramatically reduced the bargaining power of labour; the labour-saving technological shifts that have had a similar effect; the dominance of finance or "financialisation" that have put inordinate power in the hands of financial players and influenced their ability to affect economic policies in their own favour. As Taylor (2014) notes, "the recent rise of the rentier has been supported by politics and policy marshalled to drive up the share of income going to profits."

In this context, Piketty's discussion of the significance of inheritance in driving the resurgence of "patrimonial capitalism" is indeed interesting and makes some insightful points. He points out that two competing determinants of inequality drive society's attitude towards it: the "meritocratic" notion that creates a society with superstar achievers or managers; and the "patrimonial" notion that is essentially based on inheritance. The two can coexist, and indeed there is a large grey area in between, even to the point that entrepreneurs (say Bill Gates) can turn into rentiers within a generation. But this also creates a basis for greater social acceptance of inequality. "If inequalities are seen as justified, say because they seem a consequence of choice by the rich to work harder or more efficiently than the poor, or because preventing the rich from earning more would inevitably harm the worst-off members of society, then it is perfectly possible for the concentration of income to set new historical records" (p. 263).

The much greater social acceptability of inequality in the US, for example, is probably based on this and results in extraordinarily high shares of the top 1 per cent, even when compared to otherwise similar economies in Western Europe. Yet despite this supposed justification, the US and other western economies are in reality all turning into more patrimonial societies, in which inherited wealth plays an ever growing role in determining the opportunities and future incomes of individuals, and concentration is aided not only by easier tax regimes but by exploitation by the rich of tax havens and similar loopholes.

To prevent or reduce this resurgence of patrimonial capitalism, Piketty calls for global and national taxes of wealth (earned but especially inherited) and on income from wealth. This is clearly a welcome call. It is true that the political conditions for such a goal to be realised are currently far from fertile. However, it is also the case that a number of developing countries (that are only cursorily dealt with in Piketty's enormous book) in Latin America and a handful in Asia and Africa have in recent years been able to reduce top income shares and increase wage shares of national income, for example through land redistribution, raising and enforcing minimum wages and improving the conditions for workers' associations that improve their bargaining power. The secondary distribution of income in several of these countries has improved even more, through a combination of fiscal strategies and policies towards control over natural resources that increase public revenues that can then be spent on social infrastructure and services as well as social protection. All this points to the possibility of several other strategies, including macroeconomic and industrial policies as well as other more structural policies.

So it is not impossible for country strategies to change, if the social consensus shifts decisively in favour of policies to reduce inequalities. But such political conditions will never be in place without wider support for such demands from not just academics but the wider public. It is essentially for that reason that the discussions around Piketty's book and other work that highlights the different dimensions of growing inequality are timely, important and even absolutely necessary.

References

Bharadwaj, Krishna (1968) "Value through exogenous distribution", *Economic and Political Weekly*

Cohen, G.A. (2008) *Rescuing Justice and Equality*. Cambridge, Mass.: Harvard University Press.

Cornia, G. A. (2011) "Economic integration, inequality and growth: Latin America vs the European economies in transition", *UN-DESA Working Paper* 101.

Cornia, G. A. (2013) "Redistributive changes in Latin America: An overview", in Cornia, ed., *Falling Inequality in Latin America: Policy Changes and Lessons*, UNU-WIDER

Galbraith, James K. (2012). I*nequality and Instability. A Study of the World Economy just before the Great Crisis*. New York: Oxford University Press

Galbraith, James K. (2014) "Das Kapital for the 21st century? A review of Thomas Piketty's book", in *Dissent: Quarterly of Politics and Culture*.

International Labour Organization (2008) *Income Inequalities in the Age of Financial Globalization: World of Work Report 2008*. Geneva: International Labour Office

IMF (2007) *Globalization and inequality: World Economic Outlook 2007,* Washington, D.C.

Khan, Azizur Rahman (2012) "Inequality in our age", *Working Paper* No 277, Political Economy Research Institute, University of Massachusetts at Amherst.

Lim, Mah Hui (2013) *Inequality and Growth Models: The East Asian Story*, South Centre, Geneva

Milanovic, Branko (2005) *Worlds Apart: Measuring International and Global Inequality*. Princeton: Princeton University Press

Milanovic, Branko (2011)*The Haves and the Have-Nots: A Brief and Idiosyncratic History of Global Inequality.* Basic Books

OECD (2008) *Growing unequal? Poverty and income distribution in OECD countries,* Paris.

Patnaik, Prabhat (2014) "Capitalism, inequality and globalisation: A review of Thomas Piketty's Capital in the 21st Century".

Piketty, Thomas (2014) *Capital in the Twenty-First Century*. Cambridge: Harvard University Press.

Rowthorn, Robert E (2014) "A note on Piketty's Capital".

Semieniuk, Gregor (2014) "Piketty's elasticity of substitution: A critique", *Working Paper 2014-8,* Schwarz Centre for Economic Policy Analysis, New School University, New York.

Sraffa, Piero (1966) *Production of Commodities by Means of Commodities*, Cambridge University Press.

Stockhammer, Engelbert (2012) "Rising inequality as a root cause of the present crisis", *Political Economy Research Institute Working Paper No* 282, University of Amherst Massachusetts, USA.

Stockhammer, Engelbert (2013) "Why have wage shares fallen? A panel analysis of the determinants of functional income distribution", *Conditions of Work and Employment, Series* No 35, ILO, Geneva

Taylor, Lance (2014) "The triumph of the rentier? Thomas Piketty vs Luigi Pasinetti and John Maynard Keynes", *Working Paper 2014-8,* Schwarz Centre for Economic Policy Analysis, New School University, New York

Wilkinson, Richard and Kate Pickett (2009) *The Spirit Level: Why greater equality makes societies stronger*, Bloomsbury.

UN (2013) *Inequality Matters: Report on the World Social Situation*, New York.

UNCTAD (2011) *Policies for Inclusive and Balanced Growth: Trade and Development Report*, Geneva.

UNICEF and UN Women (2013) *Addressing Inequalities: Synthesis Report on Global Thematic Consultation on Post-2015 Agenda,* New York.

World Bank (2006) *Equity and Development" World Development Report 2006,* Washington, D.C.

Unpacking the first fundamental law

James K. Galbraith [LBJ School of Public Affairs, University of Texas, USA]

In the early pages of *Capital in the Twenty-First Century,* Thomas Piketty states a "fundamental law of capitalism" that $\alpha = r \times \beta$, where α is the share of profit in income, β is the capital/output ratio, and r is the rate of return on capital, or the rate of profit. Thus:

$$r = \alpha/\beta$$

Using K for capital, P for profit and Y for both total income and output (which are equal in equilibrium), we have:

$$\alpha = P/Y \quad \text{and} \quad \beta = K/Y$$

so that:

$$r = (P/Y)/(K/Y)$$

The point of this expression is that r cannot be observed directly, whereas the two ratios on the other side of the equation can be. Yet (clearly) Y is unnecessary, since this expression reduces to:

$$r = P/K$$

with no loss of generality. So the measure of r requires just two things: a flow of money profits from the national income accounts, and a measure of the stock of capital.

What is K? For Piketty, K is the *financial valuation* of privately-held capital assets, including land, bonds, stocks and other forms of private wealth, such as housing. One may quarrel (as I have) with the connection of this value to prior definitions of capital, but that is not the issue here.

Financial valuation (FV) can be rendered as the *present value of the expected future returns from the ownership of capital assets;* for this a discount rate is required. Is the discount rate the same as r? Not necessarily. Keeping them distinct, we have:

$$K = FV = \Sigma_i [\, E(P_i) / (1+d)^i \,]$$

where E indicates an expected value, d is the discount rate and (i) is a time subscript.

Note that FV *depends* on d. If the discount rate falls, then the financial value of the capital stock will rise. Since the discount rate bears some relationship to the interest rate, at least in equilibrium, FV and therefore r can be pushed around by monetary policy, so long as monetary policy can influence financial valuations without also affecting current money profits. FV also depends on the current expectation of future flows of profit income, which are, in part, a psychological matter.

Clearly, this concept of capital bears no relationship to the physical construct that normally enters a neoclassical production function or the technological view of the capital/output ratio. Piketty's use of "K/Y" as notation is, in this respect, non-standard. Still, nothing prevents us from measuring r – as Piketty defines it – from the observed profit flow and the financial valuation of the capital stock.

Why, as an historical matter, would r as measured tend to be constant over long periods of time? One answer is now obvious: *the expected stream of future profits at any given time depends on current profits.* In a boom, things are good and are expected to remain so. In a slump, the reverse.

P and FV do not always move together. But they will more often than not. And so the ratio between the two observed variables – r – will normally not change very much. One can surely find exceptions – in the turning points of the business cycle, or when monetary policy drives capital valuations out of synch with current profits. But Piketty's approach of calculating decade-by-decade averages may wash those out, to some degree.

What does the long-run constancy of r have to do with physical capital, savings or marginal productivity? Nothing at all. Piketty's r is basically a weighted average of financial rates of return across the yield curve and the risk profile of privately-held capital assets. It is the artifact of current profits and of discounted profit expectations on market values. If the discount rate rises (falls), other things equal, the ratio of current profits to financial values also rises (falls). But if the discount rate is stable, thanks to long-term stability of monetary policy and of social attitudes – or even thanks only to averaging over time – then that r should also be reasonably stable over time is no surprise.

Piketty's next big assertion is that $r > g$, or that the return on financial valuation is normally higher than the rate of growth of income. And so, he argues, so long as the ownership of financial assets is concentrated, as it always is, this leads to an increasing concentration of income (and therefore wealth) as the normal condition of capitalism.

For the truth of the first sentence, we can (for the moment) accept Piketty's evidence – noting that the entire 20th century is an exception. But the first sentence does not lead necessarily to the second.

First, profits are taxed. If t is the tax rate and if r is measured before tax, then the correct measure to compare with g is not r but r(1-t). Second, part of post-tax profits are spent on consumption rather than reinvested in new capital. Then, if cc is the rate of capitalists' consumption, including charitable gifts, we could have:

$$r > g \text{ but } [r(1-t)-cc] <= g$$

Putting r at 5 percent, the tax rate at 0.3, and capitalists' consumption including gifts at a modest one-fifth of their pre-tax gain, then the left-hand-side expression falls by half, or roughly to the historic value of g. It's hard to see how this could lead to a rise in K/Y or in the share of profit in income. And in a simple model, it would not; P/Y falls if $[r(1-t)-cc] < g$.

On the other hand, even if $[r(1-t)-cc] < g$, it is still possible for changing financial valuations to generate increasing concentration of wealth at least for some time. So long as capital is unevenly held, as it always is, bubbles *in selected sectors* (technology, energy, finance) will make some people rich. True, bubbles are transient; eventually they burst. But they could be the main thing that we have been dealing with, in short cycles, in most of the wealthy world, for the past 30 years (Galbraith and Hale, 2014).

Finally, Piketty argues that a slowdown of economic growth, due to slower population growth, must inevitably lead to an increase in the capital-output ratio. This is a simple artifact of the constancy of r, alongside a drop in g. But, as Jason Furman (2014) has asked, would r necessarily stay steady if g declines? Looking back at the formula, it all depends on current profits, future expected profits, and the discount rate. If slow growth reduces either current profits or the discount rate, or both, while expectations remain stubbornly high, it's possible that r might decline even more than g.

In short, five conclusions may be drawn:

1) The alleged long-run constancy of r is an artifact of no great economic interest.
2) Even it is generally true that r > g, it does not follow that capitalist economies have a necessary tendency toward an increasing share of profit in income.
3) If the share of profit in income is not rising, there is no obvious reason for wealth to become more concentrated.
4) Yet, wealth inequality can rise in a capitalist economy even if [r(1-t)-cc] < g, due to bubbles in financial markets and capital gains that do not count as current income.
5) The effects of a demographic and growth slowdown on the relation between r and g is indefinite. It is not inexorable that slower growth increases the capital-output ratio.

None of this is to deny that rising inequality has occurred. Nor to claim that it doesn't matter. And by yanking mainstream discussion of inequality from the micro to the macro sphere – where it belongs as I have been arguing since the mid-1990s! – Thomas Piketty has done a service to economics.

But his goal was to turn the historical record into fundamental laws and long-range tendencies. Despite strong claims – accepted by many reviewers – it is now clear that this project fell short.

As a matter of the empirical record, the modern inequality data do not show any inexorable tendencies. Inequality fell sharply in the two World Wars.[1] It

[1] As for *why* inequality declined during the two World Wars, Piketty lays heavy stress on a decline in K/Y, the capital-output ratio. Numerous graphs (with odd and uneven date-spacing) illustrate this decline for major countries engaged in the wars. But the implicit case that a fall in K/Y had to do (in part) with physical destruction of productive capital makes no sense for any major country in World War I, and only for Germany and Japan in World War II. Moreover, *a pure decline in K*, whether physical or financial, *would have increased, not reduced, r,* by Piketty's own definition, and therefore it would have increased, not reduced inequality. [How could Piketty not

rose very sharply in many places beginning around 1980 or in some cases a few years before. And that increase largely peaked in 2000, worldwide. The great rise of inequality in recent years was a consequence of the debt crisis, the collapse of communism, of neoliberal globalization. It was not a long-run phenomenon. Piketty projects that it will resume and continue, but it may or may not.

Since 2000, *declining inequality* has been observed in post-neoliberal (but still capitalist) Latin America. There is new evidence of declining inequality in China, and also in Europe after 2008, at least if one takes the continent as a whole (Galbraith *et al.*, 2014). In the US, there has been a sawtooth pattern, closely related to the stock market, with inequality peaks in 2000, 2007 and 2013, but little trend since 2000 (Galbraith and Hale, 2014). In some cases, income inequality may fall thanks to an old-fashioned Kuznets transition, most recently in China (Zhang, 2014).

Finally, there seems no warrant for the view that annual global capital wealth taxation is required to reduce the rise or the level of inequality. Many other measures, including higher wages, expanding social insurance, health care and housing, debt restructuring, effective estate and gift taxes to spur *in vivo* gifts, and the control of predatory finance *have worked and do work* to achieve this goal.

Perhaps Piketty's Law will vanish – as quickly as it has appeared?

---

have seen this?] Further, the fact that all belligerents saw large increases in money incomes, relative to capital valuations, also cannot explain the drop in r relative to g, since Y actually plays no role in the determination of r. (This is a point I did not quite grasp, in preparing my review for *Dissent.*) So what *did* cause the fall in inequality? The obvious answer is that money profits P (and also capitalists' consumption) were constrained in the major countries by war-time controls, as a matter of strict policy, while a rapid growth of labor incomes was allowed to proceed. This drove r far below g and so increased the labor share and equalized incomes. Contrary to Piketty's statements in several places, this was no accident. In the United States during World War II, the policy to achieve it was directed by the Office of Price Administration under the direction, in 1942-3, of an economist whose name I do not recall seeing in Piketty's text: John Kenneth Galbraith.

References

Furman, Jason, Global Lessons for Inclusive Growth, The Institute of International and European Affairs, Dublin, May 7, 2014.

Galbraith, James K., Béatrice Halbach, Aleksandra Malinowska, Amin Shams and Wenjie Zhang, UTIP Global Inequality Data Sets 1963-2008:Updates, Revisions and Quality Checks, UTIP Working Paper No. 68, May 6, 2014.

Galbraith, James K. and J. Travis Hale, The Evolution of Economic Inequality in the United States, 1969-2012: Evidence from Data on Inter-industrial Earnings and Inter-regional Incomes, *World Economic Review*, No. 3, 2014.

Piketty, Thomas, *Capital in the Twenty-First Century. Cambridge*: Harvard University Press, 2014.

Zhang, Wenjie, Has China crossed the threshold of the Kuznets curve? New measures from 1987 to 2012 show declining pay inequality in China after 2008, UTIP Working Paper No. 67, April 21, 2014.

Capital and capital: the second most fundamental confusion

Edward Fullbrook [University of the West of England, UK]

The meaning of "capital"

There is a centuries-old tradition in economics of using in the same work, often in the same paragraph and sometimes even in the same sentence, the symbol "capital" to signify two (and sometimes three) fundamentally different things. Inevitably, given the centrality of these things to the domain of inquiry, it has been and continues to be a source of elementary confusion. Piketty's great book would be even greater if it had not been conceived, at least in part, within this tradition.

Given the historical persistence of this confusion, it is worth spelling out the general principle at stake. It is the elementary one of the distinction between *an object or family of objects* (material or not) and some *property* (quantifiable or not) of those objects, such as their sweetness, temperature, weight, linear dimensions, age, density, beauty or market-value. For example, to define "pear" as the fruit from a tree belonging to the genus *Pyrus*, and to define "pear" as the weight of fruits from trees belonging to *Pyrus*, and to define "pear" as the market value of fruits from trees belonging to *Pyrus* are three fundamentally different definitions.

Economics traditionally uses "capital" to signify both a set of objects (material and immaterial) and quantities of a *property* of those objects, market-value. Such double-loading of a symbol does not necessarily lead to confusion, but it certainly invites it, and in economics very often realizes it. Piketty's book is a case in point.

Its first chapter includes a short section titled "What is Capital?". It begins promisingly.

> To simplify the text, I use the words "capital" and "wealth" interchangeably, as if they were perfectly synonymous. By

> some definitions, it would be better to reserve the word "capital" to describe forms of wealth accumulated by human beings (buildings, machinery, infrastructure, etc.) and therefore to exclude land and natural resources, with which humans have been endowed without having to accumulate them [p. 47].

In other words, Piketty is saying that in his book "capital" will signify a set of objects which he then goes on to specify more exactly. But before he has finished the paragraph "value" slips in, and on the following page after he has confirmed the meaning of "capital" as "both a store of value and a factor of production" he writes:

> To summarize, I define "national wealth" or "national capital" as the total *market value* of everything owned by the residents and government of a given country at a given point in time, provided that it can be traded on some market [emphasis added, p. 48].

The meaning of "capital" is absolutely central to Piketty's or anyone's attempts to theorize about the meaning of the amazing body of empirical data that he and his associates have accumulated. So confusions between the two fundamentally different meanings (which one are we thinking about now?) that Piketty introduces at his book's beginning doom the theoretical side of his project. Piketty leads us into a similar confusion with his use of the symbol "income". Sometimes he uses "income" to signify a set of objects as when he writes "Income is ... the quantity of goods produced and distributed in a given period" (p. 50), but most times it signifies the market-value of those goods

Henceforth the paper you are reading will signify "capital" and "income" in the sense of a set of objects with "capital-1" and "income-1" and signify "capital" and "income" in the sense of the market value of those sets with "capital-2" and "income-2". (Similarly with "wealth" which as we have seen Piketty defines as meaning for him exactly what capital means.) As in Piketty's book, capital-2 and income-2, rather than capital-1 and income-1, are this paper's primary interest. When we eliminate the double-loading of "capital" and "income", the focal point of both Piketty's book and this paper is the capital-2 / income-2 ratio which he labels β.

A ridiculous question?

Capital's chapter five, "The Capital/Income Raito over the Long Run", which is attracting the most theoretical attention, features what Piketty pretentiously dubs "the second fundamental law of capitalism"[1], β = s/g, where s = the saving rate and g = the growth rate. But despite the fact that his "law" is about capital-2 and income-2, the argumentation that he offers on its behalf (pp. 166-170) vacillates between using "capital" to signify capital-1 and using it to signify capital-2, and in some cases leaves this reader undecided as to which one, if either, Piketty thought he was referring. His key verb for explaining how the variables of his "law" change is "accumulate". In the space of four pages he uses "accumulate", "accumulated" and "accumulation" a total of eleven times, each with relation to "capital". Can "capital" be accumulated?

Obviously it can in the case of capital-1. It is also obvious that individuals and groups can accumulate capital-2, George Soros and the Citigroup being famous recent cases in point. But Piketty's argument depends on the possibility of closed economies or the global economy as wholes accumulating capital-2. *Is this kind of accumulation possible?* Is this a ridiculous question? Please read on.

Every quantitative order has a formal structure that can be described with abstract algebra. And not every quantitative order has the same structure. What is the formal or metrical structure of market-value?

To begin, how does the metrical structure of market-value (call it what you want: exchange-value, money-value, dollar-value, euro-value, etc.) compare with those of other quantitative orders? Consider some possibilities that we are all familiar with: length, weight, angle, temperature, probability. You will be immediately aware, whether you can describe them or not, that these

[1] Piketty's "first fundamental law of capitalism" α =r x β is purely definitional and thus not what in the context of science is called a "law".

quantitative orders have different formal properties. You will also be immediately aware that what one can legitimately do with their numbers differs radically between the orders. We can add and subtract weights and lengths but not temperatures. A joke credited to Diderot illustrates the point: "How many snowballs would be required to heat an oven?" [Duhem, 1905, p.112] We can also add and subtract probabilities and angles but only in limited contexts. Might it not be a good idea if we as economists became cognizant of the structure of the quantitative order with which our discipline, including Piketty's book, is foremostly concerned?

A thought experiment

Physics' concepts of length measurement numbers and mass measurement numbers emerge from comparative concepts, pairs of empirically defined relations, one equivalence, the other precedence, which have been shown to hold between pairs of physical objects.[2] Can market-values also be identified as originating with or shown to be reducible to a concept of comparative market-value in the sense of a set of relations between a pair of economic objects? We can conduct a thought experiment to find out.

Here is a simple formulation of the principle of comparative market-values.

> For pairs of commodities, there is the market-value of each commodity *relative to the other*, in the sense that quantities of the two commodities are said to be equal in market-value if they exchange for each other and to change in market-value if there is a change in the pair's market-clearing exchange ratio.

Although this statement appears to be logically coherent, the Twentieth Century taught us that the logical relations of statements are not always what they appear to be. So we are going to test the stated notion of comparative market-value against the general principle that, between any two magnitudes of the same empirical order, an equality relation either holds

[2] For a very accessible account of these fundamentals see Carnap, 1966, pp. 51-124.

or does not. Consider two commodities ***X*** and ***Y***, and whose units are ***x*** and ***y***. Let ***a***, ***b***, and ***σ*** be rational positive numbers.

Assume that the initial market-clearing ratio of ***ax:by*** changes to ***ax:σby***. Then, according to the concept of comparative market-value, the market-values of quantities of *X* relative to *Y* have changed. Any two quantities of the same order are either equal or not equal. Therefore, the market-value of ***σby*** relative to units of *X* at the new exchange ratio **is either equal or not equal** to the market-value of ***by*** at the old exchange ratio.

First assume that it is equal, i.e. ***σby = by***. Then, because at the old ratio the market-values of *ax* and ***b****y* were equal and at the new ratio the market-values of ***ax*** and ***σby*** are equal, it follows that the market-value of ***ax*** is unchanged. This contradicts the assumption that the market-values of quantities of *X* relative to *Y* have changed, and so one must conclude that this case cannot obtain.

Assume the other possibility: the market-value of ***σby*** at the new exchange ratio is not equal to the market-value of ***by*** at the old exchange ratio. If, relative to *X*, ***by*** and ***σby*** are not equal in market-value, then by the concept of comparative market-value they do not exchange for the same number of units of *X*. However, by assumption they do exchange for the same number of units of *X*. Therefore, this case also cannot hold. And this exhausts the logical possibilities.

The concept of comparative market-value generates paradoxes because it is circular. It defines a commodity's market-value in terms of the market-value of a second commodity whose market-value is defined in terms of the market-value of the first. In technical terms, this constitutes "vicious circularity" which renders the definition impredicative.

This simple but unexpected outcome of the test for logical coherence shows that, as a quantitative order, market-value has unexpected properties.

A false similarity

Confusions, like the one unearthed in the previous section, come easily when thinking about market-value because in two respects it bears a false similarity to familiar physical magnitudes.

First, the notion of market-value as a relation between two commodities exhibits a superficial resemblance to comparative concepts of mass and length. These physical concepts, however, are not predicated as relations between individual masses and lengths. *It is only their measurement numbers that are conceived in this way.* Instead, Newtonian physics predicates mass and extension as properties possessed by bodies independently of their relations to other bodies. This independence saves concepts of comparative length and mass from impredicativeness [Carnap, 1966, pp. 51-61].

Second, and related to the first, although market-value numbers are expressed on a ratio scale like mass and length numbers, they are generated in a profoundly different manner. Physical measurement numbers refer to physical phenomena, called concrete quantities, which have been found to have a structure isomorphic to the system of units and numbers (abstract quantities) by which they are represented. A cardinal point is that these concrete physical quantities do not come into being as the result of humankind's invention of processes of numerically representing them. If a means of numerically representing the weight of your body had never been invented, you would experience its weight all the same. The existence of the properties of extension and mass are independent of the processes by which they are measured or compared. In contrast, the quantitative order of market-value does not exist independently of the process which assigns market-value numbers. Without market exchange there is no exchange or market-value. *Market exchange, in other words, is the process by which the market-value order, not just the numbers which describe it, comes into being.*

The fact that the process that determines concrete market-values also assigns numbers to represent them invites conflation of concrete market-values and market-value numbers. The latter, stripped of their units, belong to *R*, the set of positive reals which defines a Euclidean space. Thus the conflation of concrete and abstract market-values leads smoothly to the unsupported conclusion that a "price space" is a Euclidean space [Debreu, 1986, p. 1261].

It is on the basis of this presumed "fit of the mathematical form to the economic content" [Debreu, 1986, p. 1259] that the whole neoclassical edifice, not just general equilibrium theory, has been constructed. At every point it presumes – through the convenience of its conflation – that a system of exchange- or market-values has the same structural properties, i.e. Euclidean, as do the numbers that represent them. But this subconscious presumption, the most fundamental *hypothesis* of neoclassicalism, is easily tested when the conflation between concrete and abstract quantities is avoided.

A purely empirical question

Diderot's jest quoted above, illustrates three verities of quantitative science:

1. profound structural differences exist between various quantitative orders;
2. their structures may diverge radically from that of everyday arithmetic; and, most important,
3. the structures of empirical quantitative orders are autonomous vis à vis human will and imagination.

In a more positive vein but to a similar purpose, Bertrand Russell identified the principle by which science applies mathematics to empirical phenomena.

> "Whenever two sets of terms have mutual relations of the same type, the same form of deduction will apply to both." [Russell, 1937, p. 7]

Application of arithmetical addition to mass, length and time are familiar examples. Yet, in such cases, where one set of terms is logical or mathematical and the other set is not, the existence of a homomorphism between the two sets is, as Diderot's jest illustrates, *a purely empirical matter*. It presumes the discovery of a set of extra-mathematical relations which repeated testing, not a set of axioms, shows to be structurally analogous to the arithmetical ones of =, <, > and +.

Elsewhere, using abstract algebra but offering a full verbal explication as well, the metrical structure of market-value has been investigated at length and found to be, as would you if you were to investigate it, Boolean rather than Euclidean. [Fullbrook, 2002. This paper can be downloaded for free from www.paecon.net/Fullbrook/IntersubjectiveTheoryofValue.pdf.]

Counter-intuitive

The Boolean conclusion is of course counter-intuitive, a way of thinking that we economists are even more adverse to than were physicists prior to the Twentieth Century. It is counter-intuitive because on the micro level of consumerism and business that we experience every day of our lives, market-values are Euclidean phenomena. But it is a characteristic of Boolean metrical structures that at a defined micro level, such as adding the probabilities of drawing individual cards from a given deck of cards, that they may include Euclidean characteristics.

To bring the metrical issues into focus it may help to very briefly compare two well-known quantitative orders, mass and probability. The property of mass is understood as a function of micromasses, whose existences are independent of the larger mass with which they are grouped. A body's mass is the totality of the masses of that body's parts, and its mass will increase if more parts are added to it. With quantitative properties of this type, each magnitude is *the aggregate of its parts*, the direction of determination running exclusively from the micro to the macro level.

But quantitative properties are not always of this type. Theoretical probability provides a relevant example. Certainty not only defines an upper bound for magnitudes of probability, but also serves as a *whole* in relation to which the probabilities of events in the probability space are conceived as *parts*. In other words, certainty, or the certain event, provides a *unique* standard of measurement for probability, with all other probabilities in the space being defined as *parts of that "whole" probability*. Furthermore, because of its Boolean structure, to increase in a given space the probability of one event decreases the probability of one or more others and vice versa. Likewise for market-value. Every market-value exists only as a part of an integral and interdependent system of market-values.

Although our everyday metrical perceptions of market-value are dominated by phenomena consistent with Euclidean structure, there is one Boolean market-value phenomenon with which we are all familiar both professionally and otherwise – inflation. Increasing the number of standard weights used in weighing operations does not decrease the mass of those weights. But increasing the quantity of money exchanged, that is, the number of standards of market-value used in measuring the market-value of the component sets of the aggregate endowment, not only decreases the market-value of existing money tokens, it also decreases each one's value by the same proportion. This alone shows that as a quantitative order market-value has a metrical structure radically different from mass, length and arithmetical addition.

Mesoeconomics

Our thought experiment has shown us that the concept of market-value is impredicative when defined as a relative concept *in the sense of a set of relations between a pair of objects.* But on the other hand we are aware that unlike mass and extension – quantitative properties possessed by objects independently of their relations to other objects – that the market-values of objects exist only relative to the market-values of other objects. So we are, despite the negative result of our thought experiment, still committed to the belief that market-value is a relative phenomenon. But if not pairs of objects, *what are the ultimate terms of the market-value relation?* It is, strangely, the relation upon which Piketty's great book turns.

Generally it is only when considering market-values at meso and marco levels, as with inflation, and as Piketty does in considering distributions of wealth and income, that market-value's Boolean structure comes strategically into play.[3] In Piketty's analysis it is almost visible, and it takes only a rearrangement of his simple equations to bring it into view.

We are working with the following symbols:

K' = capital-2 stated in currency units
Y' = income-2 stated in currency units
Γ' = K' + Y'
K = K'/Γ'
Y = Y'/Γ' so that
Γ = K + Y = 1
β = capital-2' / income-2' = K'/Y' = K/Y
α = capital-2's share of income-2,
r = rate of return on capital-2
s = savings rate
g = growth rate (of income-2)

Piketty's capital-2 / income-2 ratio is one way of comparing two quantities of market-value. But given that market-values only exist relative to other market-values, these two quantities, capital-2 and income-2, when considered together have a special metrical property that remains hidden when they are expressed as a ratio. Capital-2 + income-2, that is, Γ' and Γ on their different scales, comprise *all* the market-value that exists in the economy in a given year. Therefore, metrically Γ is the equivalent of certainty with respect to theoretical probability. As is the convention with probability's certain event, we can assign to Γ the value 1.

So that given β = K/Y and Γ = K + Y, we can write
K = β / β +1 and Y = β – (β – 1) / β +1], so that
K + Y = Γ = 1

For example, if β = 8, then K + Y = 8/9 + 1/9 = 1.

K + Y = 1 is the fundamental relation that underlies the market economy.[4] It is the relation that intriguingly lies behind Piketty's data but which he, blinded

[3] It is, however, the Boolean structure of market-value that makes all demand curves ultimately downward-sloping. See Fullbrook 2002.

by Euclidian preconceptions, fails to unveil. In the Piketty context, the most profound revelation of this unveiling is that *any increase in the market-value of either K or Y decreases by an equal amount the market-value of the other and visa versa.* That is why it is a profound error to speak, as does Piketty, of accumulating or of the macro accumulation of capital-2, i.e. of K or K' where K + Y = 1 or K' + Y' = Γ'. It is not an accumulation that takes place when capital-2 increases, but rather an *appropriation.* More about this in a minute. The theoretical implications of market-value's Boolean structure for understanding Piketty's data are profound, but here there is space only for very brief considerations.

Upper limits

Piketty speculates about relations between β, r, s and g and fancies that by writing β = s/g he has discovered a fundamental law. There is in fact a law to be discovered here although it is not quite fundamental. The law is that *for any K there is a maximum value for r, the rate of return on capital-2, and vice versa.* Why? Because the return on capital-2 comes out of income-2, and the greater K the smaller Y and the greater r the less Y there is for labour. Where α = capital-2's share of income-2, this law may be written:

$$\boldsymbol{\alpha + r\alpha \leq 1}$$

Consider a numerical example. Pretend that K is .9 and r is .12. Then K + rK = .9 + .108 = 1.008. But a K of 1.008 in the real world is no less impossible than it is for a body to travel faster than the speed of light.

In the real world the absolute outer limits of the *distributional variables* will never be reached, instead we can expect movement toward those limits to slow as approached and maybe reverse suddenly. These limits exist through all of history and so provide a universal basis for framing the economy's future.[5]

---

[4] The Boolean discovery reveals that value and distribution are the same thing.
[5] From the Boolean structure of market-value it follows that market economies as a whole have to be continuously changing since any change in the market-value or quantity of anything bought and sold changes the market-value of everything else. In

Two kinds of saving

In talking about the savings rate and the growth rate, Piketty is not comparing to like to like. His **s** refers to a *portion* of the *market-value* of a country's output. His **g** on the other hand refers to *two levels of real output* compared on the basis of what their market-values would be if the market-value of money had remained constant.

Assuming 2% growth and 12% saving, and that all of the 12% goes into investing in *existing* assets, then Piketty's reasoning is broadly correct, because there will be asset inflation. But if all of the 12% goes into investing in new real assets, then the story is quite different from the one Piketty describes. In that case, the effect of the 12% savings on capital-1 market-values depends on the elasticities of demand for various capital goods. With real investment (i.e. in new capital-1) of the 12%, a decrease in the market-value of capital-1 relative to the market-value of income-1, or in Piketty's terms, a decrease in the capital/income ratio, is highly plausible. And of course an increase in the **g** would also become a possibility.

g, **s** and **β** are interconnected but not in the way that Piketty's acute confusion regarding "capital" and "capital" has led him to believe. The missing relevant quantities are:

> s_v = the percent of savings going into existing assets,
> s_r = the percent of savings going into new assets, where
> $s_v + s_r = s$.

It is $\mathbf{s_v}$ that inflates assets prices and leads to an increase in **β**, whereas $\mathbf{s_r}$ is likely to have the opposite effect.

---

short, barring a total price and quantity freeze by a totalitarian government, equilibrium is an impossible condition.

Plutonomy economics

These days some, and maybe even the lion's share, of the most influential theorizing about the economy takes place in secret. And when you stop to think about it, it is difficult to image how it could it be otherwise. Aristotle's motivation for studying economies may have been purely intellectual, but historically the dominant motivation has been to learn how to make economies function better for us humans. But your palace is not my palace, and "therein lies the rub". It is nice to increase the size of the pie, but some people find it even nicer to increase the size of their slice. And just as economics can sometimes be used to increase capital-1 and income-1, economics can also be used – and it is happening with great effectiveness this very minute – to increase and maintain a group's portion of capital- 2 plus income-2.

In recent years there have been a few leakages of the applied economic theorizing carried on behind locked doors on behalf of the-one-percent, some of which, despite frantic efforts to have them suppressed, remain available.[6] What is noteworthy, in the present context, is that, although the economists of the-one-percent are not so unworldly as to ponder algebraic structures, they appear in some degree to implicitly understand the Boolean structure of capital-2 plus income-2. Before looking at one of these one-percenter contributions which was inspired by the appearance of Piketty's great book, we need to introduce both the reality and the idea of *meso inflation*.

Whereas the symbol "capital" is used sometimes to mean this and sometimes that and sometimes something else, all of them of course legitimate, but which without explicit clarification lead to acute theoretical confusion, the symbol "inflation" has, in the main been used to designate only a subset of price level increases. In recent years the term "asset inflation" has become quasi-common, but "inflation" by itself is still perceived by most humans as referring only to the inflation of income-2. Let us, at least momentarily, break with that tradition and *define "inflation" as including both*

[6] Three are currently available here: http://delong.typepad.com/plutonomy-1.pdf, http://delong.typepad.com/plutonomy-2.pdf, http://delong.typepad.com/plutonomy-3.pdf.

income-2 inflation and capital-2 inflation. Metrically and in terms of the measurement unit, say euros, they refer to the same phenomenon: an increase in the number of euros it takes to buy a given basket or briefcase of market exchangeables. Because traditionally economics has terminologically blanked capital-2 inflation, the economy's *overall inflation rate* and its relative *meso inflation rates* have with rare exceptions gone unobserved.[7] But with our new definition we can speak of the inflation rate for the whole economy, that is including both asset markets and goods and services markets. We can also speak of the income-2 inflation rate *relative* to the capital-2 inflation rate. Once we have these simple ideas at our command we have a means of understanding and describing in part *the causality* behind shifts of the capital-2 / income-2 ratio that are less mystical than Piketty's semi-traditional one.

Changes in capital-1 and income-1 are not required to bring about large changes in the capital-2 / income-2 ratio. Instead all that is needed is to exploit the Boolean structure of market-value by changing the captial-2 inflation rate relative to the income-2 inflation rate. The leaked documents from the one-percent's economists show that they see the manipulation of this structure as the primary means by which their paymasters' fortunes can be maintained and increased. For carrying out this manipulation they identify two primary sets of tactics.

One, much discussed by Michael Hudson, Steve Keen, Dean Baker, Ann Pettifor, James Galbraith and others, is to channel huge amounts of credit for the buying of particular categories of existing capital-1, thereby causing capital-2 inflation and causing it in chosen segments of the capital-1 market. Given the Boolean structure of market-value, *creating the possibility of* redistributing capital-2 and income-2 in this way is not a matter of pondering $\beta = s / g$, but of manipulating political decision making. For the last forty years, the one-percent's informed manipulation of political systems, "democracies" and otherwise, has taken place and continues to take place at both administrative and legislative levels.

---

[7] For example, what was the overall inflation rate the US economy in 2010? Quite computable no doubt, but never or almost never stated.

The aftermath of the Global Financial Collapse of 2007 is a good example of the former. In the United States and elsewhere historically unprecedented extensions of credit were almost exclusively directed toward the inflation of capital-2 rather than toward income-2 or toward increasing capital-1 or income-1. These decisions took place even in the face of the USA's decayed infrastructure.

But since 1980, the-one-percent has also excelled at bringing about changes in the law, some aimed at reducing labour's direct claim on income-2, others to enable the-one-percent to raise the capital / income ratio through engineered meso inflations. Recently there briefly leaked a new report by Bank of America-Merrill Lynch entitled "Piketty and Plutonomy: The Revenge of Inequality".[8] When it comes to Picketty's theoretical explanation, the plutonomists are laughing all the way to the bank. A chart and its introduction exhibit how they in private account for changes in the capital-2 / income-2 ratio.

> Drawing on our earlier work, and the research of Thomas Philippon and Ariell Reshef we highlight *the importance of financial de-regulation in engendering plutonomy.* Figure 42 delineates the history of financial regulation in the USA [emphasis added].

---

[8] http://www.businessinsider.com/bofa-merrill-lynch-backs-piketty-2014-5 This is one of many articles published a few months ago about the Bank of America report, but the report itself, as is often the case with one-percenter research, has now disappeared from the web.

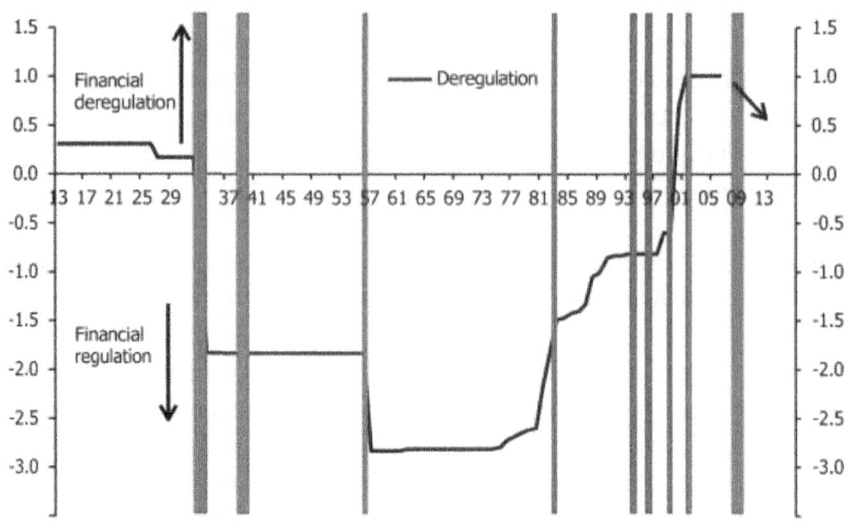

Regulatory legislation
1933 Glass-Steagall Act
1933 Securities Act
1934 Securities Exchange Act
1939 Trust Indenture Act
1940 Investment Advisers Act
1956 Banking Holding Company Act

Deregulatory legislation
1982 Garn-St. Germain Depository Institutions Act
1994 Riegle-Neal Interstate Banking & Branching Efficiency Act (repeals parts of Bank Holding Co. Act)
1996 Investment Advisers Act amended
1999 Graham-Leach-Steagall & parts of Bank Holding Co. Act

Regulatory legislation
2002 Sarbanes-Oxley Act
2008 Economic Stimulus Act
2008 Housing and Economic Recovery Act
2009 American Recovery and Reinvestment Act
2010 Dodd–Frank Wall Street Reform & Consumer Protection Act

Source: BofA Merrill Lynch Global Research, Philippon and Reshef (approximation) (http://pages.stern.nyu.edu/~tphilipp/papers/pr_rev15.pdf), WSJ

Note how well the legislation curve above fits the redistribution curve of income including capital gains for the-one-percent shown below.

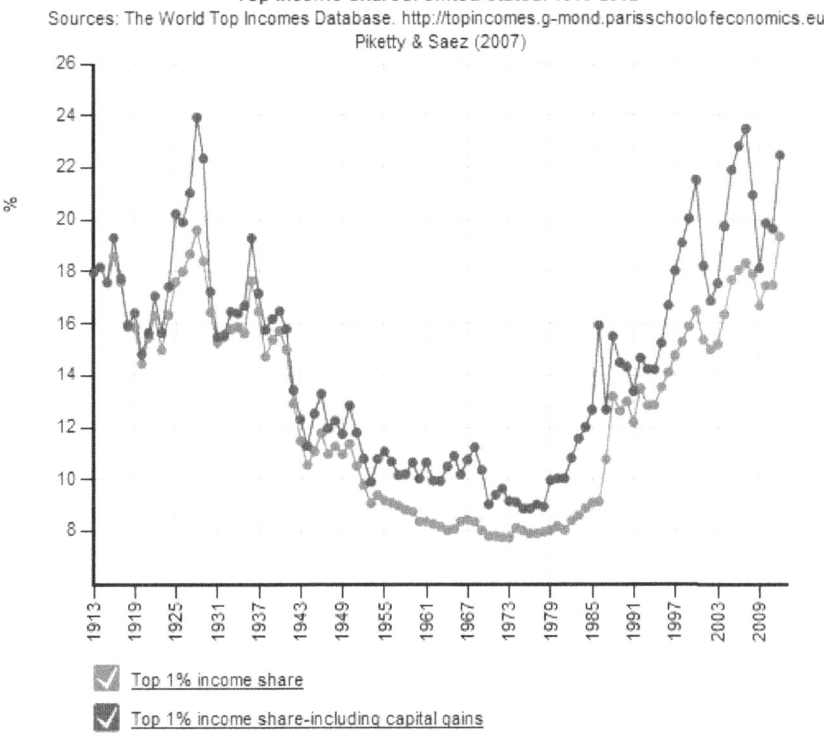

For better or for worse

Today in many high-income countries and most English speaking ones, governments maintain two sets of interconnected policies: one designed to deflate labour's share of income-2, the other to inflate capital-2 and capital's share of income-2. The political feasibility of this dominant and general plutonomist policy of increasing and maintaining high capital-2 / income-2 ratios is greatly enhanced by the economics profession's almost exclusive use of models that exclude *the central Boolean dimension of market economies* and thereby hide not only from the economist's view but also, and more importantly, from the public's view the dominant economic dynamic of our age. As Michael Hudson notes, the traditional and prevailing models fail:

> ... to distinguish between creating money to spend on employment, production and consumption in the "real" economy (affecting consumer prices, commodity prices and wages) as compared to creating credit (or simply Treasury debt) to give to banks to buy or lend against assets in the hope that this will bolster prices for real estate, stocks and bonds. The latter policy inflates asset prices but deflates current spending.
>
> The $13 trillion increase in U.S. Treasury debt in the post-2008 financial meltdown was not spent in product markets or employment in the "real" economy. It was balance-sheet help. Likewise for the ECB in 2011 ... [where] new money and debt creation has little interface with the "real" production-and-consumption economy, except to burden taxpayers [Hudson, 2011].

In writing *Capital in the Twenty-First Century,* Thomas Piketty has done humanity an enormous favour. He has achieved what many of us have tried and failed to achieve for years, in some cases decades: to place the huge upward redistributions of capital and wealth into public consciousness and to make it socially acceptable to talk about them.[9] Achieving this was always to be the first and most difficult step in de-accelerating and eventually stopping the global predations of a tiny minority. It is now done.

---

[9] The conclusion of Fullbrook 2002 points to the paper's usefulness:

> . . . for understanding two significant current problems.
>
> One is the need to bring ecological considerations into economic decision-making. . . . .
>
> The second problem is the redistribution of income and wealth from the poor and middle-classes to the rich and super-rich now taking place both intra- and internationally at a rate and on a scale unprecedented in human history. No adequate theory exists to explain and thereby to enable us to curtail, stop or reverse this radical change in the human condition. Of course it has something to do with globalization. But why should globalization have this redistributive effect? And how can the process be managed so that humans will control the direction and magnitude of the redistribution? This paper provides a theoretical framework in which to think about the problem.

But Piketty's attempt to offer theoretical explanation of his empirical findings are rooted in the axiomatic mysticisms of economics' past. Consequently there is the serious danger that his book's ultimate effect will be to tighten the Euclidian blindfold that makes invisible the hands that engineer and maintain our plutonomy economies. It is only when the profession takes off that blindfold that it will have readily at hand the understanding that the world so desperately needs.

References

Carnap, Rudolf (1966) Philosophical Foundations of Physics: An Introduction to the Philosophy of Science, New York: Basic Books.

Duhem, Pierre (1977) The Aim and Structure of Physical Theory, (1905), New York: Atheneum.

Fullbrook, Edward (2002) "An Intersubjective Theory of Value", in *Intersubjectivity in Economics: Agents and Structures*, editor Edward Fullbrook. London and New York: Routledge, pp. 273-299.

Hudson, Michael (2011) "Trade and Payments Theory in a Financialized Economy", http://michael-hudson.com/2011/10/trade-theory-financialized/

Piketty, Thomas (2014) *Capital in the Twenty-First Century*. Cambridge: Harvard University Press.

Russell, Bertrand (1937) *The Principles of Mathematics*, 2nd edition, London: George Allen.

Piketty's policy proposals: how to effectively redistribute income

David Colander [Middlebury College, Vermont, USA]

There has been growing wealth and income inequality in the US, and people don't like it. The economics profession has provided little guidance in explaining why this is occurring, and what can be done about it; income distribution is presented as being determined by abstract "marginal productivity" market forces that are largely beyond the control of government policy.

In a recent "Economics of Attitude" column (Colander, 2014) I suggested that an important reason for the success of Piketty's *Capital* (2014) was that it provided an entré into wealth and income inequality questions that people believe should be discussed. Unfortunately, Piketty's book is not a good entré into them. It is neither revolutionary nor path breaking; it is primarily an empirical contribution to the income distribution literature combined with some rough notes on how the data relate to economic theory and policy.[1] My argument in my previous piece was that presenting Piketty's book as an entré into the income inequality debate does a disservice to readers who want a serious consideration of how to advance a pro-equality income distribution agenda. In this article I present an alternative approach.

The reason Piketty's policy discussion is not a good entré into income distribution questions is that it is neither novel nor deep. Variations of his proposed policies -- an increase in progressivity to the income tax, and a worldwide, or at least region wide, progressive wealth tax have long been on the modern liberal agenda. Politically, as Piketty recognizes, they have been difficult (essentially impossible) to implement. Piketty does not seriously explore why that modern liberal agenda has not achieved the desired ends, or how a pro-equality distribution agenda can be made workable in the future. So, after finishing the book, the reader is left with a sense that

[1] The over hyping of the book is not due to Piketty; he presents his work with appropriate modesty; the problem is with the reviewers who present the book as something that it is not.

preventing the movement toward more inequality is almost hopeless. Politically, in the US at least, Piketty's policies are nonstarters, and his policy discussion will most likely polarize views, not promote a useful dialog.

Ricardo's and Mill's theories of income distribution

The problem with Piketty's discussion is that it is based in a Ricardian, not a Millian framework in thinking about the income distribution problem. Let me explain. David Ricardo framed the income distribution question as a technical production issue. In Ricardo's model technology determines marginal products and marginal products determine income distribution.

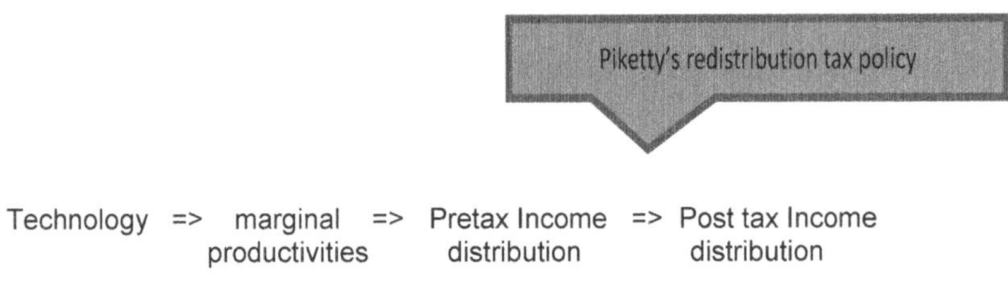

This means the policy to affect income distribution is a redistribution policy; it accepts marginal productivities, but is designed to modify the resulting pre-tax income distribution through some type of equality preferring tax policy such as a progressive income or wealth tax. Most liberal economists' discussions about income distribution have followed Ricardo, and that is the way Piketty presents the issue. The pro-equality policy agenda is seen as a *re*distributive tax policy, and conceived of as operating after marginal productivities have been determined as in the schematic above.

Because of its title, *Capital*, many commentators and reviewers have seen Piketty book as developing a Marxian approach. But that is wrong; Piketty is no Marxist, and his analysis and policy suggestions are not Marxian. Specifically, while Marx used Ricardo's analysis, he did not see a liberal policy agenda of progressive taxation as a viable one. He argued that liberal attempts to provide for a more equal income distribution with tax policy would fail because of an inherent contradiction. That contradiction was that the power structure that would be relied upon to change the distribution of wealth and income is the same power structure that reflects the existing income and wealth distribution. In Ricardo's analysis, what technology has created is almost impossible to change. Marx argued that the only solution to this contradiction was a revolution that changed the power structure.

The classical liberal alternative to Marx

The classical liberal alternative to Marx can be found John Stuart Mill's blending of economic theory with humanitarian insights and values. Mill split from Ricardo and argued that technological forces alone do not determine the distribution of wealth and income; in Mill's theory, income and wealth distribution are co-determined by technology, cultural, and social forces that become entwined with the legal and institutional structure of the economy. In Mill's model of the economy, marginal productivities do not follow from technology. Instead they follow from a much more complex process. For Mill the relationships are:

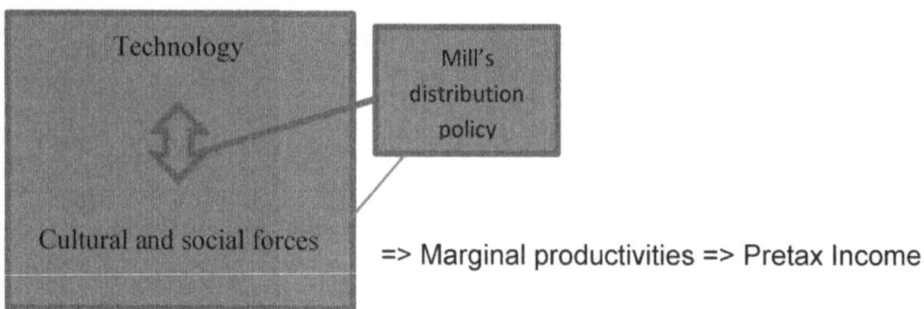

distribution =>Post tax Income distribution

In Mill's approach marginal productivities do not exist independently of cultural and social forces that create the laws. Thus, a rich person's marginal productivity is determined by the legal and property rights structure combined with technology, not by technology alone. For example, a rich author's marginal productivity is high because of the existing institutional arrangements on copyrights, and social conventions on what is proper compensation, not because he is inherently productive. That same person could have a much lower marginal productivity in an alternative institutional arrangement. Similarly with internet companies.

Mill does not take marginal productivities, and hence income and wealth distribution, as given. They are the result of policy decisions. Different property rights embedded in institutions and culture lead to different income distributions. Mill's theory provides a different approach to achieving a pro-equality income distribution agenda in which policy is designed to create a more equal distribution, thereby requiring far less redistribution to achieve the same pro-equality result. As in the schematic above, policy can be designed to make marginal productivities much more equal, by implementing policy before marginal productivities are determined, thereby avoiding the need for redistributive taxes.

Mill's belief that marginal productivities could be changed played an important role for Mill in rejecting Marx's critique of liberal policy, and his calls for revolution. Mill writes:

> The laws of property have never yet conformed to the principles on which the justification of private property rests. They have made property of things which never ought to be property, and absolute property where only a qualified property ought to exist. They have not held the balance fairly between human beings, but have heaped impediments upon some, to give advantage to others; they have purposely fostered inequalities, and prevented all from starting fair in the race. That all should indeed start on perfectly equal terms is inconsistent with any law of private property: but if as much pains as has been taken to aggravate the inequality of chances arising from the natural working of the principle, had been taken to temper that inequality by every means not subversive of the principle itself; if the tendency of legislation had been to favour the diffusion, instead of the concentration of wealth—to encourage the subdivision of the large masses, instead of striving to keep them together; the principle of individual property would have been found to have no necessary connexion with the physical and social evils which almost all Socialist writers assume to be inseparable from it. (Mill, 1848, p. 209)

Mill's approach to thinking about marginal productivity and distribution theory and policy was followed by Alfred Marshall, who, in his *Principles of Economics* specifically noted that marginal productivity theory is not a complete theory of income distribution; but is simply a part of the story. The problem for Marshall was that developing a full theory was far beyond the analytic technology of the day, so he, like Mill, emphasized that it was necessary to go beyond economic theory in thinking about economic policy and distribution theory. For Mill and Marshall, economic theory only provided half-truths and the connection between theory and policy had to go far beyond any existing models or theory. Mill's policy thinking includes thinking about how policy might influence norms, tastes, and institutional arrangements to achieve the desired policy goals. That Marshallian/Millian approach to the use of economic models in thinking about policy is quite different than Ricardo's and Piketty's.

Economists in the 1930s did not follow the Mill/Marshall "half-truths" path in which economic policy followed not from formal economic models, but from reasoned judgment that used those models but integrated their results with a broader, more expansive world view. Instead, they structured their policy thinking around narrow economic models, and as they did, the Ricardian approach to income distribution became the way income distribution policy was framed. That made taxation the primary policy vehicle they explored to achieve a pro-equality income and wealth distribution goal. It is this approach that Piketty follows in his policy discussion, and it is that approach that has not worked in the past. He correctly argues that anti-equality forces are currently winning. But he does not, as Mill did, address the question of how those policies can avoid the Marxian critique that, given the system, real change is essentially impossible because the power structure to change the income distribution is the power structure than reflects the existing distribution of income.

An alternative policy approach

Following a Millian approach to policy, there is another set of income equality policies that, in my view, offer the best hope of achieving a pro-equality income distribution goal. As opposed to trying to *change the income distribution, given marginal productivities*, in the Millian approach you use policies that change tastes, norms, and institutionally determined marginal productivities. Using this policy one structures the property rights so as to make the marginal productivities of individuals more equal, thereby making the distribution of income more equal without resorting to redistributive taxation. Here are some examples:[2]

- Property rights could have had more limited duration. Patent and copyright laws could have been designed for much shorter periods, so that the benefits of the work are passed to the broader public.
  - Intellectual property rights could have been significantly limited.
  - Institutions favoring open source software and material could have been institutionally encouraged.
  - Instead of perpetuity property rights in land, 100 year leases could have been given, with the land reverting to social wealth, and re-leased, when the lease comes due.

- Competition could have been more strongly supported by limiting government supported monopolies.
  - Regulatory structures of institutions could have allowed for narrower specialists, so that the rents created are spread more widely and more competition is created.
  - Open certification not requiring specific high-priced formal training programs, but rather "open-to anyone" certification exams.
  - At risk students could be provided with a "bottom up" educational option, in which, they receive the money that would have gone into educating them if they learn the material on their own.

- Individual's social, not materialistic, proclivities are encouraged.
  - The society could advocate and support a stronger tradition of social responsibility of the rich, so that achieving social goals becomes a favored luxury good of the rich. Andrew Carnegie's *Gospel of Wealth* could have been built into the fabric of society.
  - Institutions could have been designed to encourage social benefit, rather than private benefit, entrepreneurship.

---

[2] Further examples and expansion of these examples are given in Colander and Kupers (2014).

- Materialism embedded in the GDP goals could be countered by replacing GDP with other measures of social success such as Sen's Capabilities Index.

Why Mill's distribution policy agenda will work better than Piketty's redistribution policy agenda

A likely response to these ideas is that they are as "pie-in-the sky" as Piketty's. I agree they are pie-in the sky, but they are much more likely to be effective than Piketty's because they avoid being undermined by the "take away principle." That principle has long been known by parents, but somehow has not made its way into economist's policy precepts. The principle is:

It is much harder to take something away from someone than not give it in the first place.

There are many expressions of this principle in the popular culture: "Possession is 9/10s of the law." Or, as Mohamed put it: "The person who takes back a gift is like a dog which vomits, then eats what it vomited." Recently this principle has been given scientific backing by behavior economists' discovery of loss aversion. [3]

The take away principle has significant implications for any pro-equality distribution agenda. It explains why it is so hard to change the income distribution through progressive taxation, even when, in principle, a majority of the population favors more equality. A progressive taxation redistribution policy undermines the pro-equality sensibility of people because it frames the issue as if you are taking something away from people. People want equality, but they don't want anything taken away from them to achieve it.

---

[3] To make this general principle applicable for policy, it needs to be quantified. So here is my quantification, which is based on the ratio of time my children would cry and scream when I took something away from them (t), relative to the time they would cry and scream when I refused to give it to them in the first place (r): $t/r=7.5$, with a standard deviation of 3. Based on this estimate, it is 7.5 times more difficult to achieve an income equality goal by redistribution policy than it is by distribution policy.

Piketty's, and almost all of modern economist's discussions of a pro-equality policy agenda have failed to take this takeaway principle into account. They present that pro-equality distribution agenda as involving tax policy that is designed to *re*distribute income. That frames the policy discussion around the idea that people have earned something and that they possess it. In that frame any government pro-equality policy is designed to take it away. That framing, as Marx recognized, condemns the policy to failure because of the take-away principle. The Millian policy approach that I am advocating does not try to *re*distribute income fairly. Instead it focuses on creating laws, property rights and an opportunity space that distribute income more fairly.

Some final comments

Mill did not develop his pro-equality policy agenda in part because he felt that, with the right policies, inequality of income would not be a serious problem for future society. He believed that an affluent society would not be worried about income inequality; the concern about income and wealth distribution would fade away as society became richer and norms changed to make accumulation of wealth of far less concern.

His vision of future society was one "in which, while no one is poor, no one desires to be richer, nor has any reason to fear being thrust back by the efforts of others to push themselves forward." (Mill 1848) Given existing norms and culture, this seems a utopian dream, but those norms have been created by existing policies, not because they are inherent in human society.

Such a pro-equality outcome is possible to achieve by policy only if we stop thinking of economic policy narrowly, and start thinking about it in a much broader context. Our society is an affluent materialistic society, where materialistic goals are encouraged by policy. Given existing institutions, tastes, and culture, there is little hope to achieve a pro-equality redistribution agenda. But if we focus policy on a pro-equality distribution policy agenda – a policy that includes a norms policy, a cultural policy, and a pro-equality property rights policy that is designed to achieve as much equality as possible, and to rid ourselves of our society's current materialistic fetish, movement toward equality can be achieved in a way that would be supported by a large majority of the population on both the right and the left. It won't be easy to implement, but it will be much easier to implement than the Piketty policy proposals.

References

Colander, David (forthcoming) "Marketing Economic Ideas: The Problem with Capital" Colander's Economics with Attitude Column, *Eastern Economic Journal*.

Colander, David and Roland Kupers (2104) *Complexity and the Art of Public Policy*, Princeton: Princeton University Press.

Mill, John Stuart (1848) *Principles of Political Economy*, London: Longmans, Green and Co.

Piketty, Thomas (2014) *Capital in the Twenty-First Century*, Harvard: Harvard University Press.

Piketty: inequality, poverty and managerial capitalism

V. A. Beker [University of Belgrano and University of Buenos Aires, Argentina]

Introduction

Thomas Piketty has provided an impressive amount of data which shows that inequality, under capitalism, goes hand in hand with economic growth. In principle, one could think that Piketty illustrates with abundant data Marx's assertion that capital has the tendency for concentration and centralization in the hands of the richest capitalists. However, the French author anxiously makes it clear from the very beginning that he is not following what he calls the "Marxist principle of infinite accumulation".

His contribution is threefold. First, he argues that to the extent that the rate of capital accumulation (*r*) is higher than the rate of growth of the economy (*g*), inequality expands; the reward to capital grows faster than the payments to labour. Second, he includes a methodological innovation which consists in resorting to tax records, a source of data usually forgotten by economists dealing with distribution of income calculations. Instead, Piketty has found ways to merge tax data with other sources to produce information that complements survey evidence. Finally, he concludes with a recommendation for a progressive global tax on capital although Piketty understands that this is now utopian.

To check the accuracy of the huge amount of data included in Piketty's book is something well beyond what a reviewer can do. So, I will assume that its empirical part is correct.

As we shall see, there are some contradictions in his line of reasoning and also my feelings after reading the book are contradictory. The first one – as it happened with many colleagues – is surprise at the fact that the book has become a bestseller, something quite unusual for an economics book.

So, the first task is to try to explain the reasons for such an unusual success. Some difficulties found in Piketty's book will also be pointed out. The relationship between inequality and poverty is analysed and some implications in terms of economic policy are made explicit. A brief digression is made on the relationship of Piketty's findings with the Kaldorian model of economic growth. Finally, attention is drawn to Piketty's findings on income distribution as different from wealth distribution.

Reasons for the success of Piketty's book

What are the reasons for Piketty's phenomenal success, centred in the United States? First of all, the book's timing. Rising income and wealth inequality have suddenly become top issues in the American agenda after the financial crisis of 2008 and its consequence, the Great Recession.

However, as Tom Palley points out, they are phenomena that have been documented for years, although less comprehensively. For example, James Galbraith substantially confirmed that picture in his 1998 book *Created Unequal: The Crisis in American Pay*. Rising US income and wealth inequality was the subject of the book Edward Wolff co-authored in 2002 under the title *Top Heavy: The Increasing Inequality of Wealth in America and What Can Be Done About It*, and he insisted on this theme in his 2008 book *Poverty and Income Distribution*.

Why did the young French author succeed now where others failed before? In a nutshell, he was at the right time in the right place with the right ideas.

This shows once again that "economic ideas go through a selection process which is strongly context-dependent" (Beker, 2005, p. 18).

A second reason for Piketty's extraordinary success has been his scarce use of economic theory. He does not involve himself in theoretical discussions. His results rest on what he calls "the central contradiction of capitalism", i.e. the rate of return on capital systematically exceeds the overall rate of growth of income: $r > g$.

However, strictly speaking, Piketty's conclusions rest on $s.r > g$, not $r > g$, where s is the proportion of r capitalists reinvest. In fact, if $r > g$ but $s.r < g$, capital will grow slower than average income, contrary to Piketty's main thesis. The author seems to assume that if $r > g$ then $s.r > g$ automatically follows.

Third, Piketty has shown that growing inequality is a result absolutely compatible with neoclassical economic theory, which does not preclude at all the possibility that r may outstrip g.[1] So, his findings have become absolutely palatable for a broad fraction of mainstream economists.

However, his allegation that in the long run r is relatively stable contradicts one of the fundamental laws of neoclassical economic theory: diminishing returns to an abundant factor of production.[2] It also contradicts the Marxian law of the decreasing rate of profit. Piketty mentions this law stating that "Marxist analysis emphasises the falling rate of profit—a historical prediction that has turned out to be quite wrong". It also contradicts Keynes's prediction on the euthanasia of the rentier.

A fourth reason, pointed out by John Weeks, is that Piketty avoids any discussion of macroeconomic policy. His book is narrowly focused on inequality, trying to show that its long-run increase is just a law of capitalist development. So, he avoids any political debate.

Last but not least, his writing is very easy to read and understand. He writes in the literary tradition of Adam Smith, Marx, or Keynes and derides economists who "rely on an immoderate use of mathematical models, which

---

[1] Ray (2014) argues that $r > g$ is a consequence of *any* model of growth, provided that we insist on "dynamic efficiency". He adds that dynamic efficiency simply states that an economy does not grow so fast as to spend, so as to negate, the initial (economic) purpose of growth, which is to consume.

[2] *Piketty does not ignore this issue but he argues that the* interesting question is not whether the marginal productivity of capital decreases when the stock of capital increases – which he accepts as obvious – but rather how fast it decreases. He goes on, arguing that the decline in r is compensated by the rise in the capital/income ratio. "The most likely outcome is thus that the decrease in the rate of return will be smaller than the increase in the capital/income ratio, so that capital's share will increase". However, Piketty keeps arguing that r is relatively stable over the long run at around 4–5 per cent.

are frequently no more than an excuse for occupying the terrain and masking the vacuity of the content". Instead, he builds a clear and convincing story on the basis of a formidable database on the distribution of income and wealth from more than twenty countries. His success seems to confirm McCloskey's *dictum* that science – and particularly economic science – is persuasion and that rhetoric plays a key role in that.

Piketty defines as capital any source of non-wage income. So, he includes housing, cash, bonds, shares, intellectual property, and even the property of slaves.

In this respect, Bonnet et al. (2014) argue that once housing prices are removed from the Piketty compilation of capital, the phenomenon of rising share of capital income goes away. They remark that over the longer run the "productive" capital/income ratio has not increased at all; "productive" capital only has risen weakly relative to income over the last few decades. If so, it would mean that Piketty's conclusions are strongly determined by the secular increase in the price of a quasi-fixed factor of production as urban land is. In such a case Piketty would be bringing back to life Ricardo's land-scarcity analysis, with the emphasis now on urban instead of rural land. But, as Rowthorn (2014) points out, if the increase in the capital-output ratio that Piketty detects is mainly due to an increase, in recent decades, in the market value of certain real assets (especially housing), it may be that the truth is that there has been no over-accumulation of capital, as Piketty states, but, on the contrary, under-investment. Piketty himself remarks that real-state capital roughly represents 50% of capital in developed countries.

In spite of the weight Piketty gives in his argument to the $r > g$ relationship, he admits that "the reduction of inequality that took place in most developed countries between 1910 and 1950 was above all a consequence of war and of policies adopted to cope with the shocks of war. Similarly, the resurgence of inequality after 1980 is due largely to the political shifts of the past several decades, especially in regard to taxation and finance". But this implies that the main determinant of the ups and downs of inequality has been the changing correlation of forces – mainly between capital and labour – and not the $r > g$ relationship. This changing balance of forces has resulted in different policies over time from the welfare state of the post-war period to neoliberal deregulation. For example, until the appearance of Piketty's book, the resurgence of inequality after 1980 has been considered the direct effect of Reagan-Thatcher economic policies that, among other things, eroded union power. He admits that the inequality $r > g$ is a contingent historical proposition, which is true in some periods and political contexts and not in others. Therefore, is inequality just the result of an intrinsic trend in capitalist development or is it the consequence of policies like the ones which consisted of deregulation, weakening of the labour unions and the like? Piketty himself seems to choose a middle-of-the road explanation. He recognises that there are "powerful mechanisms pushing alternately toward convergence and divergence" as far as wealth distribution is concerned. However, he predicts that "certain worrisome forces of divergence" will prevail in the future but his forecast is based precisely on the behaviour of the United States and Europe after 1980. He maintains that "the return of high capital/income ratios over the past few decades can be explained in large part by the return to a regime of relatively slow growth". This made the rate of return on capital remain significantly above the growth rate. But the low rate of growth and the high rate of return on capital were not just the result of Reaganite and Thatcherite policies?

Nevertheless, after taking into account the different factors that he considers relevant he concludes: "the process by which wealth is accumulated and distributed contains powerful forces pushing toward divergence, or at any rate toward an extremely high level of inequality. Forces of convergence also exist, and in certain countries at certain times, these may prevail, but the forces of divergence can at any point regain the upper hand, as seems to be happening now, at the beginning of the twenty-first century. The likely decrease in the rate of growth of both the population and the economy in coming decades makes this trend all the more worrisome" because this will make sure the prevalence of $r > g$. He calls the $r > g$ relationship the "fundamental force for divergence". Once again, let us remember that he should have said $s.r > g$ not $r > g$.

Piketty's book is more descriptive than prescriptive. Its main recommendation – he himself admits – is utopian. What then is its added value?

First of all, it brings distributional issues to the fore of economic debate. According to David Ricardo, this is the "principal problem in Political Economy"[3] but it has been considered as an absolutely peripheral topic by contemporary mainstream economics. In Atkinson's words, "it has been very much out in the cold" for a long time.

Second, it follows the best traditions in economic literature. Piketty shows he is an economist with his feet on the ground who knows what value parameters may take in reality; he does not speculate with theoretical models where parameters may vary from 0 to ∞.

Third, it vindicates the need of collaboration between economics and the other social sciences: economics – he remarks – is just a subdiscipline of the social sciences, alongside history, sociology, anthropology, and political science. It also postulates a way of addressing research: to start with fundamental questions and try to answer them using the methods of economists, historians, sociologists, and political scientists, crossing disciplinary boundaries. This implies abandoning the traditional mainstream approach to economics as a "separate" science.[4] It also means to start research by choosing fundamental questions – as inequality – and not "by the possibilities of mathematically modelling the answers" (Beker, 2010, p. 19), which has been the fashion among mainstream economists.

Inequality and poverty

Let me now ask an awkward question. Should reduction of inequality or reduction of poverty be our main concern? Surely the majority of readers will rush to answer that both goals should be pursued simultaneously. However, the relationship between inequality and poverty seems to be a complex one, particularly in poor countries. The recent international experience shows that far from being complementary objectives they may be rather opposite, which poses a real dilemma for economic policy. China experienced in the last years a strong reduction in poverty simultaneously with a significant increase in inequality. There may also be widespread poverty in a society with low

[3] Ricardo, D. (1817). Preface.
[4] See Hausman (1992) on the concept of "separate" science.

levels of inequality. A decrease in inequality can also be accompanied by an increase in poverty.

Poverty has not been a great concern for mainstream economic policy. Only in 1969 Economics of Poverty was identified by JEL as a distinct field of research.

Klasen[5], from a policy perspective, defines pro-poor growth as growth that maximises the income gains of the poor. This means that the income growth rate of the poor must exceed the growth rate of the non-poor. In such a case, reduction of poverty goes hand in hand with reduction in inequality.

Basu (2005) argues that economic policy should take as welfare criteria a normative simple rule: maximising the per capita income of the poorest 20 per cent of the population. He calls this the "quintile income" of a country.

Of course, equality is a desirable goal – this is not under discussion – but the issue is how pro-poor growth can be obtained together with less inequality. Experience shows that less poverty not necessarily means less inequality and vice versa.

Piketty practically does not address the issue of less developed economies. His analysis focuses on the experience of Western developed countries and only includes a very brief reference to emerging economies. He believes that the historical trajectory of developed countries can tell a great deal about the future dynamics of global wealth, including emergent economies.

The truth is that for emerging economies, where basic needs are often not satisfied for a huge part of the population, poverty is on the top of the agenda. Fighting poverty should be the first priority for economic policy in these countries. It would be of great help for them to have a volume as Piketty's one but devoted to poverty, its relationship with inequality, its causes, and the ways to minimise it.

[5] Klasen, S. (2007). Ch. 13, p. 196.

On the contrary, in developed countries inequality has become today the main concern. Why? Once basic needs are satisfied, people evaluate their economic well-being relative to others, not in absolute terms.

Orthodox economists reject this point of view. For example, Martin Feldstein (1999) argues that changes that increase the incomes of high-income individuals without decreasing the incomes of others clearly satisfy the Pareto principle and should be welcomed. I argued elsewhere (Beker, 2005) that a policy change that improves the situation of the upper one per cent of the population without changing the situation of the rest is undoubtedly a Paretian improvement but this does not mean it necessarily is a desirable outcome. I objected that this more efficient alternative – as it is called by mainstream economists – will be rejected in many societies in the name of *equity*. The Pareto improvement concept implicitly assumes that absolute and not relative situations are relevant. In our example, although the poor are not worse off in absolute terms they are in relative ones; this may make them feel poorer as if they had lost part of their income. To learn that reckless bank executives take home million-dollar bonuses in the middle of the Great Recession is undoubtedly scandalous for jobless and homeless people. It is society and not economists who should decide what weight should be given to efficiency and what weight to equity: it is typically a value judgment.

From Kaldor to Piketty

During the fifties, Nicholas Kaldor (1955, 1957) developed a model of economic growth and income distribution in order to explain the constancy of the capital-output ratio, the rates of profit on capital and the distribution of income. At that time, Kaldor maintained that these three ratios were constant over time, according to the data for the United Kingdom and United States economies.

In his model, the capital-labour ratio was driven to a steady-state equilibrium value by the different savings rates of capitalists and workers: if K/L rose above its equilibrium value, the wage-to-profits ratio would also rise. With workers' savings assumed to be lower than those of capitalists, this led to a decline in the rate of capital accumulation, driving K/L back down towards equilibrium.

Concerning the distribution of income, Piketty finds that the capital-labour split varied widely over the course of the twentieth century. He advises to focus on the analysis of the evolution of the capital/income ratio as a way of measuring wealth accumulation over time.

According to Piketty, the capital/income ratio has followed over the course of the century just past a "U-shaped curve". In fact, in Britain and France this ratio fell between 1914 and 1945 but then sharply increased in the period 1945–2012. He finds that the general evolution of the capital share of income is described by the same U-shaped curve as the capital/output ratio. Finally, as far as the rate of return is concerned, he maintains that it is relatively stable at around 4–5 per cent (it never falls below 2–3 per cent, he remarks). Finally, he states that once $r-g$ surpasses a certain threshold, inequality of wealth will increase without limit. In this respect, Piketty, in spite of his disclaimers, resembles Marx in his prediction of an increasing concentration and centralization of capital.

As far as Kaldor is concerned, Piketty rejects his assumptions: neither the capital/output ratio nor the distribution of income is constant over time. Moreover, above a certain threshold there is no equilibrium distribution. Only the rate of return is relatively stable in the long run.

Inequality and top wage earners

Although his analysis is centred on capital accumulation, Piketty argues that the rapid increase observed in inequality in the United States, which started in the 1980s, largely reflects an unprecedented explosion of very elevated incomes from labour. He attributes this phenomenon to the fact that top managers by and large have the power to set their own remuneration, in some cases without limit. This phenomenon is seen mainly in the United States and to a lesser degree in Britain while the tendency is less marked in other wealthy countries although the trend is in the same direction. So, he finds a growing concentration of income from labour and not only from capital. Moreover, the peak of the income hierarchy is dominated by very high incomes from labour. He characterises the United States at the moment as a society with a record level of inequality of income from labour. In a previous article[6] he and his co-author had already found that the composition of income in the top 0.01% in the United States is increasingly salaries, and a corresponding lower proportion is returns to capital. In this case, the control of capital seems to be more important than capital ownership from the income distribution point of view. At this point Piketty's conclusion resembles John K. Galbraith's thesis of the rising power of the technostructure. "We have gone from a society of rentiers to a society of managers", Piketty remarks with reference to France. United States inequality has much to do with the advent of "supermanagers" who obtain extremely high, historically unprecedented compensation packages for their labour, he concludes.

So it seems that in spite of the growing concentration of capital property, the main beneficiaries of this process in terms of income have been the managers who administer it. The inequality $s.r > g$ may explain wealth evolution but income distribution needs another type of explanation.

If Piketty's claim is correct, it would be a formidable empirical argument in favour of managerial theories of the firm which argue that managers maximise their own utility while satisfying shareholders with a minimum level of profit.

However, there is something puzzling in Piketty's book: if, according to him, today's income inequality is mainly the result of labour income inequality, why does he devote 90 per cent of the volume to the study of wealth distribution and only 10 per cent to income distribution? I first thought it might be because he found greater availability of data concerning wealth distribution. However, in his answer to the *Financial Times*' critique, he admits that available data sources on wealth inequality are much less systematic than what we have for income inequality. So, the question remains open.

---

[6] Piketty, T. and Saez, E. (2006).

References

Basu, K. (2005). Globalization, Poverty, and Inequality: What is the Relationship? What Can Be Done? *World Development*, Vol. 34, No. 8, pp. 1361–1373, 2006.

Beker, V.A. (2005). Is Economics a Science? A Discussion of Some Methodological Issues (July 2005). http://ssrn.com/abstract=839307

Beker, V.A. (2010). On the Economic Crisis and the Crisis of Economics. Economics Discussion Papers, No 2010-18, Kiel Institute for the World Economy. http://www.economics-ejournal.org/economics/discussionpapers/2010-18

Bonnet, H., Bono, P-H, Chapelle, G. and Wasmer, E. (2014), "Le capital logement contribue-t-il aux inégalités? Retour sur le capital au XXIe siècle de Thomas Piketty", LIEPP Working Paper no. 25, April.

Feldstein, M. (1999). "Reducing poverty, not inequality." THE PUBLIC INTEREST. Number 137, Fall 1999. http://www.nber.org/feldstein/pi99.html

Hausman, D. (1992).*The inexact and separate science of economics*. Cambridge University Press, Cambridge.

Kaldor, N. (1955). Alternative Theories of Distribution. *The Review of Economic Studies*, Vol. 23, No. 2, pp. 83-100.

Kaldor, N. (1957). A Model of Economic Growth. *The Economic Journal*, Vol. 67, No. 268 Dec., pp. 591-624.

Klasen, S. (2007). *Determinants of Pro-Poor Growth*. Palgrave MacMillan.

Palley, T. (2014). The accidental controversialist: deeper reflections on Thomas Piketty's "Capital". http://www.thomaspalley.com/?p=422

Piketty, T. (2014). *Capital in the Twenty-First Century*. Cambridge: Harvard University Press.

Piketty and Saez (2006), "The Evolution of Top Incomes: A Historical and International Perspective". http://eml.berkeley.edu/~saez/piketty-saezAEAPP06.pdf

Ray, D. (2014). Nit-Piketty. A comment on Thomas Piketty's Capital in the Twenty-First Century. http://www.econ.nyu.edu/user/debraj/Papers/Piketty.pdf

Ricardo, D. (1817). *Principles of Political Economy and Taxation*. John Murray. London.

Rowthorn, R. (2014). A Note on Thomas Piketty's Capital in the Twenty-First Century. http://tcf.org/assets/downloads/A_Note_on_Thomas_Piketty3.pdf

Weeks, J. (2014). Economics for the 99% Encounter in a Taxi: The Piketty Phenomenon. http://therealnews.com/t2/component/content/article/81-more-blog-posts-from-john-weeks/2086-economics-for-the-99-encounter-in-a-taxi-the-piketty-phenomenon

Capital in the Twenty-First Century: are we doomed without a wealth tax?

Dean Baker [Center for Economic and Policy Research, USA]

Thomas Piketty has done a great deal to add to our understanding of the economy. His work with Emmanual Saez and various other co-authors has hugely expanded our knowledge of trends in inequality in the United States and many other wealthy countries.[1] *Capital in the Twenty-First Century* is another major contribution, provided us a treasure trove of data on trends in wealth distribution in the United States, United Kingdom, France, and a smattering of other countries, in some cases going back more than three centuries. This new data will undoubtedly provide the basis for much further research on wealth.

While few can question that Piketty has expanded our knowledge of wealth accumulation in the past, it is his predictions about the future that have garnered the most attention. Piketty notes the rapid increase in the concentration of wealth over the last three decades and sees it as part of a more general pattern in capitalism. He sees the period from World War I to the end of the 1970s as an anomaly. He argues that the general pattern of capitalism is to produce inequality. Two World Wars and the Great Depression gave the world a temporary reprieve from this trend as inequality fell sharply everywhere, but Piketty argues that capitalism is now back on its normal course, which means that inequality will continue to expand in the decades ahead. The remedy proposed in his book is a worldwide wealth tax, a proposal that Piketty recognizes as being nearly impossible politically. (In fairness, Piketty has been very open to other progressive policy proposals in discussions since his book came out.)

Before addressing the center of Piketty's argument, it is worth clarifying Piketty's focus. Unlike Marx's Capital, which explicitly focused on money invested for profit, Piketty lumps all forms of wealth together for his analysis. This means the focus of his attention is not just shares of stock or bonds

---

[1] Piketty and Saez – world's top incomes.

issued by private companies, but also housing wealth and wealth held in the form of government bonds. This is at least a peculiar mix since the value of these assets has often moved in opposite directions. For example, wealth held in government bonds in the United States declined from 114.9 percent of GDP in 1945 to 36.3 percent in the quarter century following World War II. Meanwhile the value of corporate equity rose from 49.8 percent of GDP in 1945 to 79.2 percent of GDP in 1970.[2]

There is a similar story with housing wealth. Nationwide house prices just moved in step with inflation over the period from 1950 to 1996.[3] It was only in the period of the housing bubble that they began to substantially outpace the overall rate of inflation. While they have fallen back from their bubble peaks, house prices in 2014 are still close to 20 percent above their long-term trend. This pattern is noteworthy because it is difficult to envision a theory that would apply to both corporate profits (presumably the main determinant of share prices) and also housing values.

Should we believe that in a period of high corporate profits that Congress could not possibly limit the tax deduction for mortgage interest or take some other measure that would lead to a large hit to house prices? Again, housing wealth and wealth in equity have diverged sharply before, so if we are to believe that they will move together in the future then Piketty is claiming that the future will be very different from the past. And, the course of house prices will have much to do with the pattern of future wealth distribution. At $22.8 trillion, the value of the nation's residential housing stock was not much smaller in value at the end of the first quarter of 2014 than the $27.8 trillion value of outstanding equity of U.S. corporations.[4]

---

[2] These data are taken from United States Government, Office of Management and Budget, Historical Tables, Table 7.1 [http://www.whitehouse.gov/sites/default/files/omb/budget/fy2015/assets/hist07z1.xls] and Board of Governors of the Federal Reserve System, Financial Accounts of the United States, Table L.213 [http://www.federalreserve.gov/releases/z1/Current/data.htm].

[3] Robert Shiller's data show house prices just staying even with the overall rate of inflation since the late 1990s.

[4] Board of Governors of the Federal Reserve System (2014), Table B.100, Line 3 and Table L.213, Line 2 plus Line 4 [http://www.federalreserve.gov/releases/z1/Current/].

Future trends in corporate profits

If we assume for the moment that Piketty does not want to predict the future of house prices, nor the course of public debt, his claim about the growing concentration of wealth comes down to a claim about the value of corporate stock. His claim is a strong one. He argues that wealth will grow relative to GDP. This hinges on the claim that the rate of profit will remain constant even as the ratio of wealth to GDP rises.[5] This means that profit will comprise a growing share of income through time.

There are two paths of logic that could generate this result and Piketty has chosen both, even though they are in direct opposition to each other. The first path is the one of neo-classical economics in which profit is the marginal physical product of capital. This is a technical relationship. The other path is one based on institutions and the distribution of power. In this story profit depends to a large extent on the ability of owners of capital to rig the rules in their favor. As Piketty comments the recent rise in the capital share of output is:

> "consistent not only with an elasticity of substitution greater than one but also with an increase in capital's bargaining power vis-à-vis labor over the past few decades" (p 221).

Piketty sets the stage for the first course when he briefly discusses the Cambridge Capital controversy. He pronounces Cambridge, MA the winner, even though the leading figures on the U.S. side conceded their defeat (Samuelson, 1966). Contrary to the treatment in Piketty, this was not a battle between England and its former colony, nor was it an empty exercise in economic esoterics. The real question was whether it made sense to talk about capital in the aggregate as a physical concept apart from the economic context in which it exists. This is not problematic in a one good economy, but as the Cambridge, UK economists made clear, it is not possible to aggregate types of capital without already knowing the interest rate.

---

[5] Using wealth as the key variable his claim would have to apply to housing wealth and holdings of government debt as well as shares of stock, but for simplicity and the reasons explained above, I am leaving these assets out of the discussion.

This matters for Piketty's claim because the Cambridge U.K. side established that the standard neo-classical production function did not make sense even in theory. The notion of an aggregate production function is logically incoherent. In his "Essay on Positive Economics," Milton Freidman famously argued that it was reasonable to use simplifying assumptions in analyzing the economy even if they do not closely match reality. His model was the study of gravity where he said physicists would assume a vacuum, even though a perfect vacuum does not exist in the world.

The outcome of the Cambridge capital controversy would be the equivalent of showing a vacuum does not even make sense as a theoretical concept. The aggregate production function is simply not useful as a tool for economic analysis.

This is important for Piketty's argument because in the neo-classical strain of his argument, the basis for the increasing capital share is Piketty's claim that the elasticity of substitution between labor and capital is greater than one. However if aggregate production functions are not a sensible concept, then it would not be possible to derive this conclusion from determining the technical rate of substitution between labor and capital. Instead we would have to look at institutional and political factors to find the determinants of profit rates.

As a practical matter this seems the only plausible path forward. It is difficult to see how the length of a drug company's patent monopoly or Microsoft's copyright monopoly could be determined by the physical tradeoffs between labor and capital in the production process. The same would hold true of other factors that play a large role in determining aggregate profits. The decision by the United States to have its health care system run largely by for-profit insurers rather than a government agency surely is not technically determined. Nor is the decision to rely largely on private financial companies to provide retirement income for middle class workers. Similarly, the point at which the Federal Reserve Board clamps down on growth to prevent unemployment from falling and wage pressure from building is not determined by the technical features of the production process.[6]

If we want to assess the whether it is likely that profits in the future will continue to rise as a share of output it is probably most useful to examine the recent trend in profits across sectors. Table 1 shows the sectors that have seen the largest rise in profit shares between 1979 and 2012, the most recent year for which industry level profit data are available.

Finance is the sector with the largest increase in profit shares, rising from an 18.4 percent share of domestic profits in 1979 to 29.1 percent share in 2013. Retail had a near doubling of its share from 4.7 percent in 1979 to a 9.3 percent share in 2013. This is presumably a Walmart effect as there was both some shift from wages to profits, but probably also a substantial reduction in the proprietorship share of retail, as chain stores replaced family run businesses. The category of "other non-financial" business includes a variety of industries, but it is likely that education and health care services account for much of the growth over this period. Finally, the last bar shows the growth in receipts of profits from the rest of the world (these are gross, not receipts).[7] This increased 17.1 percent in 1979 to 31.1 percent in 2013. While some of this increase undoubtedly reflected the expansion of U.S. firms into other countries, it is likely that a substantial portion of this rise was simply an accounting maneuver for income tax purposes. It is a common practice to declare profits at subsidiaries located in low-tax countries, even if may not be plausible that the income in any real way originated in those subsidies.

---

[6] Baker and Bernstein (2013) show that a sustained one percentage point decline in the unemployment rate is associated with a 9.6 percent increase in the wages of workers at the 20th percentile of the wage distribution and a 4.6 percent increase at the median. While some of this increase in real wages likely comes at the expense of higher income workers, some of it almost certainly comes at the expense of corporate profits.

[7] The figure for foreign receipts is expressed as a share of all corporate profits rather than as a share of domestic profits.

Table 1

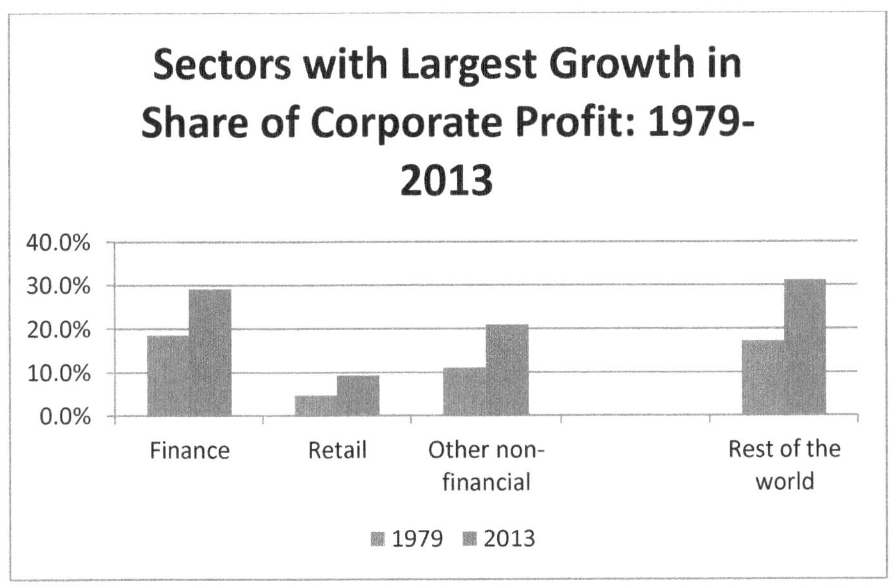

Source: Bureau of Economic Analysis, National Income and Product Accounts, Table 6.16B and 6.16D

If these sectors that drove the rise in profit shares are examined more closely, it is easy to envision policy changes that would reverse some or all of this increase. In the case of the financial sector, a policy that limited the size of financial firms coupled with taxes imposed on the financial sector that equalized taxation with other industries would likely take much of the profit out of the sector. The International Monetary Fund (2014) recently estimated the value of implicit too big to fail subsidies for large banks at $50 billion a year in the United States, almost 5 percent of after-tax corporate profits.[8] To equalize tax burdens across industries the I.M.F. (2010) recommended a tax on the financial sector equal to roughly 0.2 percent of GDP ($35 billion in the U.S. economy in 2013). These policies alone would go far toward bringing the financial industry's profits close to their 2010 share. Other policies that would further reduce its share would include simplifying the tax code to reduce the profits to be made by tax avoidance schemes and expansion of welfare state protections such as Social Security or public health care

[8] The same analysis put the annual value of too big to fail subsidies in the euro zone at $300 billion.

insurance that would reduce the need for services provided by the financial sector.

The soaring profits of the retail sector are in part attributable to the low wages in the sector. If wages rose through a combination of tighter labor markets, successful unionization measures, and higher minimum wage laws, it is likely that a substantial portion of the increase would be at the expense of corporate profits. Labor compensation in the retail sector in 2013 was roughly $530 billion.[9] If this was increased by one-third due to the factors noted above, and one third of this increase was at the expense of profits in the sector, then profits in retail would fall by almost 30 percent, retreating most of the way back to their 1979 share.

While the “other” category would require a more detailed analysis than is possible with the published NIPA data, it is clear that the profits in the education and the health care sector depend largely on the government. If the government either reduced payments in these areas, or directly offered these services themselves, as is the case in most other countries, then the profits earned by the firms operating in these sectors would fall sharply.

Finally, there is the rapid growth in the foreign profit share. This also involves a variety of factors, but a substantial part of the picture is the use of foreign tax havens. This is especially important for industries that heavily rely on intellectual property like patents and copyrights, since it is a relatively simple matter to locate the holder of these claims anywhere in the world. Hence Apple can have a substantial portion of the profits from its iPhones or other devices show up in low-tax Ireland. In such cases the growth in foreign profits is actually growth in domestic profits attributable to intellectual property claims.

The existence and strength of intellectual property is of course very much a matter of government policy. And it is likely to have a large impact on profits. The United States spend $384 billion on pharmaceuticals in 2013.[10] Without patents and related protections, it is likely that the cost would have been 10-20 percent as high. The difference of $307 billion to $346 billion is equal to

[9] National Income and Product Accounts, Table 6.2D, Line 38.
[10] National Income and Product Accounts, Table 2.4.5U, Line 20.

18.1 percent and 20.4 percent of before tax profits in 2013. While it is important for the government to have a mechanism to finance the research and development of new drugs, the patent system has become an extremely inefficient way to accomplish this end.[11] More efficient alternatives to patent protection are likely to lead to considerably lower profits in the drug industry.

Similarly weaker patent protections in the tech sector, where it patent litigation has become a mechanism for harassing competitors, is likely to both enhance innovation and reduce profitability in the sector. The same would be the case for overly strict and long copyright monopolies held by the software and entertainment industry.

In short, profits in large sectors of the economy can be substantially reduced by policies that would in many cases actually increase economic efficiency. In all cases industry groups would fight hard to prevent the basis of their profitability from being undermined, but that doesn't change the fact that it is the adoption of policies that were friendly to these business interests that led to the increase in profit shares in recent years, not any inherent dynamic of capitalism, as some may read Piketty as saying.

Furthermore, even if these power relations are viewed as in some sense endogenous, there is still the obvious point that they can be changed – or least are more likely to be changed than a policy that attacked the whole capital class, like Piketty's wealth tax. In other words, it seems more plausible that we can get legislation that would end patent support of prescription drug research, than an annual tax of 2.0 percent on wealth over some designated minimum. If the latter can be done without violent revolution, then surely the former can also be done.

In short, it is difficult to accept Piketty's projection of a future of growing inequality. This is certainly one possibility, but that is a prediction of the politics that will set policy in coming decades in the United States and elsewhere. It is not a statement about the fundamental nature of capitalism.

---

[11] Baker (2004) outlines various alternative mechanisms for financing the research and development of new drugs.

References

Baker, Dean and Jared Bernstein, 2014. Getting Back to Full Employment: A Better Bargain for Working People, Washington, DC: Center for Economic and Policy Research, accessed at http://www.cepr.net/index.php/publications/books/getting-back-to-full-employment-a-better-bargain-for-working-people.

Baker, Dean, 2004. “Financing Drug Research: What Are the Issues?” Washington, DC: Center for Economic and Policy Research, accessed at http://www.cepr.net/index.php/Publications/Reports/financing-drug-research-what-are-the-issues

Board of Governors of the Federal Reserve System, 2014 Financial Accounts of the United States, Washington, DC: Board of Governors of the Federal Reserve System, accessed at http://www.federalreserve.gov/releases/z1/

International Monetary Fund, 2014. “How Big is the Subsidy for Banks Considered Too Important to Fail,” in Global Financial Stability Report, Washington, DC: International Monetary Fund.

International Monetary Fund, 2010. “A Fair and Substantial Contribution by the Financial Sector,” Final Report to the G-20, Washington, DC: International Monetary Fund.

Piketty, Thomas, 2014. *Capital for the Twenty-First Century*. New York: Belknap Press.

Samuelson, Paul A. 1966. “A Summing Up.” *Quarterly Journal of Economics*. November, 80:4, pp. 568–83.

U.S. Department of Commerce, Bureau of Economic Analysis, National Income and Product Accounts, accessed at http://www.bea.gov/iTable/index_nipa.cfm